Egypt: Politics and Society 1945–1990

Egypt: Politics and Society 1945–1990

DEREK HOPWOOD

St Antony's College, Oxford

London and New York

First published 1982 by George Allen & Unwin
Second edition 1985, Unwin Hyman Ltd
Third edition 1991, Harper Collins Academic

First published 1993
by Routledge
11 New Fetter Lane, London EC4P 4EE

Simultaneously published in the USA and Canada
by Routledge
29 West 35th Street, New York, NY 10001

Printed and bound in Great Britain by
Mackays of Chatham PLC, Chatham, Kent

British Library Cataloguing-in-Publication Data
A catalogue record for this book is available from the British Library.
    Hopwood, Derek
        Egypt, politics and society, 1945–1990
    ISBN 0–415–09432–1

Library of Congress Cataloging in Publication Data
has been applied for.

Contents

List of Maps

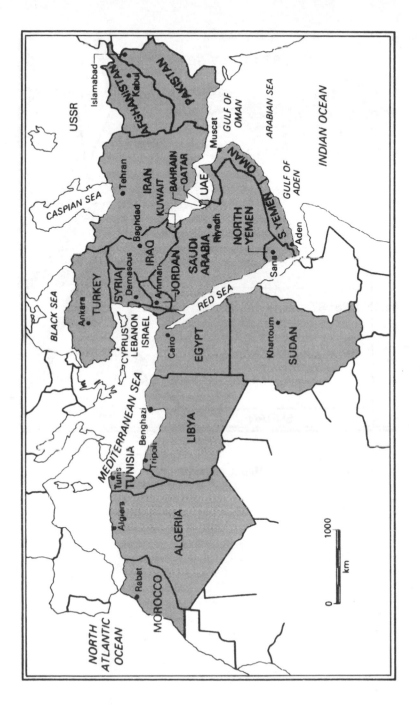

Map 1 Egypt's neighbours

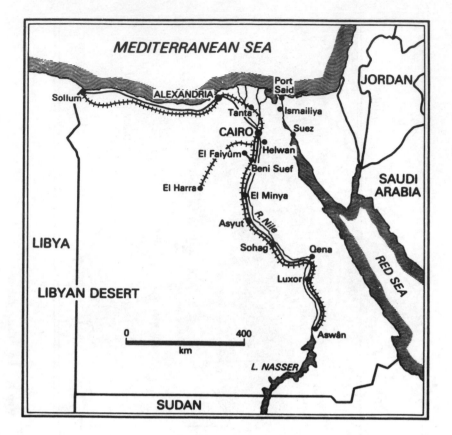

Map 2   Egypt

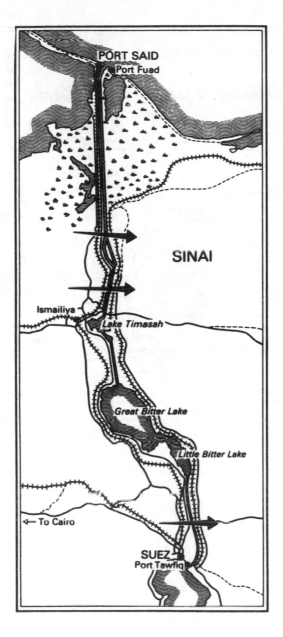

Map 3 The Suez Canal (arrows denote the first Egyptian crossings in October 1973).

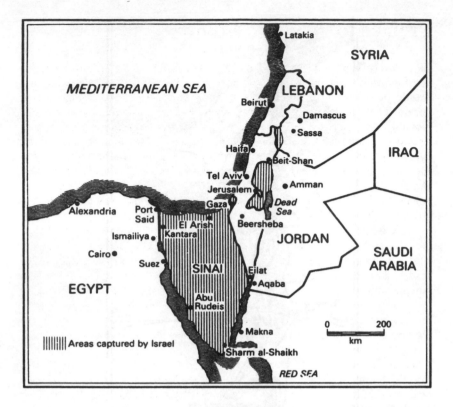

Map 4   Areas occupied by Israel after the 1967 war: Egypt's 'setback'.

Preface to the Third Edition

It is surely legitimate to ask why an outsider should write about Egypt. An Egyptian must by definition know more about his own society and he would be able to write one kind of book, an authoritative picture from the inside. There is also room, I believe, for the outsider's point of view, a view possibly not accepted or even recognised by the Egyptian, which should try to interpret what the observer sees with a sympathy and understanding which do not blind him to faults and short-comings. The problem for the British writer attempting such a study is to clear away the legacy of the Anglo–Egyptian imperial relationship, to grasp what British domination meant to the Egyptian and to understand how he tried to emerge from this shadow. This can on occasions be a sobering experience.

The British came and went in Egypt and they distorted the course of politics and society for over seventy years. The Egyptians are a forgiving and a tolerant people and, politics aside, welcome the stranger in their midst. This book could not have been written without the help, perhaps unconsciously given, of innumerable Egyptian friends and colleagues. I have also been fortunate enough to visit Egypt regularly since 1959 and have been offered endless hospitality. I have benefited from talking to Egyptian and other colleagues and students in Oxford and elsewhere and from listening to them lecturing, discussing and arguing or just conversing. I would mention a few of the many: Roger Owen, Robert Mabro, Nazih Ayubi, Samir Radwan, Muhammad Wahby, Muhammad Abd al-Wahhab and especially Mustafa Badawi a stimulating companion in Egypt and Oxford, and George Scanlon, a tireless host and a fund of knowledge in Cairo. Their views, written and spoken, are reflected in these pages and I hope they are not unfairly distorted. In the end, however, they are transmitted through my personal focus and the resultant work is my responsibility.

This book was written for the person who may have no previous knowledge of the Middle East or Egypt, whether university or college student or general reader interested in history, politics or social studies, to help him to gain an impression of a non-European country developing and changing in the face of great odds. It may also help in the study of Third World politics and development in general or be an introduction to further study of Egypt itself. If written in French it might claim to be a work of 'vulgarisation' with not much to say to the specialist. With some misgivings, I have omitted footnotes, feeling academically naked and hoping that the bibliography will partially remedy the omission. It is intended both to list the sources used and to point to further study. It should be clear in the course of the book how much I have relied on the original research of other scholars and the inclusion of their studies in the bibliography is meant as acknowledgement. Egypt has occasioned the production of numerous excellent pieces of research. Although Arabic sources have been consulted they are not included unless translations exist, especially of literary works. Wherever possible I have quoted the words of Egyptians themselves writing about their own problems.

In the third edition it has been possible to extend the period of coverage up to 1990 in a section on the first years year of office of President Mubarak. The achievements and failures of Sadat's regime are now clearer and it is possible to make a firmer judgement that it was three years ago. I have not been able to alter the main text of the book very much although I am grateful to colleagues and critics who have made suggestions for improvements and corrections. As I feared I have been taken to task for omitting footnotes and I apologise to those readers who may have wished to trace the source of the quotations.

The history of any country is incomplete. More than ever, decisions being made now in Egypt will influence both future developments and the interpretation of the past. We can only wait to see whether Mubarak's policies will bear fruit.

Derek Hopwood
Oxford 1990

Egypt: Politics and Society 1945-1990

1   *Egypt and the Egyptians*

> They have worked their way through history by
> tenacity. (Louis Awad)

> Our Egyptian civilization — which dates back 7000
> years -- has always been inspired by man's love of,
> and attachment to the land. (Anwar Sadat)

Geography and Society

Egypt is a country overburdened with history and geography — a history
overwhelming yet inspiring, a geography restricting yet lifegiving. She
cannot develop as a nation without looking back over her shoulder at the
past, nor develop as a country without taking the Nile into account. Egypt
has been the prisoner as well as the gift of the Nile. Historically, the
Egyptian people have been 'ed to the Nile valley and delta and have
drawn their sustenance from he waters of the river. The Nile valley was
rather closed and self-contained and although foreign rulers have come
and gone, the people have preserved themselves and a way of life for
thousands of years without much break in continuity. Egypt has often
participated in Middle Eastern events and has been affected by them but
has never lost an essential Egyptian identity, integrating whatever was
received or imposed, asserting continuously her own character. Egypt is
part of Africa linked physically to Asia by the Sinai peninsula. A long
coastline and the port of Alexandria have drawn her into the Mediterranean
world. The Nile pulls her down into Africa and the control of its head-
waters has been of primary concern to Egypt's rulers. The country is thus
uniquely situated to participate in several worlds, the African, the Arab
and the Mediterranean.

    Lower Egypt consists of the area from Cairo northwards which includes
the Delta where the Nile splits into several branches. This is the most
fertile, populous and cultivated region. To the east and west lie deserts
and further east Suez and Sinai leading to the frontiers of Israel, Jordan
and Saudi Arabia. Upper Egypt is mainly the river with cultivated strips
of land on either side varying in width from two to fifteen miles. The
cultivated area stops abruptly and is replaced by arid desert which on the
eastern side reaches the Red Sea and in the west merges into the Sahara.
There are five scattered oases in the Western Desert. The area of the whole
country is some 385,000 square miles of which less than 5 per cent is
cultivable land. On the map this resembles a flying kite — the triangular
delta attached to the long string of the Nile. The climate is mostly arid
and hot with little rain except on the Mediterranean coast. The desert is
virtually rainless; Cairo has about 1·3 inches of rain a year. Aswan which

nce rainless now on occasions experiences mist and cloud and even caused by the proximity of the artificial lake formed behind the High Dam.

Apart from the northern coast the seasons vary little, except for the intensity of the heat. Far more important and central to Egyptian life was the annual flooding of the Nile in autumn. This was a sign that Egypt could live a further year; a low flood could mean a 'lean' year. Life centred round the river, a benefactor which bestowed or withheld an annual bounty. It provided the rhythm of life and rarely could the thoughts of the peasant have been far from the Nile and the incessant work it demanded. Whereas ancient Egyptians worshipped the Nile, modern Egypt calls it 'the sea' as a token of its greatness, and the cultivable land on its banks is 'the mud'. Prayers were said to encourage the annual flooding and when this was too low prices rose, land dried up and a general feeling of malaise easily spread. The river together with its canals also provided a convenient means of transport, while from its mud were made bricks to build dwellings. Now because of the High Dam the river will no longer flood; water is released regularly and 'scientifically'; the old flood levels are pointed out, the fall in the height of the river is wondered at. Can such a radical change fail to affect the attitude to life itself?

Extreme heat is an inescapable feature of life in the Middle East. The sun, which to Northern Europeans is something to be welcomed and enjoyed, is something to be shunned and escaped from into shade or air conditioning. It is a constant factor of life which can enervate and lead to indifference, or fray tempers. The lack of rain causes an all pervasive dust in most Middle Eastern towns and a wind raising the dust on a hot day can make life well nigh unbearable. Heat determines modes of life, regulates the day's work and its effects must be reckoned with in an account of Arab society. Egypt is not the hottest of Arab countries, but summer temperatures in Cairo rise to 40°C and in Upper Egypt to 50°C. For those who can afford it the Mediterranean coast is a welcome relief in summer. Another escape is the shuttered, curtained house or flat which keeps out the worst effects of heat and light.

Whereas the Nile and its villages have been a very slowly changing aspect of Egypt, the capital city, Cairo, bears witness in stone to a long involvement with other peoples and cultures. Most foreign rulers and dynasties have left some evidence of their stay in civil, military and religious architecture. Cairo (the name is the European version of the Arabic, *al-Qahira* – 'the victorious' – given to celebrate the entry of a new ruler), founded in 969 near the site of another city more than three centuries older, is sited just south of the barrage (completed in 1861) that regulated the flow of water into the Delta through the two branches of the lower Nile. It stands astride the gateway to the Delta and has controlled its destiny but is open to attack from the north, east and west and has been subject to a long series of invaders from the Arabs to the British. It has dominated the country as its capital and one out of every six Egyptians lives within the metropolitan area, which also contains most industry, universities and colleges, and central government and financial offices. It is the centre of economic, cultural, religious and intellectual life and acts as a magnet to the rest of Egypt and to parts of Africa and Asia. It is a great and lively city and a city having to struggle with all the modern problems of housing, servicing and transporting a multitudinous population.

The original Arab city of Fustat was founded as a military encampment in about 640 on the eastern bank of the Nile by invading Muslim forces. A series of other invading forces gradually moved the focus of the city, the most important being the Fatimids from North Africa. Their city of *al-Qahira* took over from Fustat, which gradually fell into ruin. Their most notable monument is the university mosque of al-Azhar. Great city walls and a citadel were built under the rule of Saladin in the twelfth century, while all the time urban domestic and economic quarters were growing, usually in the traditional Middle Eastern manner of grouping trades together. The following centuries, dominated by other foreign rulers, Circassian and Turkish, added other monuments which still stand today — mosques, houses, mausoleums, bazaars. In the fifteenth century Cairo was probably greater in extent and population than any city in Europe and excited the wonder of European visitors.

A change was brought about when Egypt fell in 1517 to Ottoman Turkish rulers from Anatolia. Cairo became a provincial capital subordinate to Constantinople, which attracted to itself the intellectual and artistic talents of the Ottoman Empire. Arab civilisation and Arabic fell into the doldrums. Cairo declined in population and to some extent economically. The city in a sense withdrew into itself until Napoleon arrived with his army in 1798. While the French were there too short a time basically to alter the face of the city, the invasion so disrupted the existing state of affairs that it can justly be considered a turning point both in the history of Cairo and of Egypt. The French withdrawal led to the establishment of a new dynasty of Albanian origin which ruled Egypt until 1952. Avowedly westward looking, they were responsible for introducing into the country ideas of westernisation and modernisation. As far as Cairo was concerned a new city patterned on European lines was built alongside the existing mediaeval one. The French had begun to impose a new street system on the city, mainly for military reasons, but it was two rulers from the new dynasty, Muhammad Ali (1805–48) and Ismail (1863–79) who undertook the development of Cairo. By the end of the nineteenth century the city consisted of two parts which symbolised the new departure in Egyptian history. The western type city was growing separately from the older eastern Islamic, just as new ideas were entering the country and developing alongside deeply held older convictions. Moreover the population of the new areas held a large proportion of European immigrants whose presence was to affect subsequent Egyptian history.

In the new city which stretched to the Nile streets were widened, paved and lit, new bridges built across the river, swamps, ditches and ponds filled in. Paris was the model emulated, with its boulevards, squares and parks, opera house and hotels. New quarters were developed for residential, business and government purposes, and until the end of the century Cairo grew largely in the way determined by the planners of Ismail. The population reached about 600,000, still split into two fairly separate entities. The mediaeval city gradually filled with immigrants from the countryside, while the new European style city spread outside its boundaries remaining socially and physically distinct from the old.[1]

The new century brought great changes. New tramlines opened up new areas which gradually coalesced into the city. The population increased dramatically until it had reached 6 million by 1970. The city spilled over into surrounding districts engulfing villages and rural areas, creating new districts such as Heliopolis, a middle class suburb, and continually crowding more people into existing ones, imposing strains on all the existing municipal services.

Egypt's life is tied to the Nile, and much urban development outside Cairo is also on the Nile. In the far south Aswan has developed around the dams built there. Luxor is chiefly a tourist centre built near the sites of ancient Thebes and Karnak. Of the numerous other towns between Luxor and Cairo, Asyiut, Minya and Sohag are among the largest. The Delta from Cairo to the coast is a densely populated and cultivated area. The Delta road north from Cairo is a complex mix of local rural traffic, donkeys, bullocks and carts, and lorries and cars on inter-city journeys.

Egypt's second largest city, Alexandria, lies off the Nile and was for long a city of the Mediterranean rather than of Egypt. Built on a Greek site, its population was a mixture of Greeks, Italians, Maltese, Lebanese and others, together with the Egyptians. The foreign minorities tended to predominate in many aspects of the city's life such as trade, banking, tourism and culture and it developed a way of life described as 'Levantine'. Manners, customs and taste were based on an imitation of certain aspects of a European life-style implanted in an Eastern Mediterranean setting. It has been best described in the novels of Lawrence Durrell and it produced at least one poet of international reputation, the Greek Cavafy. Since the revolution of 1952 the foreign population has gradually left Alexandria leaving it to the Egyptians whose numbers have been swollen by large-scale immigration.

The remainder of the urban population is concentrated in new industrial complexes such as Helwan and Mahalla al-Kubra, in one or two Mediterranean coastal towns, in the el-Arish oasis in Sinai, and in the towns on the Suez Canal. These latter were abandoned and partly destroyed when Israeli forces were on the east bank of the canal but are now being rapidly repopulated and developed. There are also plans to build new cities in various parts of the desert, which are slowly taking shape.

The geography of Egypt has moulded the way of life of most Egyptians which has changed only slowly over the centuries. For over 5,000 years peasants have drawn water from river and canal to irrigate their plot of land. Their lives have been days in the field and evenings in the village, the women working alongside the men. Life has been harsh and the earth indifferent. Their society has been formed by the twin influences of Egypt and Islam which have imposed on them a pattern of existence resistant to change. Not totally isolated but often remote from the centre of authority, the changes of ruler have left them largely unaffected. This and a long history have given the Egyptian a certain melancholy and lack of excitement in the face of change, as though few were ready to plunge the country into chaos to risk the anxiety of facing a new unknown life. The weight of history, which may sometimes provide an excuse for inertia, also gives to Egyptian life a compassion lacking in other nations. A leading critic and journalist, Louis Awad, has written of the fundamentally moderate temper of the Egyptians who

...look with suspicion on all forms of extremism, fanaticism and intoxication. They have worked their way through history by tenacity and not by passion or violence. This is what gives the stamp of permanence and indeed timelessness to our life and institutions...We have known the weariness of longevity and the drabness of immortality, but at least we have shunned the follies of more youthful nations which burn themselves to ashes with the fire of fickle fantasies and follow the paths of glory though they lead to the grave.

Presumably the peasant in the field does not view life in terms formulated by an intellectual but perhaps he senses that he is part of a greater whole that has had a long historical existence and that his life is shaped by forces over which he has little control. Despite large-scale migration to the cities the peasants still form just under 60 per cent of the population and further migration must harm Egypt's agricultural production and add to the urban pressures. Despite quoting Awad above, such generalisations must be taken with caution. Some Egyptians are impatient with inertia and the constraints of history. The urbanised élite has often followed the 'follies and fantasies' of other nations and has been in the van of those demanding change and reform. The members of this élite and the intelligentsia have had an ambivalent attitude towards the peasant, as was the case in nineteenth-century Russia. They see him as part of the soil, the authentic expression of the land, but have an aversion to the dirt and poverty of the village. They have despised and misunderstood him, having little patience with his acceptance of his lot and his apparent 'stubbornness'.

It is in the towns that the élite has flourished, government officials, military officers, businessmen, intellectuals and, until recently, big landowners. Wealth, occupation and education have fixed a gap between rich and poor, well-to-do city dweller and the urban and rural poor, widened by the greater contact of the city with Western techniques and education, which tended to disrupt those traditional values which had provided a point of contact between the two. It is in the towns that the 'isms' of our time have blossomed – fascism, Marxism, fundamentalism – and more importantly where the concepts of nationalism have been nurtured, abused and glorified. No modern nation can tolerate this division of the people by wealth, education or culture and it will be shown later what efforts have been made to create a unified nation and to try to eliminate such a gap.

Another feature of life given to Egypt by its geography has been a centralised government. In a society based on a river – a hydraulic society – the ruler is indispensable for controlling the supply of the water. In such a society he is the intermediary between man and the river. The people's lives depend on water and proper irrigation and on order imposed by the government. A bureaucracy imposes itself to oversee the development and maintenance of canals and ditches. Only in a centrally organised bureaucratic society could such supreme monuments as the pyramids have been built. But life also depended on co-operation. Water had to be shared and had to flow from the river to irrigate the land of all. No peasant could monopolise the supply or prevent its passage to land of neighbours. The need for co-operation and strong government could easily lead to an acceptance of despotism and to servile submission. An Egyptian student has written: 'He does not know Egypt's history who denies that despotism and oppression from one side, submission and flattery from the other, are among the deepest and worst features in Egyptian life throughout the ages, that they are the sad leitmotiv in the drama of Egyptian history'. Submission, a belief in the futility of opposition, and the other side of the coin, the moral value attached to patience, have given rise to a number of proverbs which express the peasants' feelings, such as 'Water will not run uphill'. At the same time complaint is a constant feature of Egyptian life. In Egyptian songs 'complaint' is expressed with deep sadness and an awareness of the futility of the complaint. 'To whom shall I complain, when all are suffering injustice?' Nevertheless the peasant has not always accepted his lot and when driven too far has risen in revolt, although the geography of the country and a strong government has made the suppression of revolts relatively easy.

Islam

The influences on Egyptian society discussed above have themselves been modified by another important factor – the Islamic religion. Islam was first proclaimed by the prophet Muhammad during the early years of the seventh century in the towns of Mecca and Medina in present day Saudi Arabia. His message was that of a simple faith, obedience to God (Allah) and his prophet, strict observance of the duties of prayer and almsgiving, pilgrimage to Mecca, and the promise of punishment or reward in the next world. By force of circumstances, Muhammad found himself the leader of a community in Medina for which he had to establish a system of government, laws and institutions. Henceforward, Islam became a total way of life, regulating society and government, family and private life. Unlike Christendom, no distinction was made between church and state, and no church with rituals and hierarchy was ever established. For thirteen centuries this religion has influenced the life and society of Egypt. Islam brought radical and lasting changes, not only in religious practice but in the whole of life. Egypt has been one of the leading centres of Islamic teaching in the world with the mosque of al-Azhar in Cairo the focal point. No visitor to Cairo can fail to be struck by the number of mosques, the number of people praying, the call of the muezzin (or in these days tape-recordings) and the celebration of various religious festivals, especially during and after the fast of the month of Ramadan. All these combine to give a noticeable religious flavour to Egypt. In the older parts of Cairo during the festivals there is the feeling of being in a city of religion just as much as in Rome or Jerusalem.

Islam is deeply embedded in Egypt and demands a response on the part of the people. As in the West, religous festivals can be observed with little religious conviction but at least until recently Islam has been widely and sincerely observed and there are now clear signs of a revival of observance. In Cairo the intellectual tradition has had a leading position through the dominance of al-Azhar university mosque, although in certain poorer quarters of Cairo and in provincial towns and villages a more popular form of religion, often connected with mystical orders, has been prevalent. Local saints' days have been the occasion for great popular festivals, sometimes frowned upon by the more orthodox. Most Egyptians would recognise Islam as a bond in their life and a factor uniting them, although there have been and are those who question the place of Islam in society, who have tried to find ways of bringing into religion the scientific, social and economic ideas of the twentieth century, and those who have abandoned the attempt and have turned to secularism. (An interesting and perhaps significant fact is that some of those who are openly secularist or agnostic still call themselves Muslim − using the term in an exclusively cultural and social context.) Opposed to the secularist and reformist trend there has been a strong current of religious fundamentalism, sometimes in an organised movement, of those who preach that the only remedy for a society afflicted by non-Islamic ideas and goals is a return to the pure form of Islam as practised by the early Muslims. Such movements appeal to deep feelings in an Islamic country, in Egypt or elsewhere, and can strike responses in those who suspect that their society erred when it admitted the West, whether Christian or secular-scientific, into its midst. Thirdly, there are those Muslims, either scholar-clerics (*ulama*) or lay-believers, who continue to practise their religion according to the tradition of their forefathers, little troubled by doubts or questioning, clinging to religion as an unchanging rock in a changing world. The certainty of faith can be seen both in the faces of those women who visit saints' tombs in the hope of fertility and of those dignified *ulama* who walk the streets of Cairo in the assurance of an unshakeable faith.

History to 1945

In 1962 President Nasser presented to the Egyptian people a National Charter. Its first section was a general introduction which characterised Egyptian history as a 'constant struggle for a better life' during 'centuries of despotism and injustice'. Being an Egyptian and a nationalist it was natural for Nasser to see the history of his people as a continual series of invasions and foreign rulers, but it was historical licence to view the reaction of the people as an unending struggle against the invader. Once the native Egyptian rule of the Pharaohs had collapsed it is true that, strictly speaking, foreigners ruled the country, but often only in the sense that the successors of William the Conqueror were not native Englishmen. It is more rewarding to view Egyptian history as a long series of accretions of different peoples and dynasties which left their mark on the country, modified by two factors: first, foreign rule left village Egypt largely untouched, except for taxation and the acquisition of estates, and in a very real sense the villager is the descendant of the Pharaonic Egyptian; and, secondly, while rulers might change, a bureaucracy continued which handed on a tradition and which ran the country. Incoming rulers relied on the bureaucracy of their predecessors.

The most significant date in Egyptian history after the fall of the Pharaohs is 642, the date of the Arab conquests. After the death of the prophet Muhammad, Arab warriors inspired by their new faith had swept out of Arabia into surrounding areas, and conquered Egypt with little opposition. On to the basic Egyptian character of the country was grafted a lasting Arab character: Arabic gradually became the major language, Islam, the faith of the Arabs, the major religion, and Egypt's destiny was henceforth linked to that of the Arab world. For fourteen centuries it has been an Arab country, with a unique heritage and character more deeply rooted than that of any other Arab country. The native inhabitants at the conquest had been non-Arab Christian Copts, speaking their own language and following their own brand of Christianity. They gradually adopted Arabic as their language and Islam as their faith. A minority resisted conversion and their descendants still live in Egypt as Arabic-speaking Christians with their own 'pope', church and liturgical language.

Rule by outsiders, whether the Ottoman Turks governing from Constantinople (Istanbul), or Napoleon himself, could not radically alter the Egyptian character. Napoleon's imperial gaze had been drawn to Egypt as a means of threatening the growing British power in India. He saw the country as a stepping stone on the route east. He reached Egypt but it is difficult to believe that he planned a long French sojourn there. Although France gained little, Egypt was deeply affected, and at least two major changes took place. The Ottomans were never again able to exercise real power in the country and Egypt was the first Arab country to reassert its virtual independence from the Ottoman Empire. This brought a certain responsibility to Egypt's rulers, a new character to the country and the necessity to pursue a recognisably independent policy. Egypt was early in the line of countries gaining independence from imperial powers, so early in fact that she had time to fall into another imperial orbit. In a sense Egypt gained independence too early, which led to a near disaster for her later in the century.

The other major change was the rise of a ruling dynasty which lasted from 1805 until 1952 (although it officially lingered until 1953). Because of these two changes modern Egyptian history is usually dated from the Napoleonic invasion which brought Egypt to the notice of Europe, beginning that process of European intervention in the country which has never really ended. The French were expelled from Egypt by a combination of British and Ottoman power, and left behind a confused situation in which it was possible for the commander of the Albanian forces nominally in the service of the Ottoman governor to rise to power in 1805. This was Muhammad Ali. He was not an Egyptian, having been born in Kavalla, and used the country to further his own ambitions. Egyptians have an ambivalent attitude towards him. He did bring a certain independence to Egypt and introduce a number of reforms, but he was the founder of a foreign dynasty which was later hated and despised, especially in the person of King Farouk.

Muhammad Ali was a formidable man, one of those figures in history strong enough to change the life and direction of a country – for good or ill – and to put his stamp upon an era. He led a breakthrough for the country, turning his back on the past and introducing new and irrevocable changes. It was ironic that he was not a native Egyptian. He worked for an economic revolution in the country, building factories, digging canals for irrigation and transportation and introducing cotton cultivation in the Delta. He also attempted to redirect education and training in engineering and medicine by sending students abroad and by inviting training missions to Egypt.

All these facts are well known. What is astonishing is that an unlettered, inexperienced soldier should have had the vision of a modern powerful and independent Egypt. His military ambitions were equally great and he built up a standing army which at one point challenged Istanbul itself.

He was halted only by the opposition of the European powers, but succeeded in having his family recognised as hereditary governors of Egypt. When he died he had changed the country but had also brought about the problems which led directly to trouble later in the century. Through his overambitious projects he subjected Egypt to great economic strain and through his financial and agrarian policies he led to the creation of rich landowners, a large bureaucracy and a growing number of foreign merchants and traders. The excesses of these latter were fundamental causes of the 1952 revolution, while the problem of a top-heavy bureaucracy has still to be solved.

The death of a great man always leaves a vacuum. Muhammad Ali, not a beloved or popular figure, rather an alien dictator, founded a dynasty which provided a line of more or less able rulers. The next four, Ibrahim, Abbas I, Said and Ismail, followed policies which plunged Egypt deeper and deeper into debt and allowed foreigners more and more say in the running of the country. Each of the rulers followed different policies, and while they had certain ideas about the future of the country they were not basically concerned with the welfare of the vast majority of the population, something for which later Egyptians strongly condemn them.

Said's greatest claim on history is his relationship with the French engineer, Ferdinand de Lesseps, who sold him the scheme of building the canal across the isthmus of Suez to join the Mediterranean and the Red Sea. From the start it was more of a foreign concession than an Egyptian interest, which was run from Paris for the benefit of foreign traders and investors. It had originally been built in the face of the implacable opposition of the British who preferred the railway across the isthmus and who correctly foresaw that it would drag them into Egyptian affairs. The Canal soon became something more than itself; to Britain a lifeline of empire, to the Egyptians a symbol of hated foreign domination. Once objects are surrounded by myths and beliefs they are clung to and fought for all the more tenaciously. Suez was considered essential to British imperial life, the key to the passage to India. To Egyptians the processions of liners taking servants of empire about their business were a constant reminder of that civilisation which laid claims upon their country. (It will be seen later that Nasser's nationalisation of the Canal had a great symbolical quality.) The Canal had been built with French and Egyptian money, but in 1875 because of Ismail's financial irresponsibility the Egyptian shares were purchased by the British government under Benjamin Disraeli.[2] So was Britain's interest in Egypt strengthened.

Ismail, although a talented man, as a ruler brought disaster upon his country. He gained recognition from the Ottoman Sultan as a virtually independent sovereign (*khedive*), yet independence was to prove illusory. Through a combination of his own financial recklessness and of outside factors and predatory foreign investors, Ismail loaded Egypt with ruinous debts. If he had no compunction in squeezing the last piastre from the peasant, he was still prepared to spend a great deal on development. New parts of Cairo were built, railways, roads, bridges, telegraph and postal services brought to the country, education improved. His desires and wild tastes were exploited by others and despite his contributions to the development of Egypt his debts ensured its subjection to Europe and eventually to Britain. In part, he was subject to the stream of events begun by Muhammad Ali and he was not strong enough to swim against the tide. In 1876 he ran out of means of raising money and postponed payment on his debts. A European Debt Commission was imposed to attempt to safeguard foreign interests – the beginning of an intervention in Egyptian affairs which finally led to occupation. The Commission's authority was soon strengthened by the appointment of two Controllers, a Briton and a Frenchman, who established what came to be known as the Dual Control. They acquired such wide economic and financial powers that their regime has been called a 'veiled colonial administration'. Ismail was blamed for the country's predicament and was called upon by Britain and France to abdicate. He appealed for 150,000 volunteers to save the country from the infidels, but the country had had enough of him. The Ottoman Sultan deposed him and he went into exile in June 1879.

While Ismail was the leading figure of his era in Egypt, his son and successor, Tewfik, had to share the limelight with a number of other actors. The most notable of these was Ahmad Urabi, whom Egyptians honour as the first real hero of their struggle for national independence. He was an army officer of peasant background (and thus a native Egyptian) and representative of a mood of discontent with the growing European domination of his country and with the reactionary nature of the government and the weakness of Tewfik, who had neither the strength nor the will to oppose the British and French. In May 1880 Urabi presented a petition to the government for the redress of certain of their grievances and, emboldened, he went as far as to demand the dismissal of the unpopular minister of war. He was arrested, freed by the action of the army which had risen in revolt, and was himself appointed minister of war. As a popular hero Urabi naturally opposed European interference and the British feared that their influence would crumble under nationalist pressure. They began to speak in terms astonishingly similar to those used by Anthony Eden of Nasser in 1956 during the Suez crisis. The British government claimed that no 'satisfactory or durable arrangement of the Egyptian crisis was possible without the overthrow of Arabi [Urabi] Pasha'.

The so-called crisis was simply the British (and to some extent French) fear of losing influence and financial control, especially as over half the holders of the bonds of the Egyptian debt were in England. In 1882 a large proportion of the Egyptian revenues went to European creditors. British officials on the spot pressed the British government to intervene in order to save British interests. They systematically denounced the Urabi regime as a military despotism and foretold dire consequences for Egypt. British politicians were pushed by British financial interests into believing that intervention was essential to preserve Egypt from anarchy and to ensure the safety of the Suez Canal. Even the French were convinced for a time that intervention was essential, and in May 1882 British and French warships appeared off Alexandria. In June fifty Christians were killed in rioting in the city and England held Urabi responsible. The powers were now anxious to end the whole nationalist movement and in July a British fleet bombarded Alexandria, landed an army and defeated Urabi and the first Egyptian nationalist movement at the battle of Tel el-Kebir. The British entered Egypt declaredly to restore financial stability and good government and to protect the Suez Canal. (The French had lost heart and abandoned the enterprise.) The invasion was described as a 'duty', 'a point of national honour', and has to be viewed in the political atmosphere of the time.

The right to intervene was not questioned by most Victorian politicians if British interests were thought to be threatened. The invasion was justified as an attempt to save the Egyptian people from a military dictator and to protect the Khedive from opposition — 'To desert him', wrote one English newspaper, 'would be an act of treachery of which England is incapable'. The British public was accustomed to reading such remarks which clearly spelled out the effortless superiority of the British over lesser breeds. A quotation from a book on Egypt and the Sudan written by G. W. Stevens at the time and which went into at least fourteen editions may give the flavour of such thinking. 'The Egyptian may feel the sun; the Englishman must stand up and march in it. You see it is his country, and he must set an example.' This kind of attitude was tempered somewhat by the British public school tradition of fair play and a genuine desire to impart British qualities and by the ideas of those few Englishmen who were opposed to imperialism and its methods. Even Lord Milner, an arch-imperialist, wrote, 'British influence is not exercised to impose an uncongenial foreign system upon a reluctant people. It is a force making for the triumph of the simplest ideas of honesty, humanity and justice, to the value of which Egyptians are just as much alive as anybody else.'

Egypt thus became effectively part of the British Empire exposed to the benefits of British civilisation, although never officially a colony. (It is important to note that French influence remained strong in the country.) For the next three quarters of a century political power became a tug-of-war between the palace, the British and Egyptian politicians. The British claimed they had no intention of staying longer than necessary, but necessity always seemed to impose itself. In Egyptian eyes the period of British rule was a time of 'humiliation', a negation of dignity. From 1882 until 1954 the British opposed Egyptian demands and only grudgingly and under pressure gave ground. It is difficult to understand and sympathise with the growth of Egyptian nationalism without first appreciating the depth of the resentment felt against the British occupiers who, in the words of an Egyptian scholar, were 'a loathsome presence'. Anwar Sadat was equally forthright in his view of the British:

> Many things annoyed me in Cairo. There was, for instance, the *odious* sight of the typical British constable on his motorcycle tearing through the city streets day and night like a madman – with a tomato-coloured complexion, bulging eyes and an open mouth – looking like an idiot, with his huge head covered in a long crimson fez reaching down to his ears... I simply hated the sight of him, and often wondered what had brought this ugly alien to our city.

The resentment during the period until the First World War centred on three men, three pro-consuls of empire who bore merely the titles of British agent and Consul-General – Lord Cromer, Sir Eldon Gorst and Lord Kitchener. They personified the British presence, yet were each of rather different character. Cromer, an autocrat by nature, conceived his first task to be the achievement of financial solvency for Egypt. This he did skilfully despite the anomalies of his own position. He was able to service the debt and to balance the budget and spend money on agriculture, irrigation, railways and public services. He encouraged further specialisation in cotton production and the productive area was considerably expanded after the construction of the first Aswan Dam in 1902. He abolished the *corvée* (forced conscription), and introduced fiscal and administrative reforms which created new incentives. The expansion of foreign banks made credit available to the farmer. Cromer was optimistic about the future prospects of the Egyptian economy, but he has been criticised for neglecting industry and the development of education. British officials were brought in to help to run the country and the British army was always the obvious clue to where ultimate authority lay.

On the death of the Khedive Tewfik Egyptian nationalists opposed to British rule hoped for a leader in his successor, Abbas, but he was too weak and too young to stand up to Cromer. The nationalists, mainly lawyers and journalists, fought the British through the spoken and written word demanding independence, a constitutional government and more educational opportunity, but failed to wring any substantial concessions from Cromer. Even moderate nationalist policies often foundered on the rock of his obdurate refusal to admit that the Egyptians had a right to a major share in the running of their country. Their cry became 'Egypt for the Egyptians' and 'evacuation'. He never really changed his position and on leaving Egypt in May 1907 he said of the country: 'I shall deprecate any brisk change and any violent new departure'.

His successor, Sir Eldon Gorst, had the difficult task of taking over from an exceptionally strong personality. Cromer had had the clear objective of restoring financial stability. Gorst had the less clear task of maintaining British rule which by then had become a habit and was not really questioned; and yet some kind of policy had to be followed. Few Englishmen in Egypt were prepared to conciliate the nationalists; the foreign communities wanted firm rule and security in the country. Gorst felt he had to try to co-operate with the Khedive Abbas in creating a moderate nationalist opinion which would help to govern the country in accordance with British intentions, but the Muslim nationalists became ever more demanding, refusing to make any compromise over indepen-dence. The British considered any concessions to the nationalists as signs of weakness and as a cause of the deteriorating security situation in the country. Gorst was caught, unable to satisfy either side.

He was already fatally ill when in 1911 the British government had decided to replace him by another strong man, General Lord Kitchener, the soldier who in 1898 had avenged General Gordon's death in Khartoum. Although a tough ruler (he severely enforced press censorship, criminal conspiracy and school discipline acts) he realised that coercion would not encourage Egypt along the road to self-government. In 1913 he helped to introduce a new constitution which gave the country some representative institutions locally and nationally with certain powers. Some nationalists chose to work through these institutions while others waged an unrelent-ing opposition. Whether Kitchener's methods would have led to greater co-operation between rulers and ruled will never be known as on the outbreak of the First World War in 1914 he was summoned home to become secretary of war.

The war, although primarily a European event, had a deep and perma-nent effect on the Middle East. It signalled the end of the Ottoman Empire, which had thrown its lot in with the central powers, and the direct involve-ment of Britain in the affairs of more Arab territory. When Turkey had joined the Germans the Egyptian government called for co-operation with the British although Egypt was still nominally part of the Ottoman Empire and the Turks were fellow Muslims. Britain regulated one part of this situation by declaring Egypt a British protectorate – a device which gave Britain a decisive say in the running of the country but was of little advan-tage to the Egyptians. In fact the country became a war base and a garrison populated with British, Australian and other troops, Little attention was paid to Egyptian aspirations during the war and anti-British resentment increased. The Khedive Abbas was deposed and the eldest member of the line, Husain Kamil, was appointed Sultan. Many Egyptians were recruited for transport and other duties in Palestine, Syria and even France.

Although the Egyptians did not actively hinder the war effort, it did not mean that they were any more favourably disposed towards the con-tinuance of the British presence. While the British had concentrated on winning the war, a strong National Party was emerging together with another Egyptian national hero – Saad Zaghlul. Like Urabi of peasant stock, after having failed to co-operate with the British he despaired of moderation and turned to and became the leader of the nationalist move-ment. He personified the resentment felt against the British – a resentment deepened by the fact that at the Peace Conference the victorious Allies were discussing and determining the fate of smaller nations. Zaghlul asked that the Egyptian case should be heard but the British refused and in January 1919 he demanded complete independence for his country. To the Egyptians this seemed a reasonable demand at a time when the American President Wilson was preaching his doctrine of self-determination and sovereignty for all states. Zaghlul and his party continued to agitate, publishing protests and demanding to be allowed to go to the Peace Con-ference. The British responded by deporting Zaghlul and his colleagues to Malta. Egypt flared up in a revolt which was only put down by armed forces, and Lord Allenby was sent in March 1919 as High Commissioner and strong man to deal with the situation.

The period from Allenby's arrival until 1936, the date of the Anglo–Egyptian Treaty, is a complex story of the triangular relationship between the British, Egyptian politicians and the palace – a three-legged stool according to one British official. The Consul-General under the protectorate had become High Commissioner and his splendid residence by the Nile was believed by Egyptians to be the real source of power in their country. A number of politicians came to the fore during the period, the leader for a short time being Zaghlul and his party the Wafd. On the whole poli-ticians rose through royal favour and British support and fell when these were withdrawn. The ruler, now titled king, played a dubious role, pitting politicians against each other and trying to assert his own authority *vis-à-vis* the British. King Fuad (1917–36) was not very popular and considered to be virtually a foreigner by the Egyptians. He had lived abroad for a long time and spoke Italian better than Arabic.

The British high commissioners differed in character and in the policies they pursued. Field Marshall Viscount Allenby, despite his reputation as a soldier, was willing to make concessions. Lord Lloyd (1925–9) was more in the mould of Cromer and the new British Labour government decided to replace him with the more flexible Sir Percy Loraine (1929–36). Sir Miles Lampson (1936–46), later Lord Killearn, is remembered as a strong pro-consular figure who tried to dominate Egyptian politics. King Farouk wrote of this overbearing man: 'I consider it the greatest pity that Lampson should have represented Britain in Cairo during those extremely hazardous years of [the Second World] War...He never at any time in his term of office made the slightest move of friendship, tolerance or man-to-man understanding with me'.

In 1919 the British issued the report of a mission sent to Egypt under Lord Milner which had been asked to recommend arrangements whereby Egypt could be given a semblance of independence while Britain retained control. Although the report was rejected by Egypt, the British nevertheless decreed the end of the Protectorate in 1922, reserving to themselves four points: security of communications, the defence of Egypt and foreign nationals in Egypt, and the Sudan. In the period 1919–36 there were twenty governments and eight sets of negotiations in which the Egyptians ceaselessly tried in the face of British reluctance to whittle away British privileges. In 1936, largely because of the fascist Italian threat from Libya and Abyssinia, the two sides finally came together to sign the Anglo–Egyptian Treaty. This gave the country a certain independence, but not enough to satisfy all Egyptians, as Britain still retained responsibility for the defence of the Suez Canal and was able to station troops there. The fundamental question of sovereignty over the Sudan was postponed. Several groups, radicals, army officers, students, the Muslim Brothers, continued to work for full independence. The Second World War interrupted for a time the course of Egyptian history, as the country became once again a military base with the British imperial presence all too evident. Although there were those who saw in the initial strength of Germany and Italy a hoped-for escape from British domination, the Egyptians once more did not seriously try to hinder the Allied cause.

One incident during the war has passed into Egyptian history as an intolerable example of British high-handedness. It is important to cite it as for Egyptians it typifies the whole Anglo–Egyptian relationship, the opposition of strength to weakness. In February 1942 the British believed that the Egyptian government, including the young King Farouk (who had succeeded Fuad in 1936) was, to quote a letter from the British Ambassador Sir Miles Lampson (the High Commissioner had become Ambassador in 1936 after the signing of the Treaty) 'not only unfaithful to the Alliance with Great Britain but actually working against it and thereby assisting the enemy'. The abdication of Farouk was demanded unless he was willing to appoint a new prime minister acceptable to Britain. On 4 February Lampson set out for the palace in Cairo with (according to his diary) 'an impressive array of specially-picked stalwart officers armed to the teeth' to present an ultimatum to the King. Tanks and armoured cars surrounded the palace and Lampson (he was a large man) 'brushed aside' the chief chamberlain and 'entered the King's presence without more ado'. Farouk in his version of the incident claimed that he had armed guards in the room pointing their revolvers at Lampson in case he went too far. Lampson insisted on a change of government or abdication. The King was rather offended by the paper he was asked to sign. 'But this paper is dirty, crumpled and soiled and unfit to sign', he complained. 'Read it', said Lampson. Farouk had no option and asked Nahhas Pasha, the British choice, to form a government. A hypocritical exchange of letters followed, guaranteeing Egyptian sovereignty.

'The policy of H.M.G. is to secure sincere collaboration with the Government of Egypt as an Independent and Allied country in the execution of the Anglo–Egyptian Treaty, without interference in the internal affairs of Egypt or in the composition or changes of her Government.' Lampson admitted he signed this letter 'with my tongue in my cheek'. The Egyptians considered the whole incident 'brutal aggression' and it was reported that 'certain sections of the Egyptians were considerably outraged'. Lampson confided that he 'could not have more enjoyed' the affair and the British Foreign Secretary, Eden, congratulated him on his 'firmness' − a phrase which gains significance later during the Suez crisis in 1956.

If ends justify means then Egypt did remain faithful during the war to her undertakings to Britain, but such pressure and humiliation could not be forgotten or forgiven, and served to strengthen the resolve to gain independence.

Economy and Society to 1945

Economists have divided the history of the Egyptian economy into three overlapping phases. The export economy phase lasted from the 1850s until the 1920s; this was followed by a period of import substitution (that is, producing locally goods previously imported) which reached a peak in the 1950s. The final phase was the post-revolutionary period of planned development. To these three must now be added the period after 1970 of the liberalisation of the economy.

After Muhammad Ali's early experiments in industrialisation Egypt became an economy based largely on one exportable crop − cotton − which entailed the integration of the country into the world economic system. The British occupation strengthened this tendency, keeping Egypt both as a market for British manufactured goods and as a cotton plantation to service the Lancashire mills. Egyptian writers see in this period the origins of the underdevelopment of Egypt, when Britain actively discouraged industrialisation and favoured a policy of *laissez-faire*. Capital accumulated in this process tended to be spent on consumption or reinvested in the system but not in industry. Also a great part of the export surplus was still used to redeem the Public Debt − some 30 per cent of export proceeds were used in this way in the 1900s.

Two other factors reinforced these tendencies, the emergence of an Egyptian bourgeoisie dependent on landownership, and the privileged position of foreigners in the country. One of the most important developments in the Egyptian economy was the growth of private landownership and the emergence of a class who acquired a disproportionately large share of the land. By 1914 small peasants represented over 90 per cent of all landowners and yet owned only a quarter of the land. The large owners formed a group with common economic interests and landownership gave them a privileged position at the top of Egyptian society. Their main interest was to maintain and improve their status and the gap between them and the rural poor was vast. They used their income to purchase more land or property but rarely to invest in other activities. The other privileged group in Egypt was the foreign residents who were protected by the Capitulations — the legal agreements which gave them the right to be tried in their own Consular Courts.

The period of the economy from the 1920s to the 1950s was characterised by an import-substitution industrialisation brought about by three main factors. During the 1920s and 1930s there were three agricultural crises which culminated in the Great Depression of 1929–32. There was a severe slump in world demand for cotton and this brought into question the traditional reliance of the Egyptian economy on one export crop. The national movement had stressed that industrialisation was a basic component of national independence. The educated élite began to think of industrialisation as the basis for modernisation and this led to a certain amount of national enterprise. New industries and new companies began to appear, symbolised by the establishment of the Bank Misr, an Egyptian foundation which eventually promoted a large number of enterprises. The success of the Bank encouraged some of the large landowners and merchants to invest in industrial concerns. Companies developed in fields such as textiles, building materials, insurance and transport. The Bank's success also showed that there was a local bourgeoisie prepared to help Egyptian industry and this fact succeeded in breaking the monopoly of foreign investors but failed to alter fundamentally the colonial nature of the economy. The government, however, was now under some pressure from the nationalists and local industrialists to change its opposition to industrial development. This it did by tariff reform in 1930 which increased the duty on imported goods.

The Second World War further stimulated Egyptian industry. Imports had to be greatly reduced and the spending of Allied troops, which at its peak represented some 25 per cent of the national income, boosted the demand for industrial products. Some 200,000 Egyptians were employed by the British army, while others were engaged in supplying various goods and services.

The position of the underprivileged did not improve during this period. The population increased from 10 million in 1897 to 19 million in 1947, an increase not matched by a comparable growth in habitable or cultivable land. Population density in 1927 was 420 to the square kilometre and this had risen to 845 in 1966. Annual per capita income has been estimated at £E12·4 in 1913 and £E8 in 1937. The increase in the man-to-land ratio naturally had a depressing effect on average income and low incomes prevented Egyptian villages from expanding. Mud huts by their very construction had to remain of one storey and agricultural land was too expensive to purchase. Overcrowding incited people to migrate to the towns and the population of Cairo increased threefold. The illiteracy rate remained high despite the spread of schools and universities. The peasants at the bottom of the scale continued to suffer from debilitating diseases, poverty and undernourishment. The Second World War disrupted the normal cycle of agriculture. Because of lack of shipping, there was a need to produce more grain and less cotton (a change the peasant did not welcome) and by 1943 there was a fall of 25 per cent in total agricultural production. After this there was a gradual improvement until by 1952 production was some 10 per cent above the level of 1934–8.

At the top of society came the large landowners, conservative in outlook and inclined to accept British rule if it guaranteed them prosperity and stability. The growing urban middle class such as lawyers, doctors, journalists and officials resented British domination and kicked against it. The peasants, the bulk of the population, had no political voice. The Copts of the towns occupied a large number of government posts and were generally more prosperous than the Muslims. They gradually began to accept the nationalist movement, although they were noticeably more favourably inclined towards the British. The commercial middle class which was almost entirely foreign – they were Jews, Syrians, Armenians and Europeans – controlled industry, finance and even some of the smaller trades.

For the British, life in Egypt was on the whole good. Service abroad was both the penalty and reward of belonging to the British Empire. As in India, men served in Egypt with devotion and dedication, seeing it their duty to educate the Egyptian into British ways and standards, innured to the heat, the squalor and the flies, and looking with a fairly good humoured tolerance upon the 'natives'. The compensations were often a higher standard of living and higher positions than could have been expected in England. Life was eased by numerous servants, by polo, tennis and gossip at European clubs. Social life centred around the British residency and the honour of being invited to dine was much coveted. Several long-time British residents have written with humour and affection, and at times sarcasm, of their life in Egypt.

Leisure of an Egyptian Official was but one book which dealt, in terms amusing to the Englishman but offensive to the Egyptian, with the facts of life in Egypt.

2 *The End of the Old Regime: 1945-1952*

At the end of the Second World War the British and the Egyptians were poised for their final struggle. An Egyptian looking at the victorious British Empire might have felt despair at facing an enemy more powerful than ever, but appearances were deceptive. The British army was stretched to its limit and thousands of conscripts were counting the days until demobilisation. Although Britain ended the war as victor, victory was based on the illusion of power. It had been American and Soviet military might which had won the war. It took the British many years to come to terms with this fact and many years of searching for a practical policy. The will to govern large areas of empire was gradually diminishing especially among members of the new Labour government. The main imperial decision to take was that of giving independence to India. Once that had been taken it was possible to begin to think in terms of relinquishing other parts of the Empire. In the Middle East there were British troops in bases stretching from North Africa to the Gulf. In Libya they were the occupiers after having ousted the Germans and Italians; in the Gulf they were serving local rulers; in Aden they were policing a colony; in Palestine they were hopelessly attempting to impose a policy unacceptable to Jews and Arabs; in Egypt they were there to guard the Suez Canal and the large British base.

Political Groupings

On the Egyptian side there were a number of political actors, parties and movements taking part in a struggle against the British and against each other. At the head of these stood King Farouk, who had come to the throne as a popular ruler of whom much had been expected. As early as 1937 Sir Miles Lampson had sounded a far-sighted warning note in a report to the Foreign Office:

It would be unwise to overestimate the appearances of popularity which is unfortunately giving King Farouk an exaggerated opinion of himself. The chances are that the Egyptian people in the long run will revert to its fundamental dislike of the family of Mohammed Ali...he is credited by various qualified informants with being at present uneducated, lazy, untruthful, capricious, irresponsible and vain, though with a quick superficial intelligence and charm of manner.

There is more than a little truth in this prophecy and Farouk was not the man to lead Egypt to independence. He had a flawed character, surrounding himself with corrupt advisers and flatterers, and his private life became a scandal. If the British were the hated occupiers, Farouk became the symbol of the corrupt old regime. The first task of a revolution was to rid Egypt of both.

The politicians were divided into several movements and factions. The Wafd, the party founded by Zaghlul, had often been in power and had a political machine which could win a freely held election, but a struggle for power had led to the withdrawal of some of its best members and the autocratic nature of Mustafa Nahhas, its leader, and the corrupting influence of people close to him deprived it of real moral authority. It was probably as reactionary as and less efficient than other possible governments. Some four other groupings of traditional politicians also provided government members and prime ministers, including the Saadists (the breakaway group from the Wafd), the Liberals and the Independents.

There were, however, other groups who stood apart from the traditional politicians and, while having basically the same aims, advocated more violent policies. One of the groups was the Society of Muslim Brothers, known as the *Ikhwan al-Muslimin* or the *Ikhwan* (Brothers). They were representative of the age-old trend in Islamic history which claimed that all difficulties in Islamic society stemmed from a deviation from the ideals of early Islam. All foreign and other corrupting elements in Egypt had to be eliminated. The *Ikhwan* were equally eager to expel the British but wanted to replace them and the politicians with an uncorrupted Islamic society. They were founded in 1928 by Hasan al-Banna, a gifted religious leader with talents both as preacher and organiser. He quickly built a following and a movement organised under himself as General Guide with nation-wide cells, battalions, youth groups and a secret apparatus for undercover activities. The aims of the Society were clearly stated by al-Banna to his followers:

> You are not a benevolent society, nor a political party, nor a local organization having limited purposes. Rather, you are a new soul in the heart of the nation to give it life by means of the Quran... When asked what it is you propagate, reply that it is Islam, the message of Muhammad, the religion that contains within it government... If you are told that you are political, answer that Islam admits no such distinction.

Islam was seen by the *Ikhwan* as a total system, complete in itself and the final arbiter of life in all its aspects. Banna defined the scope of the movement: 'The idea of the *Ikhwan* includes in it all categories of reform', and they had firm attitudes towards politics, economics, education, the role of women and culture. Reform entailed fighting two kinds of imperialism

– 'external' imperialism, the brute force of the occupying power, and 'internal', those forces which by deliberate neglect of or by indifference towards the needs of the Muslim community served the interests of that power. This 'internal' imperialism spread moral defeat and diverted Egyptians from their traditional faith.

The methods employed by the *Ikhwan* to further their aims were good organisation, propaganda, regular meetings and a militancy which was always inherent in such Islamic movements and rationalised in the concept of *jihad* or struggle against non-believers or opponents. *Jihad* meant both intellectual and physical struggle culminating, if necessary, in death and martyrdom. The secret apparatus was formalised as the instrument for the defence of Islam and the Society. It began to assume the role of defender against the police and the governments of Egypt and to infiltrate the communist movement which the *Ikhwan* considered one of its principal enemies. The Society also attempted ordinary political activity with little success as it was prevented from having its official candidates elected to the parliament. It inspired great devotion amongst its followers and spread amongst most sections of society, the urban middle class, peasants and students. At its peak it had about 2,000 branches with a membership of some 500,000.

Another activist political grouping was that of Young Egypt (*Misr al-Fatah*), a right-wing group founded in 1933 by a lawyer, Ahmad Husain. It became a political party in 1938. It had fascist overtones, its young members being organised in a paramilitary movement, the Green Shirts, who demonstrated against any manifestation of European influence in Egypt. Its programme was similar to that of the *Ikhwan* – no privileges for foreigners, no occupation, Egypt as leader of the Islamic world, the will of the people was God's will. The party largely recruited students in the main towns who were attracted by its militancy, its organisation and its uncompromising stand against the British. It admired Nazi achievements and methods and as German power grew its anti-British tone increased. Together with the *Ikhwan*, Young Egypt were the radicals of Egyptian politics in the period 1945–52 and they even adopted the description of socialist. These two were the movements which some Egyptians hoped would create a new Egypt, cleansed of foreigners and corruption, and a more just Islamic society.

Students at school and university played an active role in politics during the period. Most parties or movements had student or youth sections and universities were a major focus of discontent. Student support was mainly divided between the Wafd and the *Ikhwan*, with communist support given to the former and the *Ikhwan* often joined by Young Egypt. They were all united in their basic demands – evacuation (of the British) and unity of the Nile Valley (Egypt and Sudan). Politics and personalities clashed and on occasion led to internal fighting, but on the whole their efforts were devoted to forming joint committees, formulating demands, leading strikes and demonstrations, burning and rioting and at times attacking British forces. Universities and schools were often closed in retaliation or because their students were on the streets. Many students of the period can relate stories of marching through the streets, hurling stones at property and persons or battling with the police. In the tense atmosphere of the time such events were almost daily occurrences which became less frequent only when examinations were approaching.

The communist movement was small and largely ineffective. There was no large industrial working class to appeal to and the movement was headed by a small number of intellectuals. An attempt was made to create a federation of trade unions but they were themselves weak and without much influence. The Egyptian Communist Party, founded as early as 1922, really emerged after the Second World War. Many of its members served prison sentences and after release in 1949–50 they tried to become active again. The party was, however, split into small factions and, although it played a role in the national struggle, mainly in alliance with other groups, it was hindered by the fact that many of its members came from minority or foreign groups, Greeks, Italians and Jews. The communist in Egypt, as in other Arab countries, also faced the problem of reconciling an ideology based on foreign teaching and conditions with the needs and reality of Egypt, and with the conflicting demands of the Islamic way of life. Communism had a limited appeal, and was considered by its opponents as a European anti-Islamic movement. By 1952, however, the various communist groups claimed several thousand members.

The movement destined to have most impact on the course of Egypt's history was by its very nature compelled to be clandestine – the Free Officers' movement, which was to execute the coup in 1952. Little official attention was paid to this small group of army officers bound together by the conviction that the British had to be expelled from Egypt and the corrupt regime of politicians replaced. They had contacts with other political groups but were not identified with any of those in power nor did they take part in acts of terrorism.

Anglo–Egyptian Dissensions

It is easy with hindsight to see that the years 1945–52 were the end of an era both for Britain and Egypt. For the latter the pressure of those years, with disturbances, tension, extremism, terrorism, the failures of the King and politicians, was something that had eventually to explode. It can now be seen as one of those periods of desperation that inevitably lead to radical change. The British, although they perhaps did not know or did not care to admit it, were fighting a losing battle. Anwar al-Sadat (one of the Free Officers) described the period:

From the national point of view one can say that from May 1945 to July 1952 Egypt lived in terror, with the severest restrictions of the freedoms of meeting, speech and the press. She was in a pre-revolutionary situation. It was one of the saddest periods in her history, when she was to be desolated by a terrible cholera epidemic, and was to have the experience of international isolation, of unpopularity abroad, of defeat and anarchy at home.

Each section of the population participated in and viewed the period according to its own interests and aims. In general it was in the towns that ferment was most obvious and the British presence most irksome. Foreign residents, the richer members of the minorities and the Egyptian upper classes continued to lead a pleasant life, visiting Alexandria and Europe for the summer, spending time in clubs and at the races and on the whole enjoying a higher standard of living than they would elsewhere. Most other Egyptians saw this as corrupt and unjust, a way of life, typified by the behaviour of the King, which was inexcusable given the general poverty of the country. Many intellectuals, doctors, lawyers and teachers, trained in Europe or in Egypt, searched for a solution to the country's problems. All options, violent and non-violent, of European or Islamic origin, seemed open. Discussions in books, newspapers and journals, and verbal, were endless, and few would have disagreed that Egypt had to be set on a new road once British influence had been eliminated. The poorer people of the towns, with little to lose, could easily be brought on to the street to shout slogans, to disrupt and to riot. Even the peasants, traditionally docile and passive, could on occasions become desperate enough to revolt against their exploiters. Novelists and short story writers began to use the poverty-stricken conditions of town and country as material for their work, usually portraying life there as an acceptance of conditions which the poor were powerless to change. The 'soul' of Egypt was sought amongst the long-suffering peasants, perhaps as an antidote to or an escape from the political tensions and the corruption of the city.

The election in 1945 of the Labour government with its professed anti-imperialist leanings encouraged the Egyptians to believe that Britain would change its policy. Ernest Bevin, the Foreign Secretary, had given some cause for hope when he said:

> You need us for your defence; you need us for our technical ability; you need us for many things. We need you too equally...I hope Anglo–Egyptian relationships will never, from today, carry an idea that we are the predominant partner.

> Our foreign policy is a very limited one, and can almost be resolved in these two questions...the question of evacuation by Britain and that of the unity of Egypt and the Sudan under the Egyptian crown,

replied the Egyptians. The Egyptians demanded firstly that Britain should honour its pledge in the 1936 Treaty to move British troops from the cities to the bases on the Suez Canal. They had been retained in the cities during the war as a direct contribution to the British war effort. No Egyptian government could do less than demand their total evacuation from the cities and eventually from the Suez Canal area. The union of Egypt and Sudan under the Egyptian crown became an issue on which the Egyptians took up an entrenched and finally non-negotiable position. Sudan was ostensibly an Anglo–Egyptian condominium, a meaningless concept as the governor general and his political officers were British and in control of the country. The Egyptian argument that Egypt and Sudan were 'one country and one people indivisible, inseparable' was really untenable both historically and in reality. Only a proportion of the Sudanese population spoke Arabic and was Muslim and the two countries had never been united under the Egyptian crown, although parts of the Sudan had been administered by Egypt (or by Egyptians on behalf of the Ottoman Empire) during the nineteenth century. Those with the longest historical memories could point to the Egyptian occupation of the Sudan lasting three hundred years, 2000–1700 BC. Concern over the control of the Nile waters lay at the root of Egyptian interest. Britain was on strong ground in insisting that the Sudanese must be allowed to determine their own future. There was some illogicality in the Egyptian position in insisting on total independence for themselves while denying it to the Sudanese.

The Egyptian Prime Minister, Mahmud Nuqrashi, sent a note to the British government in December 1945 demanding a renegotiation of the 1936 Treaty and the evacuation of British troops, the presence of which was 'wounding to our national dignity'.[3] The British, concerned with the postwar growth of Soviet power, replied that the time was not ripe for renegotiation. The Egyptian people who had heard this argument all too often reacted strongly. The hopes that had reposed in the new Labour government seemed to be dashed. The Egyptian government had failed and the people took to the streets to make their feelings plain. Their cries were: 'No negotiations without evacuation'. There were riots and demonstrations by students and workers in Cairo and Alexandria, which British observers saw as the work of a numerous and malicious hooligan element, but they were clearly more than this. The riots flooded over into attacks on British property and personnel, one of the few ways the ordinary Egyptian could make his real feelings known. In the riots there must also have been an element of adventure and malicious satisfaction amongst the participants in destroying the kind of property that they did not themselves possess. The British were shocked by the violence, demanded that order be restored, and urged the resignation of the prime minister. They insisted that they would not be 'swayed by the actions of irresponsible elements...whose activities if not decisively checked [might] do grave damage to Anglo–Egyptian relations'.

The new Egyptian Prime Minister, Ismail Sidqi, the strong man of the 1930s, now 71 and in poor health, agreed to try once more to come to terms with the British. He let the demonstrations run their course and then clamped down, closing some Wafdist newspapers and arresting some members of Young Egypt. In the face of Wafdist opposition he formed a delegation to enter discussions with the British in Cairo in April 1946. The Wafd, which made impossible conditions for joining the talks, was more interested in gaining power for itself than in helping Sidqi to succeed.

There were some more hopeful signs. Sir Miles Lampson, the tough British Ambassador, was sent in February to the Far East. The British Prime Minister, Clement Attlee, at least paid lip service to the principle that an alliance between Britain and Egypt should be 'as between two equal partners having interests in common'. He seemed to realise that no agreement was possible without Egyptian good will and for this was roundly criticised by Winston Churchill, the leader of the Opposition, and Anthony Eden, the Conservative spokesman on foreign affairs. They stressed above all the importance of the Suez Canal as an imperial lifeline and claimed that the vital interests of Britain and international security would be threatened by British withdrawal from Egypt. Attlee saw more clearly the realities of the situation and agreed to a plan whereby British troops would evacuate Egyptian cities and bases by September 1949.

Sidqi accepted these proposals in the hope that a 'new Chapter was opening in Anglo-Egyptian relations'. He even wrote to *The Times* in May 1946 begging the British to mend their ways and accept Egypt as an equal. His advice was that Britain should 'seek... to safeguard the dignity of Egypt, which would be a guarantee of her friendship and a guarantee of peace, rather than to remain rooted in the out-of-date and barren conceptions of a past age and a policy forever outworn'. But the two sides remained far apart and the Wafd continued to object to any kind of concession and stirred up public feelings against the negotiations. There were attacks against British troops and installations. The British, nevertheless, went ahead with the evacuations, the most symbolic being the departure from the Citadel in Cairo on 4 July.

By September the negotiations had come to a halt as the Egyptians insisted on an immediate total British withdrawal and on the unity of the Nile Valley. Although Sidqi appeared to favour a negotiated settlement he could not convince the members of his delegation and resigned in September. No other politician was able to form a government and he returned to continue negotiations with Ernest Bevin in London. Some agreement was reached but a draft treaty referred to the Sudan as being prepared for self-government rather than unity with Egypt. Sidqi, unable to fight any longer, resigned in December and was succeeded by Nuqrashi.

The Wafd had been Sidqi's main political opponents, the *Ikhwan* the most stridently active. Their journal encouraged all Egyptians to teach their children to 'detest and anathematize the British Empire, so that the British will be confronted with hearts that hate, tongues that curse, and hands that kill'. A British observer in Cairo could not understand this dislike. He wrote:

It is difficult to understand why these men should wish to make enemies of Egypt. British friendship is vital to Egypt... This does not suit the nationalists, who bear a heavy responsibility for *warping* the minds of the younger generation of Egyptians with distorted history and misrepresentation... Unfortunately, not enough Egyptians who realise the dangers, have the courage to take a firm stand against a comparatively small body of troublemakers.

This kind of reporting did not help to improve Anglo—Egyptian relations. The assumption that 'true' Egyptians needed British friendship and that opposition came only from a handful of 'troublemakers' misled the British reader.

Nuqrashi presided over a further period of disorder. The *Ikhwan* called for strikes and a full *jihad* (war) against the British. The government responded by closing down the more extreme organisations and arrested some left-wing intellectuals and some of the *Ikhwan*. In the prevailing atmosphere of unrest and opposition Nuqrashi found it impossible to negotiate and in August 1947 he referred the question of the Sudan to the United Nations. His arguments *against* the 1936 Treaty were strong (it was a 'form of subordination... a relationship which is both unbalanced and undignified'); *for* union with the Sudan less so (Sudan and Egypt were 'one country, geographically, ethnically, culturally, politically'). The UN, then as later, had neither the will nor the power to act and was moreover dominated by the large powers. Britain had withdrawn her troops to the Canal Zone and appeared in a favourable light. The matter was left on the agenda without a decision. Feeling was intense over this 'failure'; Nuqrashi was blamed; the British were blamed. There were more demonstrations and strikes. Newspapers called for the formation of guerrillas to harass British individuals, to kidnap them, flog them in public and blow up their homes. In September/October an outbreak of cholera was even blamed on the British for lax quarantine and for using outdated vaccine.

The Palestinian Factor

At this point another dimension to Egyptian politics has to be considered. March 1945 had seen the foundation of the League of Arab States as a body to co-ordinate Arab policies. Egypt played a central role in the League since its foundation. The headquarters were in Cairo and its secretaries-general Egyptian.[4] Its first secretary-general, Azzam, believed that the unity of the Arab world could only be achieved under Egyptian leadership. Nothing has caused more dissension or disunity in the Arab world than the search for unity. All Arab states hold the deep and sincere belief that the Arab world is one, united by language, culture, history and religion. All attempts to achieve practical unity (except the union of the small shaikhdoms in the Gulf) have to date foundered on disputes over policies, ideologies, rivalries and personalities. There is still a common conviction that the European powers destroyed the natural basis for unity by occupation and the imposition of mandates, treaties and boundaries.

Most Arabs also consider the State of Israel to be a Western creation and an alien disruptive growth in Arab territory. In Europe in the late nineteenth century the Zionist movement had developed. It was a Jewish nationalist movement which claimed that Palestine was a Jewish country and encouraged all Jews to migrate there. In November 1917 the British government under Zionist pressure had agreed to issue the Balfour Declaration, which viewed with favour the establishment in Palestine of a national home for the Jewish people, and the British undertook to help to achieve it on the understanding that the rights of the existing (Arab) population would not be infringed. The Arab population was not consulted about this policy and naturally rejected it and from that moment on the Arab world tried in vain to discourage and evict the growing number of Jewish settlers. In 1919 the British government further accepted the mandate for Palestine from the League of Nations in which it undertook both to fulfil the Balfour Declaration and to prepare the country for independence. The next twenty-eight years saw a series of doomed British attempts to accommodate the claims of both Jews and Arabs to inhabit and govern the same small country. By 1947 Britain admitted that it could no longer keep the Arabs and Jews from each others' throats and announced its intention of quitting Palestine. In September the Arab League decided to resist by force a United Nations plan for the partition of the country. Egypt fully backed this decision, yet was in no position to face its consequences.

When Britain terminated the mandate in May 1948 Egypt sent troops into Palestine to try to expel the Jewish settlers. Although the King and public opinion were in favour, the army was ill prepared and had no plan of co-ordination with other Arab states. Thus began the nightmare of Egypt's relationship with Israel which led to four wars, an intolerable military budget, a distortion of politics and a deep psychological wound. The Egyptian army was defeated by an enemy much inferior in numbers and initially in equipment. Although there were cases of heroic resistance and Egypt held on to a strip of territory round Gaza in Southern Palestine, nothing could disguise the defeat. There were scandals over inferior equipment and the King and government were blamed for treacherously letting down the army, in which there developed an intense feeling of shame. The ground was immensely fertile for the growth of a resistance movement.

Black Saturday

Likewise, the *Ikhwan*, whose volunteer squads had fought well in a *jihad* to prevent the Muslim land of Palestine falling into the hands of Jewish non-believers, gained in popularity and adherents. They were continuing the age-old struggle to protect the Islamic world against non-Muslim encroachment. The reaction in Egypt to the defeat was intensified by the hopes that the press had raised before the war. There were disturbances in Cairo against Jewish and foreign inhabitants, encouraged by members of the *Ikhwan*. Nuqrashi ordered the suppression of the movement which retaliated late in 1948 by assassinating him. His successor, Ibrahim Abdel Hadi, confronted the *Ikhwan* and detained thousands of them and members of the *Fatah* and communist groups in concentration camps. In February 1949 Hasan al-Banna was himself assassinated, probably by agents of the security branch of the government. Certainly the government was happy to see him go. Egypt became quieter for a time although with none of its problems solved. The King and a minority government were disliked by all the radical movements, by the Wafd and the army. Farouk continued his heedless course of political and personal corruption. It was singularly unfortunate for Egypt that when it most needed strong and efficient leadership Farouk was King, probably the worst of Muhammad Ali's line.

Abdel Hadi brought calm to the country and began to criticise the King's activities. This was not welcome. Farouk demanded his resignation and called for an election It was believed that the Wafd would win and co-operate with the King in ruling the country The British also thought that Nahhas as Wafdist prime minister might be more co-operative. In January 1950 the Wafd was re-elected as most people expected, although with a minority of the votes cast. The new government did attempt some social reform and was popular in the countryside because the Korean war brought a boom in cotton prices. But Nahhas's main effort was still directed toward enforcing a British evacuation. Field Marshal Slim, the hero of the war against the Japanese in Burma, was sent in June to emphasise the importance of the Egyptian role in regional security and the necessity of maintaining British troops in the Canal Zone. The British government showed some clumsiness in sending a soldier to convince the Egyptians that they had a role to play in Great Power security pacts. The Cold War of the time was not a struggle in which they were interested, and they would never be convinced that the presence of foreign troops could be anything other than 'a sort of occupation and incomplete sovereignty'.

In August the British Ambassador, Sir Ralph Stevenson, continued talks in which he stressed that Britain could never run the risk of the Suez Canal being closed. Eventually, in 1951, Britain offered a new treaty by which troops would be withdrawn by 1956 if Egypt accepted a number of defence arrangements and agreed to keep the Sudan as a separate issue. The offer was totally rejected, both because the withdrawal appeared to be conditional and because of Egyptian insistence on unity with Sudan. The talks collapsed and in October Nahhas put before parliament decrees abrogating unilaterally the Anglo-Egyptian Treaty and proclaiming Farouk King of Egypt and Sudan.

It was election time in Britain. The Tories were eager to resume power under Churchill. There was still a number of them who saw the world in terms of an earlier period and earlier British power. When Prime Minister, Churchill spoke of maintaining 'our *rightful* position in the Canal Zone'. Even the Labour Foreign Secretary, Herbert Morrison, had accused Egypt of 'uncompromising insistence on demands which bear no relation to present day realities'. The British were loath to admit that Egypt had the right to determine its own policies without interference from Westminster, that is until they were forced into the admission. There followed the most bitter period of tension with the Egyptians.

On 16 October 1951, the Egyptian parliament approved the abrogation of the treaty. There was an exultant mood in Egypt. Newspapers proclaimed: 'King and people break the fetters of British imperialism'; 'The helpless and hungry Egyptian horse tied to the British chariot and whipped on by a relentless and cruel driver has been freed'; 'Egyptians feel that they are free in their country and have the incontrovertible right to self-determination'. It was an act of defiance which uplifted Egyptian hearts. A state of emergency was proclaimed. Britain strengthened its troop concentrations on the Canal. The Wafd government gave way to pressure from the *Ikhwan* and leftist groups actively to oppose the British. They allowed the formation of 'Liberation Battalions' (terrorists in British eyes) and student groups. The *Ikhwan* (who were to some extent rehabilitated) and the *Bulac al-Nizam* (the auxiliary police) were given arms. The scene was set for confrontation. Food supplies to the Canal Zone were blocked and Egyptian labour was withdrawn from the Base. British troops felt under threat, although they were ordered only to protect themselves and not to provoke incidents. On occasions they overreacted to great provocation and took strong retaliatory action. Defence was viewed in terms of offensive prevention. The British commander, General Erskine, explained to his troops:

> Our job is clear. We stand on our rights. We are not going to be forced out or knocked out...With public excitement at its present level, I

must warn you that hostile and criminal elements of the population may try to attack individuals and small parties. You must be
ready to protect yourself and go to the help of your comrades
if attacked.

There were numerous occasions when clashes occurred and lives were lost,
although many Egyptian accusations of British misbehaviour were exaggerated. Two incidents provoked especial revulsion amongst Egyptians.

In December British bulldozers and Centurion tanks 'bulldozed 50
Egyptian mud houses out of the way' to open a road for the British army
to a water supply. The operation was carried out by the soldiers, according
to a British reporter, with 'their customary nonchalance'! On 25 January
1952 the police barracks at Ismailiya were attacked when its occupants
refused to surrender to British troops. The police in the barracks were
ordered by Cairo to resist the British tanks. The building was shattered
and fifty killed and a hundred wounded. The reporter now did not write
of nonchalance:

It was a sobering and disturbing sight to see the enormous firepower
of a modern military force turned upon a barracks full of policemen
who had mixed motives in resisting so strongly − motives in which
patriotism and other honourable feelings have their place.

He seemed to acknowledge that perhaps the Egyptians had a case, although
with qualifications:

Most of the *fellahin* fighters belong to the simplest class of Egyptian,
a class whose good qualities can too easily be diverted by unscrupulous
men to malicious purposes.

The attack at Ismailiya is typical of the tragedy that occurs entirely
unsought by both sides. The British soldiers were obeying orders, their
commanders giving the orders they believed necessary. The Egyptian
police resisted with the utmost bravery, motivated by patriotism and
obeying their orders, convinced that their stand was significant and necessary. In fact their resistance can be said to have directly changed the
immediate course of Egyptian history.

Egyptians were incensed by the incident. A group of police in Cairo
mutinied in protest against the death of their colleagues. They marched
to the royal palace. At the same time groups of people in Cairo began
to go on the rampage. This was the beginning of Black Saturday, 26
January 1952. At the end of that day over 750 establishments had been
burned or destroyed at an estimated value of more than £50 million, at
least thirty people were dead including eleven British and other foreigners,
and hundreds injured. The exact responsibility for the riots has never been

determined, although the British Embassy had few doubts. In its note to the Egyptian Ministry of Foreign Affairs it stated:

> Little or nothing was done by the police to prevent these outrages, the perpetrators of which were well organized and led in circumstances which strongly indicates official connivance. The British [Turf] Club was surrounded by a savage mob under organized leadership which broke into the premises... In all ten British subjects... were killed. Elsewhere gangs of fire raisers deliberately and wantonly attacked British commercial premises... The responsibility of the Egyptian Government... is rendered even greater by the fact that, until the Egyptian Army was summoned to the scene late in the day, the authorities made little or no attempt to restrain the rioters and, in some cases, the police even assisted them. There must have been official connivance otherwise why was the police guard at the Turf Club suddenly and deliberately reduced from 40 to 4 at a time when there was a high state of tension in the city?

The British could do little more than complain. An Egyptian government report accused the Wafd Minister of the Interior, Sirag el-Din, of negligence and stated that national sentiment should not have disrupted police security. If the Ismailiya incident was a main cause of the rioting there could not have been too much advance planning. The main thrust of the attacks was on British property – Shepheards Hotel, BOAC, Barclays Bank, Cooks, British car showrooms – but the mob went beyond these. Other symbols of the Western presence and, in the eyes of the *Ikhwan*, decadence, were also attacked – cafés, cinemas, bars, luxury shops. Organised or not, encouraged or not, Black Saturday was an outburst of frustrated fury, vented on the symbols of that frustration. It was the culmination of seventy years' impatience.

The next six months were only an interlude before revolution. Black Saturday was the death spasm of the monarchical regime. Farouk dismissed Nahhas and four prime ministers held office in six months. There seemed to be some attempt to restore order. Perhaps both sides realised they had gone too far. Martial law was proclaimed. The Liberation Battalions were withdrawn. The British troops withdrew to their bases. The British government even released some blocked Egyptian funds in London. But there appeared to be no real means of governing Egypt. The King's reputation fell lower. He had blocked inquiries into the Palestine disaster. The palace was full of intrigue and corruption. The Wafd had failed and Farouk had difficulty in forming new governments. Many politicians believed that he was so unstable it was useless attempting to govern, and the King was looking for a new minister of war who would root out the plotters he suspected in the army. On 22 July the Free Officers realised that Farouk might be drawing the net in around them.

They decided to strike and by the next morning seized power. Farouk was forced to abdicate. He sailed into exile on 24 July on the same yacht on which his grandfather Ismail had left for exile some seventy years earlier.

3 The First Years of the New Government: 1952-1956

Nasser's Early Life

The real leader of the Free Officers and the leader of Egypt for the next eighteen years was Gamal Abdel Nasser.[5] His father came from a small village in Upper Egypt and was a clerk in the postal service. In 1915 he moved to Alexandria where on 15 January 1918 his first son Gamal was born. The father moved several times during his son's early childhood and at the age of 7 Gamal was sent to Cairo to live with his uncle and to attend school there. He also spent some time in the family village where he became acquainted with the everyday life of the Egyptian peasant. His village was a microcosm of rural society. His family belonged to the middle layer of small proprietors and tenants, a class largely dominated by others yet from which there was some outward movement into the towns and cities through education and government employment. This class gave Nasser both his roots in the Egyptian countryside and his escape into another world.

In Cairo he went to a school in an old quarter of the city near the Azhar mosque, Khan al-Khalili, where he was able to experience at first hand the life of the bustling crowded quarters of Cairo, the other aspect of poverty in Egypt. During this early period of his life he greatly missed his mother and was deeply disturbed when he learned that she had died during their separation. He did not approve of his father's early remarriage and the resulting disillusion strengthened his independence and perhaps his introspection. It may also have implanted in him a mistrust of others which he retained for the rest of his life. He was from then on known for his serious and thoughtful nature.

After an interval with his family in Alexandria he entered *al-Nahda* (fittingly 'the reawakening') school in Cairo. He spent five decisive years from 1933–8 in the city mixing study with militant activity and demonstrating both against the British presence and Egyptian politicians. He was exposed to all the political currents of the time, including the Wafd, Young Egypt, and the National Party. He felt personally and with adolescent intensity the problems of Egypt, perhaps more intensely than his fellows. He called these days 'feverish' and a period of boiling over. 'The present situation is critical...We are just about to bid life farewell and meet death. Despair is a solid structure; and who is to demolish it?' he wrote in *The Philosophy of the Revolution*, a partly autobiographical work. A serious youth, he began to internalise the problems of his country, following the pattern of those future leaders who seem to bear within themselves all the problems of their society. He was also searching for a

pattern for his own life. Was he to be an activist, a leader himself, or
would he find someone worthy of following? He wrote:

> The truth, however, is I did not feel at ease within myself...I had
> within me a feeling of distraction which was a mixture of complex
> and intermingled factors; of patriotism, religion, compassion, cruelty,
> faith, suspicion, knowledge and ignorance.

He admired the Wafd centred around Nahhas; he occasionally marched
with Young Egypt. He believed at the time 'The Egyptian only needs a
leader who will lead him to battle'. He was sure, moreover, that the
seeds of revolt were growing in him, impelling him to respond to political
pressures.

He marched in demonstrations against the British in November 1935
and was wounded by a bullet fired by British troops. He was identified
as an agitator by the police and asked to leave his school. After a few
months in 1936 as a law student his sense of disillusion with the politicians who had 'surrendered' to the British by signing the 1936 Treaty
and with what he considered the indifference of his fellow students, led
him to join the army, which he saw as the only body capable of changing
the country. He had made his first important decision, abandoning study
for the more active life of the army. He had chosen a pattern for his
life.

In 1936 the Egyptian army opened its officer corps to sons of the
middle and lower classes. Nasser was a member of the second entry of
such men, an officer cadet at the age of 19 in the Abbasiya Military
Academy. He was attracted to the discipline and study of military life
and was quickly promoted. He later wrote: 'Throughout my life I have
had faith in militarism'. Of his future companions in the revolution he
met Abdel Hakim Amir in the Academy, and Zakariya Muhyidin and
Anwar Sadat in his first posting to Upper Egypt. It is difficult to maintain
that their plotting began at once, but being of similar age and background
they were united in their disrespect and even contempt for their senior
officers. They spent many nights discussing the problems of Egypt. Sadat
gives an interesting picture of Nasser at that time:

> My impression was that he was a serious-minded youth who did not
> share his fellows' interest in jesting; nor would he allow anyone to be
> frivolous with him as this, he felt, would be an insult to his dignity.
> Most of my colleagues, therefore, kept their distance from him...he
> had obviously erected an almost insuperable barrier between himself
> and other people.

The German successes in Libya and Egypt in 1940–1 in the Second
World War led some Egyptian officers to see in the Axis their saviours

from British occupation. Sadat actively supported the Germans but Nasser stayed aloof from making any approaches. The anger of all of them was aroused by Lampson's ultimatum to Farouk in 1942. The army felt humiliated. Nasser was ashamed that it had taken no action:

> What is to be done now that the catastrophe has befallen us, and after we have accepted it, surrendered to it and taken it submissively and meekly. I really believe Imperialism is playing a one-card game in order to threaten only. If ever it knew that there were Egyptians ready to shed blood and to meet force by force it would withdraw and recoil like a harlot [a strange simile?] ... That event had a new influence on the spirit and feeling of the army and ourselves... they all repented; they did not intervene... But let us wait. Tomorrow will soon he here.

Thus wrote Nasser to a friend in February 1942. The event which bit deep into his spirit was something he later avenged.

He remained on the sidelines of the war and in 1943 was appointed instructor at the Military Academy. During his time there he was able to make contact with a number of younger Egyptians, like him fired with the aim of liberating and reforming the country. The period after the Second World War until the revolution of 1952 was, as we have seen, one of ferment and tension. Even a personality less politically sensitive than Nasser could not have remained unaffected. He was in a sense torn between his position as staff officer and his interest in 'revolutionary' movements. He was introduced to Marxism, to the *Ikhwan* (by Sadat), and to the left wing of the Wafd. At the same time a group of officers, including Nasser, Sadat, Amir, and one or two others, began to meet regularly. These Free Officers (*al-Dubbat al-Ahrar*) did not yet coalesce as a movement. They had in common not an ideology but a common determination to reform Egypt. Nasser emerged as prime instigator, while he was working out within himself a fusion between the organising staff officer and the future revolutionary leader sampling all ideologies.

It was the war in Palestine which decisively placed the Free Officers on course toward revolution. Nasser was commanding officer of a unit of the Egyptian army which moved into Palestine. He was immediately dismayed by the inefficiency and the lack of preparation of the Egyptians who were fighting against greatly inferior numbers. The slaughter distressed him and he was himself wounded in the chest. In the battle for the Negev desert which began in October 1948 Nasser and his unit were trapped at Falluja near Beersheba and together with several other Free Officers held out against Israeli forces and were eventually able to counterattack. In retrospect he saw this episode as a symbol of a determination to pursue the real fight against all those forces which oppressed Egypt. 'We were fighting in Palestine but our dreams were in Egypt'. As they sat in the trenches they discussed endlessly how to free their country. They fought the Jews and even admired and envied their successful bid to oust the British from Palestine. Nasser became known for his part in the Falluja battle. A general also made his name for heroism in the war — Mohammed Neguib.

The army returned home bitter in defeat. The Free Officers, determined to begin the real struggle, began to meet in earnest, issuing propaganda denouncing the King, the regime and the army, infiltrating the government, and making contact with other organisations. Nine of them met in 1949 to constitute the Committee of the Free Officers' Movement. Nasser was elected chairman in 1950 and he was apparently from an early date able to direct these diverse activities and to inspire the loyalty of his colleagues. Although the Free Officers played a certain part in issuing arms and training commandos to fight the British during the Canal Zone clashes in 1951, it was largely students and the *Ikhwan* who bore the brunt of the fighting. Nasser was biding his time, conserving his energies.

First Years of Revolution, 1952–6

It is not clear what part, if any, the officers played in planning and executing the burning of Cairo in January 1952. Did Nasser again hold his hand? Did the staff officer abstain from such haphazard actions which were not directly under his control? The virtual collapse of government after January with five changes of prime minister put more urgency into the planning of the Free Officers. They had earlier clashed with the King over elections to the Army Officer Club. Traditionally the King's candidates had been unopposed but in December 1951 the Free Officers put forward their own candidates, including General Neguib for president. This infuriated Farouk and deepened his suspicions of the loyalty of the army. In early July the King and court left for Alexandria and two army units known to be favourable to the Officers were to move into Cairo on 19 July. On 20 July the Officers learned that Farouk was finally intending to arrest some of them. Nasser was meeting his friends at the time and they decided to act at once. He had, as an efficient staff officer, carefully drawn up a plan which was put into operation almost flawlessly. It followed the classical lines of an army takeover. Armoured cars encircled the military area at Abbasiya in Cairo, tanks took up position at strategic points, Sadat and assistants took over the radio station, and some twelve generals were arrested. The army and city passed into their hands with hardly a shot fired.

The figurehead behind the coup was the most respected general in the army, Mohammed Neguib, who had distinguished himself in Palestine. He was older than the other officers and the man behind whom they sheltered as a symbol of maturity and respectability. As he was older he did not have a very close rapport with them and he was more prepared to compromise. He was used by Nasser for a time but was never the real power behind the movement. He was given the position of commander-in-chief and president of the Revolutionary Command Council (RCC).

The coup was announced in the name of the army on behalf of the whole of Egypt, not of a party, a revolutionary mass movement, or an ideology. The army's first aim was to purify itself and the government of corrupt elements; apart from that no firm plans had been made. At first Ali Mahir, a previous prime minister and friend of Farouk, was asked to head the government. The most important immediate decision concerned the future of the King. The more fiery officers wanted to execute him. Nasser saw him as an already dishonoured figure, power-less and pathetic, and did not wish to make him a martyr. His will prevailed and on 26 July Neguib, after a tremendous popular welcome in Alexandria, handed Ali Mahir an ultimatum to be given to Farouk: 'The army, representing the will of the people, requires Your Majesty to abdicate ... and to leave the country this same day'. By 6 o'clock the King was boarding the royal yacht with his queen and 6-month-old son (declared king in his place) to leave Egypt for ever.[6]

Nasser, behind the genial figure of Neguib and the cloak of the politician Ali Mahir, now had power. He had to learn to utilise it. None of the Free Officers had had any previous political experience and they had to construct a role for themselves to justify their seizure of power and to legitimise their regime. (Their search for this legitimisation and for an ideology is discussed in Chapter 5.) It was a rather long-term process. There were more immediate problems involved in the day-to-day running of the country. The first broadcast after the coup on 23 July contained no precise announcement of goals or plans. It merely informed Egyptians that the army had acted on their behalf to 'cleanse the nation of tyrants and to reform the constitutional life of the country'.

It seemed at first that the army would return to its barracks once it had 'cleansed' the nation and put it on a different course. But power is magnetic and not easily relinquished. Ali Mahir naturally wanted civilian government and soon clashed with the Free Officers, who had not decided in their own minds the future form of government. He resigned in September and Neguib took the offices of prime minister, war minister, commander-in-chief and chairman of the RCC. Nasser played a rather clever game in the RCC. There had been an intense debate over whether to install a dictatorship or to stick to 'democracy'. On a vote seven officers voted for dictatorship, and one – Nasser – cunningly and insincerely (?) for democracy. He thereupon resigned and went home after warning of the dangers of dictatorship. The remaining officers immediately realised their loss and went to bring him back. He returned in an obviously much stronger position.

The regime's first declared objective had been the expulsion of the

British and negotiations began immediately over the evacuation of the Canal Zone. The direction of domestic policy was established by the agrarian reform law of September by which no one was permitted to hold more than 200 feddans (1 feddan = 1·0368 acres) of land. Thirdly, the regime set about eliminating possible opposition, the Wafd and the *Ikhwan*. In January 1953 all parties were dissolved and a mass organisation, the Liberation Rally, launched in an attempt to fill the vacuum between the people and the regime. In June the monarchy was abolished and the Republic of Egypt established. Neguib became president and prime minister, Nasser deputy prime minister and other officers took over key ministries. Direct military rule was established with the civilian and parliamentary government dismantled, although as often under military regimes a speedy return to civilian rule was promised.

The time had now come for Nasser to show his mettle. Although he had been the power behind the RCC he had allowed the limelight to fall on Neguib. A decisive split came over the future form of government in Egypt. In February 1954 some of the dissident political groupings, especially the *Ikhwan*, were coming out into the open. Neguib seemed receptive to a return to the earlier system of government and was suspected of siding with the *Ikhwan* and others, possibly hoping for greater personal power with their support. He did not realise that he could only have succeeded with the full support of the army, or that the thoughts of the Free Officers were moving in different directions. Although he was popular with the people, this was not a sufficient basis for power. Nasser and most of the Free Officers forced Neguib to resign on 23 February. But this was followed by demonstrations of popular support for Neguib and the threat of a split in the army. Nasser had made his move before purging all pro-Neguib elements from the army, and he did not possess sufficient organised support amongst the urban masses.

Neguib returned temporarily as prime minister only nine days later. Nasser was now able to demonstrate his ability. Unreliable officers (including the leftist Khalid Muhyidin) were exiled or imprisoned. The Liberation Rally was used as an organisation to persuade students and trade union members to demonstrate against a return to parliamentary life and against the *Ikhwan* and other dissident groups. There were demonstrations in Alexandria and Cairo and a general strike – proof that the Liberation Rally was in control. The armed forces expressed support for the RCC. Finally, after some manoeuvring, the RCC announced on 28 March the indefinite postponement of elections for a constituent assembly. Anti-RCC demonstrations were dispersed and on 18 April Nasser once more became prime minister with a cabinet that contained most of the leading Free Officers.

Institutionalised military rule had begun in Egypt. Nasser, who had shown his ability to outwit and outmanoeuvre his opponents, had decisively won the struggle. There was no one strong enough to oppose him.

To complete his ascendency he had finally to demolish political opposition and equally importantly to establish himself in the eyes of the people of Egypt as their *natural* leader. He had to forge that bond which unites a leader with his people. He attacked the weaker political parties first, the Wafd and others, by depriving their leaders of political rights for ten years. He silenced critical journalists, he purged student agitators and moved against *Misr al-Fatah*, the irony being obvious in his moves against the latter two groups. He left his main opponents, the *Ikhwan*, for a final showdown. They had considerable support in the country and were still propagating an extremist line.

Despite his internal preoccupations, Nasser made an effort to settle the British question. The Sudan problem had been settled by Britain and Egypt agreeing in February 1953 on self-government for the country which would within three years determine what form of association with Egypt it would have, if any. (The Sudanese parliament unanimously declared the Sudan an independent republic in December 1955 and this had to be accepted by Egypt.) The British government had to establish a new relationship with the Free Officers. The young, eager and inexperienced men were a different proposition from the King and the older politicians. The British did not know the new men and were not sure where the real power lay. Anthony Eden, British Foreign Secretary, did not have much faith in Neguib:

> His powers of leadership were... doubtful and I was disturbed to notice that in his earlier meetings with our Ambassador... he was never alone and did not appear to lead his side. There were risks in any course. General Neguib was at least a better bet than either King or Wafd.

The British made it plain from the beginning that they would not interfere on behalf of the King nor take any action unless British lives were threatened. Some goodwill was shown on both sides, although when the British government had announced in September 1952 that there was no strategic alternative to the maintenance of the base in the Canal Zone, Neguib had countered that 'we can make the United Kingdom evacuate its forces'. Eden described him as a 'constant irritant' and replied that negotiations could only proceed if he stopped his threats.

Eden was locked into his pre-war mentality of threats, capitulation and blackmail. In his opinion Egypt had to fit into a regional defence system and agreement on this point would have to precede any withdrawal from the Canal: 'If we were to evacuate the Canal Zone before making a Middle East defence arrangement we should be exposing ourselves to Egyptian blackmail', he wrote to Churchill. A man who thought in these terms could not have had much sympathy with the nationalist aspirations of the Free Officers. In America he discussed the future of Egypt with President

Eisenhower as though Egypt was still a country on whom the West could impose its will. Eisenhower was not of the same mould as Eden who criticised the President for being unprepared 'to put any pressure upon the Egyptians'. Britain was left to continue negotiations alone (although the Americans made unofficial approaches to Nasser). The beginning of Eden's hatred of Nasser can now be seen. He wrote in his memoirs of Neguib's 'restrained and civilized' policies being slowly overcome by Nasser and the Officers and of their Gestapo methods — a revealing and inappropriate phrase.

Despite these hard words Britain and Egypt were moving closer together in their positions. Egypt would only discuss evacuation and eventual administration of the Base. The British slowly began to realise the drawbacks of holding on to the Base against Egypt's will. Some compromise seemed possible. In January 1954 Nasser, still feeling his way and not yet totally alienated from the West, proclaimed that: 'the last obstacle is that the English now claim the right to keep uniformed technicians on the Base, which would symbolize, in the people's eyes, the perpetuation of the hated occupation'. Eden grudgingly admitted that the new regime seemed 'free of some of the vices of the Wafd' and that an 'agreement seemed to our advantage and worth a trial'.

In October 1954 an agreement was signed by Nasser and Anthony Nutting of the British Foreign Office, by which all British troops would be withdrawn from the Base within twenty months with the provision that it could be re-activated in the event of an attack by an outside power on an Arab League state or on Turkey. Eden saw that 'defence arrangements must be based on consent and co-operation' and Nasser called the agreement:

> the biggest single achievement in Egypt's national aspirations to date. We want to get rid of hatred in our hearts and start building up our relations with Britain on a solid basis of mutual trust and confidence, which has been lacking for the past 70 years.

Britain had finally relinquished her role in Egypt. An Egyptian newspaper commented:

> Time will give the British the opportunity to understand Egypt under her new regime...We hope that the coming days will establish that British mentality has completely changed, that the conduct of British statesmen has altered towards not only Egypt but also the Arab peoples in general.

These high hopes were to be shattered less than two years later.

It seemed also, however, that Nasser had compromised himself. He had achieved the British evacuation but had committed Egypt to Western defence interests. The agreement had a mixed reception amongst the Egyptian people. There was an enthusiastic welcome for the 'end of imperialism' yet Nasser had on several occasions to meet his critics who accused him of merely rewriting the old treaty. The chief critics were the communists and the *Ikhwan* who rather strangely condemned him for agreeing to the evacuation 'without a struggle'. The *Ikhwan* continued to foment opposition, provoking riots and calling for an end to the military regime.

On 26 October Nasser was addressing a large crowd in the main square of Alexandria justifying the signing of the agreement when at 6.30 p.m. several shots were fired by Mahmud Abdel Latif, a member of the *Ikhwan*. A light bulb above him was shattered and several people injured. Nasser was unhurt and was heard shouting: 'If I die, you are all Gamal Abdel Nassers'. Later that same evening Nasser and his colleagues made other speeches. The theme was that his escape was proof of the 'prosperity Heaven desires for Egypt'. A leader's prestige can be immeasurably strengthened if he 'miraculously survives' an assassination attempt. In Nasser's case it was confirmation of his role as leader and the real beginning of the bond between him and the people. On the following day he deliberately exposed himself to crowds in Alexandria, at stations en route to Cairo and in the capital. He was met by a reported 200,000 in Cairo and others followed him to the headquarters of the Liberation Rally. He was becoming a leader of the people able to marshal the masses behind him.

The *Ikhwan* had gone too far. Despite their valuable role in fighting the British and their undoubted sincerity, there could be no possibility of co-existence with the army regime. Their leaders were arrested, six executed including the would-be assassin, and thousands of others thrown into prison. The death sentence on their Supreme Guide was commuted to life imprisonment by the RCC. The ideas of the *Ikhwan* have remained potent in Egyptian society as indeed they must in any Islamic environment where there remains a fundamentalist current and the strong appeal of a return to a pure Islamic society. They are both an active answer to contemporary problems and a passive retreat away from contemporary difficulties. Unfortunately, their solution is usually unworkable in the context of actual politics and the fundamentalist nature of the message often leads to extreme actions and a blank refusal to co-operate.

Until the end of 1954, Nasser had been fighting for power and position in a personal struggle to emerge from the strict, rather distant staff officer into the populist revolutionary leader and in an effort to find his role in Egypt and Egypt's role in the world. As he himself wrote:

The annals of history are full of heroes who carved for themselves great and heroic roles and played them on momentous occasions on the stage. History is also charged with great heroic roles which do not find actors to play them on the stage. I do not know why I always

imagine that in this region in which we live there is a role wandering
aimlessly about seeking an actor to play it. I do not know why this
role ... should at last settle down, weary and worn out, on our frontiers
beckoning us to move, to dress up for it and to perform it since there
is nobody else who can do so.

These are the words of a man who seemingly with reluctance took up the
role on behalf of Egypt. It was certainly a role that Nasser grew into,
gradually forging and tightening the bond first between himself and the
Egyptians and then with the wider Arab world. Once his position in Egypt
was firmly established he was able to look and to venture abroad.

It was, ironically, the British who first drew him into the wider Arab
world. It was the period of pacts directed against Russia and we have seen
how Britain vainly attempted to draw Egypt into an alliance. The North
Atlantic and the South East Asia Treaty Organisations faced Russia from
two sides; the Baghdad Pact brought into alliance Britain, Turkey, Iran,
Pakistan and Iraq to complete the chain. Nasser, perhaps guilty over his
compromise agreement with Britain, reacted angrily when Nuri Said, the
Iraqi premier, brought his country into the Pact. He felt that the West
was trying to bypass him by shifting the focus of power from Cairo to
Baghdad, using the Iraqis as their stalking horse. Whereas the West looked
at the Pact in terms of defence against the Soviet Union, Nasser saw it in
terms of the Arab world — which countries would join the Pact, which
follow Egypt's lead and remain outside? The action of Jordan was crucial.
The Kingdom of Jordan under King Husain was related to Iraq by ties
of blood. Its ruler, King Faisal, was Husain's cousin. Nasser believed that
Jordan with a British general, Sir John Glubb, leading its army, was under
Western influence and he tried to bring the country into his orbit. He thus
entered Arab politics.

Anthony Eden met Nasser in Cairo in February 1955 to attempt to
persuade him to join the Pact. Nasser told him that 'by its bad timing and
unfortunate content, it had seriously set back the development of effective
collaboration with the West by the Arab states'. The two men disagreed,
and although Nasser tried to console Eden by pointing to an improvement
in Anglo-Egyptian relations, the British Foreign Secretary urged him to
restrain his criticisms of the Pact and sourly commented in private: 'No
doubt jealousy plays a part in this and a frustrated desire to lead the Arab
world'. This underlined Eden's total lack of sympathy with the Egyptian
leader, who far from restraining his criticism allowed the Voice of the
Arabs radio to broadcast the strongest propaganda against the Pact,
denouncing Nuri for his 'betrayal of Arabism' and for accepting 'imperialist
alliances ... The cause of Arabism will only be victorious so long as Arabs
maintain their vigilance against imperialism and its stooges'.

Nasser continued to react strongly against British pressure whenever
he felt his position was threatened or his dignity offended. Both sides were

led by obstinate men. Eden could not see that his policies were designed for situations that no longer existed and bore the illusion that Britain could organise the Arab world in its interest against Egyptian opposition. The new British Ambassador, Humphrey Trevelyan, who established a working relationship with Nasser, was put in an almost impossible position by the policies he was obliged to propound. Some politicians believed that the declining British position in Egypt was symptomatic of the decline of the British Empire as a whole and that therefore no weakness should be shown to Nasser. Trevelyan wrote percipiently: 'In the Middle East the British never saw the writing on the wall until they hit their heads against it'. Official relations deteriorated through 1955 until the crisis of July 1956 was reached.

While Nasser was finding his feet with the British and in the Arab world, he found support elsewhere. He first met President Tito of Yugoslavia in February 1955 and immediately admired the man who had stood up to a far more powerful state than Britain – Stalin's Russia. Tito had survived by aligning himself neither with the West nor the communist world. Together he and Nasser developed the concept of non-alignment, a policy that entailed the avoidance of anti-Russian or pro-Western pacts but did not debar them from receiving aid or purchasing arms from either side. Tito became a friend of Nasser and influenced his thinking in other directions, notably when he later adopted a socialist but not totalitarian communist system for Egypt.

Nasser found another friend in Pandit Nehru, the Prime Minister of India. Nehru, the older man and deeply intellectual, was sometimes frightened by Nasser's boldness, by his capacity for action, yet they had similar ideas on the role of the non-aligned nations in the world. They met in Cairo and came together again in Bandung in April at the Conference of Non-aligned Nations, an occasion organised by Indonesia as a forum to discuss such issues as the persistence of colonialism, the pressure of pro-Western pacts, and the place of Communist China. The conference was a revelation to Nasser where he found himself the centre of attention as a Third World leader and accepted as a colleague by Chou En Lai, the Chinese premier, and by Sukarno the Indonesian leader. He was greeted by crowds in the streets as the man of the day. These experiences helped to mould his ideas and he began to think in new terms. In him Egypt, growing out of its colonial past, was becoming an independent nation in its own right. On his return to Egypt crowds turned out to greet him and his identification with them deepened. The staff officer was completing his metamorphosis into a popular leader.

Other events forced him to change direction. The Egyptian army had previously obtained its arms from the West and Nasser and Amir approached Washington and London for further supplies. In return for arms the West demanded adherence to its pacts or, in the case of France, the cessation of help to the Algerian national movement, then in the second year of a nine-year fight for independence. Such conditions were unacceptable to the Egyptians to whom the Russians were beginning to make approaches over arms. The British warned Nasser that if he accepted Russian weapons none would be forthcoming from Britain. He was incensed by this 'threat' and determined never again to discuss arms with the British, for he was extremely sensitive to actions which he perceived as a threat or an insult to Egypt's independence. He thus had little alternative to taking up the Russian offer. He knew that Egypt needed a strong army to defend the country against the growing strength of Israel. In September an arms agreement with Czechoslovakia was announced. This time it was the West's turn to be seriously disturbed. The British Ambassador received instructions to remonstrate with Nasser. The United States sent an envoy with a threatening note. These moves increased his defiance and convinced him that the West would never be able to accept him as an equal.

In September he declared defiantly to his armed forces:

When I hear some spokesman declare that this [arms agreement] is a victory for Soviet or foreign influence in the Middle East or Egypt, I recall the remote past and I assert that this commercial agreement without conditions or restrictions that we have signed is not a victory for Soviet or foreign influence, but that it merely ends the long period of influence in which we have been dominated and controlled.

By the middle of 1956 it was estimated that Egypt had acquired 150 Russian-built planes, 300 tanks, ships, guns, rocket launchers and miscellaneous equipment. He received no arms from the West and Egypt thus became totally dependent on the communist bloc for military equipment. This was a new relationship for Egypt and for Nasser. Whereas the British (and to a lesser extent the Americans and the French) were a known 'devil', the Russians and their satellites were largely unknown. The West was viewed in imperialist or neo-colonialist terms as those countries which wished to retain their influence in the Middle East through pacts and bases. To the relationship with Russia was added the ideological dimension. On both sides this involved difficulties. Nasser was imprisoning Marxists while accepting Russian aid. The Russians aided Egypt while nevertheless considering him a bourgeois nationalist and anti-communist.

War over Suez

For a time Nasser was unwilling to destroy his ties with the West finally as he was unsure whether Russia could supply the kind of technical and financial aid he was seeking. The Americans had a peculiarly difficult time, offering arms and then withdrawing them, offering aid with conditions.

They were offended by Nasser's acceptance of Soviet arms and yet loath to alienate him completely. The crisis came over the Egyptian decision to build a High Dam at Aswan.

The first dam at Aswan had been built in 1902 by the British in an attempt to recycle the flow of the Nile. It was raised on two occasions to increase capacity. One of the earliest decisions of the Free Officers was to build a High Dam and by December 1954 a German design had been completed. The Dam was to be the symbol of new Egypt, to increase both electrical generating capacity and the area of irrigated land, to serve agriculture and industry. The size of the project was far beyond the financial and technical resources of Egypt and aid was needed from abroad. Two months after the announcement of the Czech arms deal the Egyptian Minister of Finance went to Washington to ask for financial aid. In December 1955 an unconditional loan of $56 million was announced together with $14 million from Britain. It was hoped that the World Bank would also contribute and in January 1956 Eugene Black, the President of the World Bank (the International Bank for Reconstruction and Development) visited Cairo and signed an agreement whereby Egypt was to be loaned an additional $200 million. Such loans from the Bank carried the stipulation that the budget of the recipient country had to be supervised by Bank officials. To Nasser these conditions were suspiciously redolent of Khedive Ismail and the Debt Commission of the 1870s. Would not the acceptance of such a loan return Egypt to the days of Western domination? Feelings on both sides were strong. Nasser admitted that he had grave doubts about the West's sincerity, and in the West doubts were expressed about the possibility of constructing the Dam. In a BBC interview in 1966, Nasser in answer to the question whether he had expected American aid replied (perhaps with hindsight?) 'No I did not. I was sure that Mr. Dulles would not help us by financing the Aswan Dam'.

It seemed to the West that Nasser was doing his best to alienate them. The French believed that he was still aiding the Algerian national movement and the British that he was responsible for the dismissal in March 1956 of General Glubb from the command of the Arab Legion in Jordan. The Americans disliked his recognition of Communist China in May, and the diehard members of the US Congress were not pleased with his approaches to the Soviet Union. The Russians were offering increasing amounts of aid to Egypt in several forms including a loan to finance the High Dam, and the Americans announced on 19 July the withdrawal of their own loan. They did this in the worst possible manner. A communiqué was released to the press, without prior warning to Cairo, stating that an

> important consideration bearing upon the feasibility of the undertaking of building the Dam, and thus the practicability of American aid, was Egyptian readiness and ability to concentrate its resources

upon this vast construction program. Developments within the preceding 7 months have not been favourable to the success of the project, and the US Government has concluded that it is not feasible in present circumstances to participate in the project.

Even Anthony Eden regretted this precipitate action and showed some understanding of Nasser's character:

> We were informed but not consulted and so had no prior opportunity for criticism or comment...We were sorry that the matter was carried through so abruptly...Timing and methods...were quite as important as the substance. At this moment Colonel Nasser was in Brioni [he was in fact on the way back] at a meeting with Marshall Tito and Mr. Nehru, and the news was wounding to his pride.

Nasser was furious. Zakariya Muhyidin, Minister of the Interior, told Humphrey Trevelyan: 'It is not so much the withdrawal of the money which we mind...It is the way in which it was done'. Nasser in the same BBC interview said: 'I was surprised by the insultive [sic] attitude with which the refusal was declared. Not by the refusal itself'. Britain followed America in withdrawing the offer of aid, having been left little choice. Selwyn Lloyd justified the action on economic grounds in that Egypt was undertaking too many other commitments (arms and industrialisation) to be able to give the Dam the necessary priority.

Nasser was furious:

> If a shameful clamour, raised in Washington and devoid of all principles of international usage, announces by lies, deceit and delusion that the Egyptian economy is impotent and unstable, I look at them and tell them: 'Die in your rage. You shall not dominate or tyrannize over us... We shall not permit the domination of force and the dollar'.

He had been elected president for six years in June with 99·9 per cent of votes under a new constitution which gave him the powers of both head of state and of government. He felt doubly insulted, personally and as the chief representative of Egypt. He had prepared his reply. To the astonishment of the world he announced that Egypt was nationalising the Suez Canal. This was the final step in Egypt's liberation, claiming as her own the symbol of and the reason for past imperial domination.

Nasser prepared the takeover very carefully. In charge of the project to occupy the premises of the Suez Canal Company in Port Said, Suez and Ismailiya he put Mahmud Yunis, an engineer who had earlier impressed him. He chose his ground carefully for the announcement. On 26 July 1956, the fourth anniversary of Farouk's exile, he appeared in Muhammad Ali Square in Manshiya in Alexandria where twenty months earlier the assassin had attempted to kill him. An immense crowd gathered and at 7.40 p.m. he began a three-hour speech given from a few notes jotted on the back of an envelope. It was broadcast live and he spoke partly in classical Arabic and partly in colloquial in order to emphasise the intimate nature of the relationship between him and the people and of what he was telling them. It was a rambling speech covering both recent political developments and earlier history. It was Nasser's great opportunity to cock a snook at the Western world which he did with relish in a speech of great defiance and self confidence. Apart from the main message there were several revealing touches. It signalled the end of the British era: 'Never shall anyone stand up in the British parliament and speak of the British sphere of influence... in Egypt', and he finally exacted his revenge on Sir Miles Lampson (Lord Killearn) for his humiliation of the Egyptian army:

> Lord Killearn and we all know Lord Killearn − stood up in the British House of Lords and began insulting Egypt... In March I met the British Ambassador at my house and told him... we would not accept an insult... uttered by MPs and Lords − and in particular Lord Killearn.

Nasser then spoke of the financial negotiations to finance the building of the Dam with Britain, America and the World Bank and its president, Eugene Black: 'I started to look at Mr. Black, who was sitting on a chair, and I saw him in my imagination as Ferdinand de Lesseps'. This seemingly irrelevant mention of de Lesseps was the codeword for Yunis to start his operation. The Canal was soon in Egyptian hands: 'Today we greet the fifth year of the revolution and in the same way as Farouk left on 26 July 1952, the old Suez Canal Company also leaves us on the same day'.

The reaction in Egypt was naturally ecstatic − not in London. To Eden, now Prime Minister, it was 'theft' and Nasser would have to be made to 'disgorge' (Dulles's word). Eden complained at a Cabinet meeting: 'This is the end, we can't put up with any more of this. By this means he can blackmail us... I want to seize the Canal, and take charge of it again.'

There were four parties chiefly concerned with Egypt − Israel, the United States, France and Britain. Other countries were involved but not to the same extent. Israel had her own worries − the three Western allies were primarily concerned with the Canal. America seemed at first to have the same apprehensions as Britain although the Canal was not as important to American as to European shipping. Dulles, the Secretary of State, played a dubious role and during the crisis changed his position from support with strong words for decisive action to final condemnation of the Anglo−French plan. Eden and Dulles were on bad terms and Eden was convinced that he was not receiving the American backing he deserved. France was fighting her own battle with Nasser over his support for the Algerians and was determined to put him down. The national-isation of the Canal was the pretext.

Anthony Eden was in many ways fighting a personal battle. As a young Foreign Secretary he had bravely opposed concessions to Nazi Germany and the need to oppose dictators was firmly rooted in his personality. Observers noted a change in him when he became Prime Minister: 'He started being extremely severe, a very strong disciplinarian. He frightened people.' He saw Nasser as another dictatorial tyrant, as a potential Hitler: 'Nasser has followed Hitler's pattern, even to concentration camps and the propagation of *Mein Kampf* among his officers. He has understood and used the Goebbels pattern of propaganda in all its lying ruthlessness.' He saw Nasser as the potential ruler of an empire stretching from the Atlantic to the Gulf. Such an attitude was absurd. Egypt was a poor country with an embryo army, struggling to assert and maintain its own independence. To believe possible an Egyptian hegemony in the Arab world was to inflate the capabilities of Egypt and her president out of all proportion. Eden's convictions led him to take actions which proved disastrous both for his own career and for Britain's position in the Middle East.

Nationalisation of foreign-owned assets has become commonplace since 1956. The Suez Canal Company was an international company with headquarters in Paris and there were immediately discussions on the legality of Egypt's action. Eden had made his position clear – it was 'theft'. Unless Nasser could be persuaded by international pressure to agree to a new formula, nothing short of military action could force him to 'disgorge'. Eden wanting to launch such action immediately was equally quickly informed that British forces were in no position to do so. Instead a British radio station on Cyprus began broadcasting anti-Nasser propaganda in an attempt to persuade the Egyptians to rise against their president. In a slightly more temperate atmosphere representatives of Britain, France and America met in London at the beginning of August and agreed to summon a conference of Canal users. Both France and Britain had frozen Egyptian financial assets in their countries and were increasing their military preparedness in the Eastern Mediterranean. Those who saw Nasser at this time reported that he was relaxed and carefully moderate. No retaliation was taken against British interests. The West was making no attempt to negotiate with him although he was invited to the users' conference. He was about to accept when he heard of Eden's attack on him on television – 'Our quarrel is not with Egypt, still less with the Arab world; it is with Colonel Nasser alone' – and he refused to go. The conference had to take place without its leading character.

It opened on 16 August in London and was attended by twenty-two countries. Two plans were proposed – by America and by India. The American plan, adopted by a large majority, called for the creation of an international body to supervise the running of the Canal and for a treaty which would recognise Egyptian sovereignty over it. India and Russia opposed these proposals calling them a restoration of the old Canal Company under a new name. Robert Menzies, the Australian premier, was deputed to take them to Cairo to negotiate with Nasser. Menzies was given an impossible mission as Nasser clearly felt that there was nothing to negotiate and that any international supervision would entail foreign intervention in Egypt's internal affairs. Menzies implied that there would be trouble if he refused the proposals. This Nasser took as a threat and closed the discussions. At the same time President Eisenhower declared at a press conference that America would never use force to settle the issue, and Dulles moved yet further away from Eden's position, saying that the Canal was not 'primarily of US concern'.

These developments only served to strengthen Eden's determination and that of the French to force a satisfactory solution. The French and the British continued to meet to discuss methods of coercing Nasser, including the use of military force. An attempt failed to establish a Suez Canal Users Association (SCUA, known in Egypt as the skewer with a blunt point) and Dulles incensed Eden by stating on 2 October that SCUA had no teeth and that there were fundamental differences between American and Anglo–French policy over Suez. He implied that Britain and France had a colonialist approach to the problem. But there were also signs that Nasser was ready to negotiate a settlement which would not in any way endanger Egyptian sovereignty. The dispute was referred to the United Nations with an Anglo–French complaint about the nationalisation and a counter complaint by Egypt about the build-up of Anglo–French forces in Cyprus.

The debate in the Security Council began on 5 October. The Egyptian Foreign Minister, Mahmud Fawzi, offered compensation to Canal shareholders, pointed to the fact that the Canal was still functioning and urged a settlement based on co-operation. Some progress was made in private talks between Fawzi, Selwyn Lloyd and Christian Pineau, the French Foreign Minister, on the basis of recognising Egyptian sovereignty and insulating the Canal from the politics of any one country. After a meeting on 12 October Pineau announced that there was no basis for negotiation but Anthony Nutting, Minister of State at the Foreign Office who later resigned because of disagreement with Eden over his policy, alleged that the statement was false and that Pineau had acted in bad faith as he wanted deadlock to continue so that France could fulfil plans with Israel for military action against Egypt.

In the Arab world Nasser's action had been greeted with great satisfaction. He was the symbol of the overall struggle against Western domination and the takeover of the Canal was symbolic of the gradual reclamation by the Arabs of their heritage. Several Arab leaders proclaimed their solidarity with Egypt, notably King Saud of Saudi Arabia, President Kuwatly of Syria, and the prime minister of the Sudan. The League of Arab States on 13 August declared that it fully supported Egypt, that the Canal was

Egyptian property and that an aggression against any Arab state would be considered aggression against them all — brave words but in practice meaningless as Egypt bore the burden alone. The Federation of Arab Trade Unions called on oil workers to stop production and destroy installations if there was an attack on Egypt.

The atmosphere had remained calm in Cairo. On 9 August Nasser had ordered the formation of a National Liberation Army of 50,000 men in addition to the regular army of 100,000. Production of small arms was increased and the Red Crescent Society (the Egyptian Red Cross) was mobilised. Both Nasser and Amir made speeches stressing that any attack on Egypt would be fiercely resisted — 'war against us will not be recreation, as is believed by those who dream of it'. In early September Nasser admitted, in the face of the growing Anglo—French military build-up, that if attacked he would ask for help — from Russia if need be. On 15 September Egypt had finally taken over the full running of the Canal recruiting its own pilots, who successfully guided ships through the narrow waterways. (There had been much self satisfied comment in the West that no pilots, especially Egyptians, would be able to do the job of the experienced employees of the Company. This was soon disproved.) There was one discordant note. The irrepressible *Ikhwan* opened a clandestine radio to take advantage of any political difficulty that Nasser might encounter: 'Egyptian people', they said, 'be very careful; the mad actions of Nasser will lead Egypt to the abyss and to a new occupation... you want to get rid of this tyrant who exploits Egypt... wait very little for the free sons of Egypt will liberate Egypt.'

By an unhappy combination of circumstances the nationalisation of the Canal drew another participant into the conflict — Israel. Since the humiliation of 1948 she had been a prime target for Arab revenge. Egypt had sought arms largely to confront her. There had been several violent incidents between the two countries and Egypt had made a practice of halting Israeli-bound cargoes in the Canal. In the Gaza Strip — the piece of Palestinian territory governed by Egypt — there was a population of some 200,000 Palestinian refugees. A large number of clashes took place in the area and a mixed armistice commission vainly tried to keep the two sides apart. Egypt began to train *fedayeen* (commandos) to make raids into Israel, and every raid was repaid with a reprisal. In obtaining Russian armaments Nasser had announced that one purpose was to achieve the level of equipment of the Israeli army, but such parity was never reached. Whenever Israel or America spoke of the military balance in the Middle East, they meant a balance weighed heavily in Israel's favour and the USA was always ready to supply arms.

In November 1955 Ben-Gurion, the Israeli Prime Minister and a very belligerent character, announced to the Israeli parliament:

Egypt has openly declared that a state of war continues between Egypt and Israel ... Egypt has violated basic international law governing the freedom of shipping through Suez ... The armistice lines are opened by them to saboteurs and murderers ... This one-sided war will have to stop ... We shall reserve freedom of action.

This determination was at the root of Ben-Gurion's attitude — force was to be met by force. Retaliation was always inevitable. Israel felt threatened by the Egyptian arms build-up and by Arab statements such as 'We must strengthen ourselves ... so that we may be able to restore to the people of Palestine their rights to freedom and national existence'. Ben-Gurion shared with Eden and the French an obsession with Nasser. The greatest danger to Israel, he said, came from 'the Egyptian dictator' and he was afraid that Israeli shipping would be permanently barred from the nationalised Canal. On 15 October he spoke of certain favourable developments, meaning that meetings had taken place with the French to discuss a concerted attack on Egypt. This was the beginning of what became known as 'collusion' or in Egypt as the 'tripartite aggression'.

Tripartite Collusion

The Conservative government and party have always been extremely embarrassed by charges that it used Israel as an excuse for attacking Egypt and have never formally admitted collusion. Neither Eden nor Harold Macmillan is open in his memoirs, nor has the other main British participant Selwyn Lloyd, been completely frank. There was speculation as early as 1956 and the full truth gradually became known as books by French, Israeli and British participants were published. Eden and Lloyd concealed their actions from colleagues, from British diplomats and from the Americans. Meetings were held at which minute-taking was forbidden. Lord Mountbatten, First Sea Lord at the time, records that a report produced by the Suez Naval Force Commander let slip some facts which proved collusion. This was pointed out to the Cabinet which ordered that certain pages of the report 'be redrafted so as to conceal the fact that there was any collusion and the originals ... be burnt. This was done.' The British were embarrassed and made poor conspirators, while the Israelis and the French seemed to be enjoying themselves. Dayan, the Israeli Chief of Staff, reported that Lloyd seemed to regard the whole exercise as 'something dirty that he did not want to touch'.

On 14 October Eden met Albert Gazier, a French minister, and General Maurice Challe of the French air force at Chequers where Challe outlined a plan of action which would enable Britain and France to gain physical control of the Canal. The plan called for Israel to attack across the Sinai desert and when near the Canal for Britain and France to issue an ultimatum for an Egyptian and Israeli withdrawal from both sides of the Canal. An Anglo–French force would then occupy the Canal to prevent further fighting and to keep it open to shipping. Eden met the French two days later and agreed to use military force if Nasser would not accept the UN plan. On 22 October Lloyd met Ben-Gurion outside Paris and learned that Israel could not attack unless Britain and France first destroyed the Egyptian air force. The Israelis later revealed that they never intended to appear in force on the Suez Canal, only to make a smaller demonstration to Sharm al-Shaikh (in Sinai) and so to that extent the British themselves were double-crossed.

The British and French were now playing a game, agreeing to further discussions in Geneva at the end of October, when Nasser received through the Americans news that a British general, Keightley, had been appointed to command an invasion of Egypt. He had several other warnings – large troop movements on Malta and Cyprus, concentrations of warships and landing craft and hints from Nuri Said. Haykal reported that Nasser refused to believe in the possibility of collusion with Israel and withdrew most of his army from Sinai to the Canal: 'Nasser just could not bring himself to believe that Eden ... would jeopardize ... Britain's own standing in the Arab world by making war alongside Israel on an Arab nation'. A Middle East News Agency report of 30 October was very near the mark although wrong in interpretation: 'It was recently revealed to official circles that France has kept on asking the British authorities to use Israel for this role of attacking Jordan until they have been persuaded ... There is a big plot'. Despite further confirmation from a source in Paris Nasser was still not convinced. He had misplaced ideas of an Englishman's sense of honour.

On 29 October Israeli troops crossed the frontier into the Sinai peninsula in order, it was alleged, to destroy the bases of the Egyptian commandos. By the following day the attack had widened and Israeli forces were reported to be within twenty miles of the Suez Canal. On the same day the Egyptian Ambassadors to Paris and London were called to the French and British Foreign Offices where they were handed the Anglo–French ultimatum which demanded that Israeli and Egyptian troops withdraw a distance of ten miles from the eastern and western banks of the Canal. At that moment the Israelis had not yet reached the Canal and the Egyptians were on both sides of it! Egypt was also requested to accept the temporary occupation of key points on the Canal by Anglo–French forces. Non-compliance would result in intervention by Britain and France. Eden declared that the purpose of the ultimatum was to separate the combatants and to protect the Canal. Nasser, still hardly believing in Eden's complicity, firmly rejected the ultimatum informing the British Ambassador that it was a threat of unjustified aggression. On 31 October the Israelis reached the Canal, accepted the ultimatum, and withdrew ten miles from its banks. At the same time the Anglo–French invasion fleet had begun to trundle across the Mediterranean, sailing at the speed of the slowest ships and taking longer to cross from Malta to Egypt than did Nelson a century and a half earlier.

Haykal draws a vivid portrait of Nasser during these days, of the conflicting and bewildering emotions to which he was subject. As his first disbelief evaporated he began to prepare to resist the invasion. After arguing with Amir who wanted to attack in Sinai, he had withdrawn part of the army to defend the Canal. He also made preparations for a popular war to harass the invaders once they had landed. Messages of support came to him from other Arab leaders and the Syrians went further by blowing up the oil pipelines belonging to the Iraq Petroleum Company which crossed their country. In the Canal block ships were sunk to prevent transit. Already Eden was defeated in his professed aim of keeping the Canal open.

The British planes began to bomb military targets near Cairo and elsewhere. The British radio in Cyprus broadcast appeals to the Egyptians to rid themselves of Nasser and advance warnings of the targets to be bombed. Trevelyan mentioned this advance notice in his memoirs and incidentally underlined the two-faced nature of the whole enterprise:

> When we received the first telegram 'en clair' announcing the targets for the first night's attack, we believed that a mistake had been made and immediately telegraphed about it. Our forces were behaving in an humane way; Egyptians knew that when the RAF told them their objectives in advance, they could trust their word and their ability to do what they said

– a strange misuse of the words 'humane' and 'trust'. The bombing destroyed the Egyptian air force and on 5 November British and French paratroopers were dropped over Port Said and Port Fuad. Casualties were suffered on both sides, especially in the fighting to capture Port Said. At the same time the Israeli army pressed on to capture the whole of Sinai down to Sharm al-Shaikh, the site which commands the entrance to the Gulf of Aqaba at the head of which stands the Israeli port of Eilat.

The Anglo–French action caused considerable loss of life and property in Port Said. The official British report praised Egyptian resistance:

> These Russian guns were most skilfully handled and caused us considerable trouble; the fighting here was hard and the Egyptians made good use of their dug positions...Egyptian resistance was very stubborn...The Garrison and populace of Port Said were encouraged to resist by loudspeaker vans which toured the town...At the same time arms were distributed to civilians.

At one point the Egyptian local commander decided to surrender but he was overruled by Cairo and ordered to resist. The British report somewhat unfairly blamed the Egyptians for the damage caused to Port Said by their refusal to surrender. British troops, brought in by sea on 6 November, had to occupy the town street by street. By dusk organised resistance had ceased. Some 2,700 Egyptian civilians and soldiers had been killed or wounded, and 140 British and French soldiers, and a large number of buildings destroyed or damaged. And the Canal was blocked.

Egypt had been invaded by two major powers and one well-armed smaller opponent and could not have been expected to withstand such a tripartite attack for long. Yet it can be justifiably claimed that Egypt and Nasser emerged as victor. The French by their support for Israel and their unrelenting war against the Algerians found no favour in Arab eyes. The Israelis were the natural enemies and had gained little by their attack. As for the British, they virtually disappeared from the Egyptian scene. The British Ambassador left in a despondent mood having tried to establish a relationship of trust with Nasser only to be totally undermined by Eden's action. In Egyptian eyes the British were now despicable. Nasser said:

> If Eden had come with the British Navy and tried to invade Egypt I think the Egyptians would have forgiven and forgotten once it was all finished. Even if he had come with the French we would have said that perhaps he needed an ally. But to bring the Israelis into an adventure against the Arabs was very foolish. We were used to hating British policy but then we began to despise British policy. I hate to use the word despise. But it is the only one.

Egypt was saved by the intervention of the United Nations, the United States and the Soviet Union and the threat of the collapse of sterling. The Russians, who were busily engaged in suppressing the Hungarian uprising, threatened Britain and France with rocket attack if they did not withdraw from Egypt. America refused to co-ordinate policy in any way before the withdrawl of Anglo–French and Israeli troops. The members of the Baghdad Pact likewise demanded withdrawal. Other, non-aligned, countries condemned the aggression. Opposition was almost total and Nasser drew comfort from this general support. Britain and France under severe condemnation at the United Nations agreed to a ceasefire at midnight on 6 November. Their troops were halted just as it was claimed they were poised to advance down the length of the Canal. A United Nations Emergency Force (UNEF) was established, the leading elements of which arrived in Egypt on 21 November. During the period of Anglo–French occupation a number of incidents occurred, as the Egyptians were waging a minor guerrilla war. It was very reminiscent of 1951. The final evacuation took place on 22 December. Eden's verdict: 'Suez was a short-term emergency operation which succeeded'. Most of the rest of the world was of a different opinion. Eden fell ill as a result of exhaustion from over-work. The mental strain he had suffered worsened his physical condition and he resigned soon afterwards. His opponent emerged as victor.

Two problems remained from the crisis — the re-opening of the Canal and the withdrawal of Israeli troops. The Canal was blocked by over fifty sunken ships. Mountbatten arranged for several salvage vessels to go to Suez but to British dismay after the withdrawal the Egyptians would not allow them to be used. Eventually, with United Nations help, the Egyptians opened a channel and the first convoy passed through in March 1957. The Canal was completely opened in April. Egypt free from international pressure ordered the dues for passage to be paid in advance to its Suez Canal Authority, an autonomous Egyptian organisation. In May the new British prime minister announced that British ships should use the Canal, paying tolls to the Authority in sterling. A few carping unimportant reservations were made — Britain did not accept 'the Egyptian declaration as a permanent and satisfactory settlement' — but these were meaningless nods in the direction of Britain's former policy. The Canal was run smoothly by Egypt, open to all ships except those of Israel, until it was once again closed by the 1967 Arab–Israeli war. Reasonable arrangements were made for compensation for the assets of the old Suez Canal Company and the frozen funds abroad of the Egyptian government were released in May 1958. For a short ten years the Canal left the political scene.

The Israeli forces were occupying most of the Sinai peninsula. The United Nations on 7 November called for their immediate withdrawal and Ben-Gurion reluctantly agreed. He would have preferred to use withdrawal as a bargaining counter in a future peace settlement. As it was there was prolonged negotiation over the status of the Gaza strip and Sharm al-Shaikh. As the Israelis withdrew from Sinai they carried out a scorched earth policy, destroying roads, railways and military installations. The United States, especially President Eisenhower, placed great pressure on Israel to give up all its territorial acquisitions and even threatened sanctions. In March 1957 United Nations troops took over control of Gaza and of Sharm al-Shaikh. The Egyptians together with the UNEF began to administer Gaza with the assurance that further *fedayeen* raids would be stopped. The UN troops on the Gulf of Aqaba were there to ensure the free passage of Israeli shipping to Eilat. They remained until 1967 when their removal materially contributed to the outbreak of war.

The Suez affair left Nasser in a relatively strong position. Although the Egyptian army had been defeated and much equipment captured, Russia soon began to make good the losses. He now stood as the man who had successfully defied the two old colonial powers on behalf of Egypt and the Arab world. Russian, American and United Nations pressure on the invaders to withdraw was not emphasised. In a way this was not important as the Egyptian will to resist had not broken and was not finally put to the test. Britain's position in Egypt was essentially destroyed and had to be slowly rebuilt. Diplomatic relations were broken off until December 1959. A large number of British and French nationals were expelled, others were interned and property was sequestrated. Some 11,000 Jewish residents in Egypt were expelled or left, forced out by the considerable anti-Jewish feeling in the country. Their property was confiscated. Unfortunately, some Jews were identified with Israel whether they proclaimed their allegiance to Egypt or not.

4 The Unfinished Revolution: 1956-1970

Nasser and the Arab World

Eden had assessed the Suez expedition as a short-term success, not as something that put paid to Nasser's ambitions: 'the chances of a Nasser empire were scotched, not killed'. In fact, Nasser's very success bore within itself the seeds of danger. He was entering a period of great popularity, a hero of the Arab world, yet in Haykal's phrase he was 'the lion chained' — chained by his assumption of the leadership of Egypt and that wider Arab world, drawn into unending inter-Arab projects and problems. He was never free again to concentrate solely on Egyptian affairs. In the Arab world his aims were to influence the course of events, to sustain leaders in power favourable to his policies, to oust those who were not, to eliminate all traces of colonialism, and to work towards Arab unity and prepare for the struggle against Israel. Each of these aims involved him in a continuous effort, establishing alliances and unions, breaking them, in military involvement directly or indirectly, broadcasting propaganda, courting the Soviet Union for military aid, wooing the United States for economic assistance. As his friend Haykal wrote: 'These were the historical conditions that formed his destiny and laid on him a burden too great for any one man to bear. Arabism took him for its hero and lifted him out of Egypt into an inter-Arab international role.'

The countries of the Arab world in 1956 were at different stages in their political evolution. Arab unity, their proclaimed objective, was difficult to achieve because of rival regimes and ideologies and colonial rule. Egypt was the natural centre and Nasser the natural leader. There was no other Arab political figure remotely approaching his stature. Morocco with its King Muhammad V had just gained independence from the French. The Algerians were in the midst of their struggle against the French. Bourguiba led Tunisia to independence in 1956. Libya was an impoverished state dependent on foreign aid, under a religious leader King Idris. Sudan had become fully independent on the first day of 1956 and had opted out of union with Egypt. It had a parliamentary system of government. Lebanon was unique in the Arab world, with a population finely balanced between Muslims and Christians, and an elected Christian president and Muslim prime minister. It was a small prosperous country concerned with its own internal problems, but tempting outside interference. Jordan began to shake off British tutelage in 1956 and was ruled by its hereditary monarch, Husain, a member of the Hashemite dynasty which had originated in Arabia. Husain's father, Abdullah, had been given the throne of Transjordan by the British in 1920 and had been assassinated by a Palestinian in 1951. He had annexed the remnant of Palestine left in Arab hands in 1950. Iraq was ruled by King Faisal, Husain's cousin, and by an elderly experienced politician, Nuri Said. In Saudi Arabia the strictly religious Saudi royal family held supreme power. The head of the family was a rather inefficient man, King Saud, who was trying to cope with the changes in his society brought about by large oil wealth. Yemen had another religious leader, Imam Ahmad, and was virtually a closed mediaeval society. Southern Yemen and Aden were still a British colony and had not yet begun to fight for independence, although there were signs of future trouble which were happily exploited by Egypt (the British wanted it as a military base to replace Suez). The states of the Gulf, all formally independent, were closely tied by treaty to Britain. Oman was in a troubled state facing a virtual civil war with the British supporting the Sultan and the Egyptians and others fomenting opposition.

Syria, omitted from the above list as it was to become of immediate concern to Egypt, has had an important position in Arab history and Damascus, the capital, has played a significant role in Arab politics. Its frontiers have not always been as clearly defined as those of Egypt and the Syrians are not a nation with as long a historical identity as the Egyptians. The Arabic name for the area, *Sham*, means both Damascus and Greater Syria, that is the area covering Syria, Lebanon, Palestine/Israel and Jordan. It was in this region that early ideas of Arab nationalism and unity were developed, and especially in the 1940s by Michel Aflaq and Salah Bitar, two Syrians who founded the Baath (renaissance) party. The basic aim of the party was Arab unity; it asserted the existence of 'one Arab nation with an eternal message' and claimed that all those whose language was Arabic and who lived in an Arab country were united by ties stronger than local or sectarian differences. The party had gained some influence in Syria and elsewhere.

At heart Nasser disapproved of those of his fellow leaders who were reactionary, conservative, anti-revolutionary or too pro-Western. His relationship with King Husain veered from attempts to overthrow him to establishing a joint military command. When Jordan broke its long-standing connection with Britain in March 1957 it seemed that Nasser's more radical policy was succeeding, though not for long, as Husain began to fear for his own position and soon dismissed pro-Egyptian politicians in his government. Diplomatic relations between Jordan and Egypt were broken in June because Egypt had been broadcasting such virulent propaganda against Husain. Saudi Arabia and Lebanon also felt threatened by Nasser's growing popularity. Iraq still had pro-Western rulers. As a result Egypt and Syria found themselves rather thrown together. The latter country had a broad national front as government in which the Baath ideology was the dominant influence although the Baath leaders did not have supreme power. The communists were gaining influence in the army and consequently in the government as the army largely determined the character of the government. The President of the republic, Shukri Kuwatly, an older politician in the National Party, shared with the Baath a fear of the growing influence of the communists. The Baath party considered Nasser a successful Arab leader with whom an alliance could be of benefit. They had the ideology, he the power. Events moved quickly. In January 1958 leaders of various Syrian groups went to Cairo to urge on Nasser the advantage of a union between Syria and Egypt. He was faced both with enormous pressure and enormous temptation. The Syrians stressed that only union would save the country from outside (communist) interference. Nasser was tempted by the prospect of the beginnings of Arab unity and of greater power.

He imposed stringent conditions on the Syrians – abolition of political parties including the Baath and the exclusion of the army from politics. The Syrians willingly agreed and an agreement was signed. The United Arab Republic came into being.[7] It was a hasty almost foolhardy union with no previous planning or preparation, the result both of political convenience and ideological conviction. It was unfortunately a perfect example of marrying in haste and repenting at leisure.

The honeymoon was blissful. A new constitution was drawn up and Nasser was elected President of the UAR with 99·9 per cent of the votes cast. Syria and Egypt were metamorphosed into the Northern and Southern Regions and there was one cabinet with a vice-president from each region. Nasser was given an overwhelming welcome when he visited Damascus. Thousands came out to greet him, the most popular Arab leader in modern times, and Arabism was at its zenith. Underneath, however, problems were already present. The Syrians are a proud and sensitive people and Egypt was preparing to impose on them a police and army regime which was Nasser's solution to the difficulties of unity. There was no possibility of merging the two political systems – Syria had an unstable, fragmented system, Egypt its one party and supreme leader. In addition to the dissolution of Syrian political parties, army officers were dismissed and Egyptian security officials sent to Syria. Nasser attempted to impose his will on the Syrians, paying little attention to their sensitivities and attitudes. He believed that his own popular appeal was a guarantee of success.

The union and Nasser's consequent popularity caused a ferment in other parts of the Arab world. The two Hashemite rulers of Jordan and Iraq saw a threat to their thrones and hastily fabricated a federation which had no impact on public opinion and was widely regarded as a face-saving move. King Saud offered nearly £2 million to Abdel Hamid Sarraj, the Syrian intelligence chief, to assassinate Nasser. Instead he took the cheques to Nasser and the scandal forced Saud to yield authority to his brother Prince Faisal who was more prepared to tolerate Nasser.

In Lebanon President Shamoun and his foreign minister shifted from neutrality in Arab affairs to a more pro-Western and consequently anti-Nasserist position. This aroused tension between Christians, who were broadly pro-Western, and Muslims who on the whole supported Arab nationalism and Nasser's leadership. The tension caused disorders and eventually open conflict. Egyptian arms and money were sent to support the Muslim side and strong and continuous support was given by radio propaganda: 'The battle of the Lebanon is taking more definite shape. It is a battle between the ruler and the people who are revolting against tyranny... It is an indication of the beginning of Lebanese freedom', proclaimed Egyptian radio.

At the same time tension was rising in Iraq. Nuri Said believed the army was loyal to the regime but a group of officers had been plotting and in July a brigade favourable to these Iraqi 'Free Officers' entered Baghdad and Nuri and members of the royal family were murdered. It seemed at first that the new rulers under Brigadier Qasim would support Nasser's policy, and the position of King Husain in Jordan and of the Christians in Lebanon became grave. Both had to turn to outside help – in Jordan British troops landed to protect the throne and in Lebanon American marines went ashore. The immediate threats to both countries were thus removed. Nasser was naturally furious at these moves which he considered a despairing attempt by 'imperialism' to reassert itself in Lebanon and Jordan after having lost its hold in Iraq. In fact the new government formed in Lebanon restored normal relations with Egypt, and Husain had shown that he needed outside help to retain his throne. It seemed that Nasser's position was very strong and that his radical policies were to succeed in other parts of the Arab world.

Appearances were deceptive. The Iraqis quickly demonstrated that they were in no hurry to jump into union. Husain proved over the long term to be adept at remaining in power. The Syrians proved to be difficult bedfellows. The Baath were not able to assume exclusive leadership, and in October 1958 in a new cabinet fourteen out of twenty-one ministries (including the most important) were allotted to Egyptians. Nasser had no clear plans for union and his moves alienated a considerable section of the population, especially landowners who did not welcome agrarian reform, politicians who lost power, businessmen and the army. He realised what was going wrong and in October 1959 sent Abdel Hakim Amir as governor with orders to try and conciliate Syrian opinion. The Baath were still smarting and resigned from the government in December. Nasser relied on Abdel Hamid Sarraj as his Syrian strong man, making him Minister of the Interior and President of the Executive Council of the National Union – the organisation founded to replace political parties. Sarraj was dedicated to Nasser, efficient and ruthless, and he earned widespread dislike. Nasser tried to silence every centre of political power and Sarraj supported him with a strong security organisation. Discontent grew, especially in the army, which began to plot to take Syria out of the UAR. Amir attempted to halt some of Sarraj's more excessive police methods but it was too late. A Syrian general later complained that: 'Every Egyptian officer during the union acted as if he were Gamal Abdel Nasser, and Syrian officers felt so demoralized that ... they felt no incentive to oppose the secession'. On 28 September army units stationed outside Damascus marched on the capital where they were joined by others and a national uprising was proclaimed. Nasser's first impulse was to resist by force claiming that the mutiny was supported only by a minority. He reacted emotionally in a broadcast speech.

> If certain elements have revolted, this does not mean at all that the Army had denied the nation its aims ... This revolt was carried out by a small force ... which the people do not support. I call on every mutineer to face himself, his soul, heart and conscience ... I do not accept bargaining.

Nasser's words demonstrate his initial disbelief that the Syrians would attempt to betray Arab unity in such a way. He had committed himself to the project and his personal honour was at stake. Seven days later, however, he had been able to reflect and in a further broadcast rejected any attempt to oppose the split by force:

> I will not accept, whatever the conditions may be, seeing the people here and the people in Syria party to a battle ... I have refused military war as a means of strengthening the unity ...

He spoke frankly of his disquiet over the precipitate formation of the union:

> You know that my opinion was that unity ... was a strenuous operation. My opinion was that preparations for it should have been made gradually over a number of years ... but I had to submit to the popular Syrian will ... I feel at this moment that it is not imperative that Syria remains a part of the UAR, but it is imperative that Syria should remain as Syria ... National unity in Syria is a consolidation of Arab unity and true preparation for its realization ... This United Arab Republic will continue ....

Nasser recognised the impossibility of imposing his will on Syria but left the door open for further attempts at unity by retaining the title of UAR for Egypt.[8] His reputation suffered from this failure and the euphoria of 1958 was never repeated. To date there has been no other similar union although quite a few short-lived attempts have been made. The goal of Arab unity has never been abandoned but the practical difficulties of achieving it became much clearer after the dissolution of the Syro–Egyptian union. Political, ideological, dynastic and economic differences have to date been too great to overcome.

What was Nasser's reaction? He continued to support the aims and slogans of Arab nationalism and only a few days later Egyptian forces were fighting in Yemen, yet to some extent he turned towards internal Egyptian affairs. In a broadcast to the Egyptian people on 16 October he made some surprising admissions. Presumably after much heart-searching he had discovered self criticism, but it was still the speech of a confident leader whose decisions were not to be questioned:

> I have chosen to spend the past days thinking. I thought about our people everywhere ... I wanted my choice to be theirs, and my attitude to be an expression of theirs ... I say to you now that I have chosen ... and my choice was that the road of revolution should be our road. To proceed with all force towards revolutionary acts is the only answer to all the demands of our national struggle ... Our responsibility is to reconstruct the homeland and to liberate it.

This was the burden of his message. The ideals of the revolution and the rectification of past mistakes could be achieved only by the complete reform of Egyptian society, and to work towards these objects he would issue a National Charter, summon a congress of popular forces and form a third mass political organisation, the Arab Socialist Union (ASU). He apparently did not see or was not willing to admit Egyptian mistakes to Syria, preferring to ascribe the break-up to the plots of imperialism and reaction. His 'mistake' had been to trust the reactionaries in Syria. He still believed that there was a current leading towards Arab unity and that the people's will was more important than constitutional processes. This conviction led naturally to the conclusion that it was correct to use any possible means to enable the people to impose their will and he was led into other foreign adventures, despite his admitted previous lack of attention to internal affairs. The Arab world and Arab policies possessed an irresistible attraction for him and those fighting for independence or for changes of regime looked to him as their leader.

The Charter for National Action issued in May 1962, besides outlining the path of Egyptian development, asserted that Arab unity could only come about by exporting the Egyptian revolution to all Arab states – 'the revolutionary path is the only bridge that the Arab nation can cross to reach the future to which it aspires', and 'natural and historical factors have made the UAR ... the nucleus state in this endeavour to secure liberty, socialism and unity for the Arab nation'. Nasser was committing Egypt to 'exporting' his revolution, or to what others might regard as interference in the internal affairs of fellow Arab states. Syria was still the main objective and Egyptian agents were active there trying to bring about a pro-Nasser coup. There was an army rising in April/May 1962 in favour of union which the Syrian government put down claiming that the time was not yet ripe for re-union, and at an Arab League meeting in

August Syria accused Egypt of interference in her internal affairs. The Arab League almost broke apart over this dispute. Although the two countries continued to abuse one another it was elsewhere that Nasser faced his greatest inter-Arab trial.

One of the more bizarre attempts at Arab unity had been North Yemen's adherence to the UAR in 1958 – bizarre because of the conjunction between an Islamic theocracy in Yemen and the revolutionary leaders of Syria and Egypt. It was an improbable union from the start with no practical achievements. The ruler of Yemen, *Imam* (a religious title) Ahmad, known for his restrictive government, had little sympathy with Nasser or with the modern world in general and in any case Nasser would have been happy to see him overthrown. In March 1961 he was hit by an assassin's bullets and although not killed he was in poor health from then on. On 13 October he announced that his son, Muhammad al-Badr, would succeed him. Muhammad had slightly more liberal tendencies than his father but was still committed to maintaining the traditional regime. There were various signs of unrest during the next months and eight days after the old Imam's death on 18 September 1962 the army rose in revolt under Brigadier Sallal, captured the capital Sanaa and declared a republic. Unfortunately for them, instead of dying under the rubble of the palace as was first believed, the new Imam Muhammad escaped and joined loyal tribes in the mountainous north where he launched a counterattack in an attempt to preserve his authority. As Muhammad obtained substantial support from Saudi Arabia and Jordan, Sallal appealed to Nasser for help. Nasser, the symbol of revolution, could not refuse, as in any case he had previously encouraged the revolt. It was an opportunity for Egypt to offer practical support to a movement fighting the 'reactionaries' of the Arab world and for Nasser to regain some of the prestige lost after the Syro–Egyptian split. It was a brave move to send Egyptian troops to Yemen and one which he deeply regretted later. Haykal reports that Nasser said to Che Guevara:

In Yemen when the Revolution started... I jumped to its help... But then I discovered first that it could not be helped from outside, second, that it would take a long time and much agony.

The country was mountainous and the tribesmen could wage guerrilla war in areas where it was impossible for tanks to penetrate. Nasser underestimated both the strength of resistance and the difficulties of the terrain. For five years part of the Egyptian army was trapped into fighting fellow Arabs and into a severe sacrifice of men, money and material. The number of Egyptian soldiers increased until there were some 60–70,000 in 1965. The fighting swayed backwards and forwards across the country and no Egyptian soldier can have enjoyed fighting in the mountains, frequently in bitter cold, where it was reported that prisoners were not often taken alive. The Egyptian private soldier, usually a *fellah*, must have longed for home and could have had little sympathy for the cause he was having to fight for. In the war in general a stalemate was reached. The Egyptians did not succeed in their central military aim of destroying the royalist opposition. The Imam's forces were not able to capture Sanaa and the main Egyptian headquarters.

By August 1965 Nasser appeared convinced that the time had come to call a halt. The increasing numbers of troops were still not achieving victory. Talks were opened between Nasser and King Faisal of Saudi Arabia but neither side was willing to compromise over the future form of government in Yemen. The talks dragged on and in February 1966 Nasser threatened to keep his troops there for another five years. During this period fighting continued and the Egyptians in an attempt to cut their losses began to use poison gas in air attacks on Yemen's villages. Although in January 1967 this was denied, evidence provided by the International Red Cross after investigating a number of incidents showed that several Yemeni villagers had died after inhaling toxic gas. The report did not specifically mention Egypt but the inference was clear. The Egyptians used gas together with conventional bombing in an attempt to break Yemeni morale, and despite publicity continued to use it. Some voices in the world were raised to condemn Egypt but nothing was done officially. Other countries, it seemed, had their own reasons for keeping quiet. It was a part of the inhumanity of war and the full truth of what happened may never be known, although Nasser must have officially approved its use.

The intervention in Yemen drained Egypt financially and meant that some of its best troops were trapped there when Israel attacked in June 1967. The Israeli victory put an end to the possibility of Egyptian troops remaining there — it was too costly and they were needed on the Suez front. By the end of 1967 about 40,000 men had been withdrawn. One factor influencing the Egyptian decision was the British announcement that British troops would finally leave neighbouring Aden (Southern Yemen) in January 1968. After the Egyptians left, fighting between royalists and republicans continued until about the summer of 1969 when most royalist leaders had been defeated or had fled. Yemen has remained a republic. Nasser's intervention, which he lived to regret, certainly prolonged the fight and encouraged the Saudis to support the other side. The sacrifice of some 10,000 men killed, wounded or captured probably ensured the survival of the republic. It was a sorry episode in inter-Arab relations, when ideologies counted for more than brotherhood and solidarity.

While Arabs were killing each other in Yemen, Nasser warily kept at bay new approaches for Arab unity. He and Egypt stood alone, refusing concessions to the regimes in Syria and Iraq and opposing reaction elsewhere. He did not, however, drop his aim of exporting revolution or of seeking a unity of the Arab peoples and in a sense he prided himself on his own ideological purity. Others would have to come to him on his terms. While the Syrians and Iraqis for their part were anxious to prove that they were just as progressive and revolutionary as Nasser they had a much less secure base from which to do so. The situation changed in Iraq when President Qasim was killed in February 1963 and the Iraqi wing of the Baath took over, committed to unity and socialism. A Syrian coup followed a month later and a Baathi-led cabinet was appointed in order, it announced, to atone for the crime of 'secession' from Egypt and to lead Syria into union both with Egypt and with Iraq. Nasser agreed to hold discussions in Cairo in March and April. He was much more cautious this time, and did not have much confidence in the Baath leaders. In the talks he subjected them to severe questioning and criticism of past behaviour, which he called deceitful and opportunistic. A transcript of the talks was published and broadcast on Cairo radio and it provides a fascinating picture of the cut and thrust of argument and of Nasser's taunting, especially of the Syrians. He made it very clear that union would be on his terms according to the precepts of the National Charter. Nasser's strong personality dominated the discussions and the Syrians and Iraqis tried rather lamely to defend themselves and to ward off his attacks. He obviously enjoyed his own superiority and dominant position. His strength derived from the fact that he was the only conceivable leader of the proposed merger and that the Arab Socialist Union was by far the largest political organisation in the three countries. Little understanding was reached over the future political leadership or organisation of the union yet a formal agreement was signed on 17 April which, however, postponed full implementation of union for over two years. And the Baathists were never really reconciled to the idea of a union which would not allow them the free hand they sought in Syria. In July they bloodily put down an attempted pro-Nasser coup, which ended Nasser's patience and any attempt at dialogue between himself and the Baath. On 22 July he declared: 'We do not consider that the UAR is bound to the present Fascist regime in Syria by any common aim'. The 'Fascist regime' had been discredited and he would henceforth consider union only with the 'true' Syria — 'The Syrian people, who alone possess the right to settle the issue'.

The Iraqis under President Arif were having trouble with their own Baathis who were eventually forced out of office. Syria was isolated and Nasser, although having avoided another possible failure, had progressed no further in the cause of Arab unity. Once again he drew certain lessons from the setback:

We previously believed that progressive Arab revolutions render union probable. But nowadays the concept of union is itself in crisis... While every Arab country boasts a party, union seems utterly impossible ... For union to emerge ... we must launch a unified Arab nationalist movement which would incorporate all the nationalist movements of the Arab world.

The unspoken corollary of this was that Nasser would only consider union with those who unconditionally accepted his leadership.

At this point, January 1964, the Arab world was more divided than ever. Syria was quarrelling with Egypt and Iraq; Egypt and Saudi Arabia, and to some extent Jordan, were fighting on opposing sides in Yemen, and there were other inter-Arab disputes. Most quarrels derived from ideological differences and yet underlying everything was the continuous desire for unity. Arab leaders met at a summit conference in Cairo in January 1964 and overnight, it seemed, friendship and tolerance were re-established. This was a sign of that especial volatility of Arab politics in which sworn enemies embrace and those who have called each other traitors sit at the same table. The reconciliation fell short of settling all differences however and a specific cause had brought them together – Israel's plan to divert the Jordan river waters which was taken as a threat to the Arab nation as a whole. But since no Arab state was able to take on Israel in battle all that could be done was to utter threats. Nasser realised this and admitted that 'we cannot use force today because our circumstances do not allow us'. The summit was an effort to mend fences and while promises were made of further co-operation it also marked the end for a considerable period of attempts at political union.

Egypt and the Soviet Union

Since the Suez War Egypt had also operated in a wider world, the keystone of her foreign relations being the relationship with the Soviet Union. As acceptance of Russian arms had been a chief cause of the withdrawal of the offer of American and British aid to finance the Aswan Dam, Nasser was forced to look elsewhere for friends. The Egyptians had had no previous experience of dealing with the Russians and the relationship was far from easy. The Russians, who at that time were also novices at the game, could be very heavy-handed. Britain had been a familiar opponent with whom a certain experience in negotiation had been gained. The United States had come in on the coat tails of Britain and had suffered from British unpopularity and from the anti-colonialist feelings of Egypt. Their role at Suez had been ambiguous but the American attitude of coldness towards those states which co-operated with the communist camp drove Nasser into the Soviet embrace. Russia was the only alternative supplier of weapons. As British influence weakened Russia and America entered into competition to become the leading powers in the Middle East. America had a considerable lead with the sixth fleet in the

Mediterranean and access to bases in the area. Russia had to pursue a compensatory policy of gaining at least equivalent power. The Russian fleet was increased (with direct access to the Mediterranean through the Bosphorus Straits) and Egypt chosen as a centre of influence. In theory Russia was committed to the spread of communist ideology and Marxist revolution. In practice the demands of great power politics meant putting aside the claims of ideology, although the Russians could never forget them entirely. This sometimes led to difficulties for an atheist Marxist state in dealing with an Islamic Egypt which was imprisoning its communists. The most fascinating aspect was the relationship between Nikita Khrushchev, the Soviet Communist Party First Secretary and old-time party member, and Nasser, the Arab nationalist and much younger man.

In January 1958 a large loan agreement between Egypt and Russia was signed, which also provided for increased technical assistance in the Egyptian development programme. In October an agreement with the Russians had been reached for building the first stage of the Aswan Dam. Yet the course of Russo–Egyptian relations did not run smooth following these agreements. Nasser was incensed by the favourable treatment accorded to Iraqi communists by Qasim after the overthrow of Nuri Said and he set to work to root out the communists in Syria. He launched a bitter and open attack, referring to:

> these communists who disown Arab nationalism and believe in atheism and subservience ... The communists uttered false slogans in Baghdad, most significant of which was that of democracy. But where is democracy in Baghdad? It is the democracy of terrorism, gallows and communist courts in the streets to kill whomever fails to give in to them ... This is the most miserable kind of terrorist dictatorship, a terrorist communist dictatorship.

Nasser was speaking on the balcony of the Presidency in Damascus before a large and enthusiastic crowd. His speech was full of fire and venom directed against the Iraqis and those whom he believed manipulated them from outside. To him communists were nothing more than agents. Such words and the fact that he had acted quickly in suppressing them in Syria considerably irked Khrushchev and triggered considerable Soviet opposition. As long as Arab leaders suppressed communists discreetly and made no major issue of their anti-communist sentiments, the Russians were willing to ignore the banning of communist parties; this was a seemingly unwritten condition of Soviet–Arab relations. They could hardly remain silent in face of Nasser's open attacks. Khrushchev, addressing the 21st Party Congress, called his campaign 'a reactionary business'. He said that Nasser's views on Arab unity were totally erroneous and called him 'a passionate, hot headed young man' who 'had taken on more than his stature permitted'. While saying this, Khrushchev also emphasised that 'differences in ideological views must not interfere with the development of friendly relations between our countries' — a clear demonstration of the basic dilemma of Soviet policy.

The two leaders exchanged letters which give a vivid picture of the differences which arose. Each was at pains to convince the other of his sincerity. As quoted by Haykal, Khrushchev wrote to chide Nasser for his outspoken criticism, explaining the virtues of communism and denying that the Soviet Union ever interfered in the internal affairs of other countries. Aid was offered without conditions and it was up to Egypt to refuse Russian aid if it so wished:

> And does not the present situation, when a campaign is going on in the UAR against the Soviet Union and consequently against the Soviet people, give rise to complications for discharging our obligations under the agreement for the construction of the Aswan Dam? I hope you will understand that this is not a threat ... but 'Don't spit into the well — you may need to drink its water'.

Nasser replied in equally offended tones, maintaining that in the Arab world local communist parties with Soviet support were working against Arab nationalism and unity and that it was necessary for him to fight them even if it meant incurring the displeasure of the Soviet Union.

Despite this cool period in Soviet—Egyptian relations preparations for the Aswan Dam went forward and work began in January 1960. The Soviet—Egyptian impasse did not mean a disengagement from prior commitments or a disinclination to undertake new ones, and after mid-1961 relations even began to improve. Syria had left the UAR and consequently Nasser could no longer directly persecute Syrian communists. Russia also began to approve the new more socialist direction that Nasser was pursuing after the break-up of the UAR. In September 1961 Nasser and Khrushchev met in New York and although the meeting was cool Nasser gained the impression that some of their quarrels had been settled.

Soviet ideologues tried to help by classifying Egypt's socialism as a progressive step on the road to communism and even though they did not sound convinced in their writings, political and cultural ties between the two countries were increased during 1962—3. More aid was granted and the rapprochement was sealed by Khrushchev's visit to Egypt in May 1964 to open the first stage of the Aswan Dam. The ebullient First Secretary took part in an impressive opening ceremony at which the waters of the Nile were diverted. In his speech he congratulated Egypt on 'embarking on the path of socialist construction' and promised, apparently on his own initiative, more aid and military equipment. He probably overplayed his hand. On his return to Moscow he was more restrained in his comments but still asserting that Egypt was seeking 'to build a society on socialist principles'. In October 1964 Khrushchev was removed from power partly, it was believed, because of his behaviour in Egypt. On hearing the news Nasser reportedly said: 'Oh my God, now we have got to start all over again'.

In fact Khrushchev's fall did not deeply affect Soviet policy. His successors were rather more phlegmatic and their approach to Egypt became more pragmatic although Nasser did still at times object to Soviet heavy-handedness. On one occasion he quarrelled with Brezhnev who was asking him angrily whether he would ever accept US help in negotiating with Israel. Nasser shouted back: 'After what you've done to me I would accept a solution even if it came from the Devil itself'. Ties between the countries were increased in many ways, culturally, ideologically and militarily. Russia and Egypt went into the 1967 Arab–Israeli war together and both suffered defeat.

Egypt and the United States

Egypt's relationship with the United States was less crucial, although equally difficult. The Americans had queered their pitch in Egypt by refusing aid for the Aswan Dam and had recovered somewhat by Eisenhower's insistence on the Anglo–French and Israeli withdrawal after the Suez invasion. Nasser felt, however, that the Eisenhower doctrine of January 1957 of offering aid to countries in the Middle East threatened by international communism was meant to isolate Egypt and he rejected the American approach. When Egypt's quarrel with Russia was at its height America again approached Egypt with an offer of aid (especially of wheat) which was accepted. During 1958–9 other aid was given unobtrusively. Nasser established a working relationship with President Kennedy with whom he conducted a frank correspondence. He distrusted Kennedy's commitment to Israel and criticised his lack of pressure on the Israelis to bring about a settlement: 'It is too bad, Mr. President, that the United States has put all its weight against law and justice in this case' he wrote (as reported by Haykal). Eventually Nasser, with his deeply suspicious nature, began to suspect Kennedy's real intentions. Relations were exacerbated by the Egyptian rapprochement with Russia and by Egypt's involvement in Yemen against the ally of the USA, Saudi Arabia. Kennedy was working for a disengagement in Yemen and irritated by what he saw as Nasser's reluctance to withdraw. Kennedy's assassination prevented a further deterioration of the relationship but, according to Haykal, Nasser had little sympathy for President Johnson whom he considered rough and insensitive.

Several things soured US–Egyptian relations. Important segments of public opinion in America were reported to have become increasingly indignant over the employment of German scientists – some ex-Nazi –

on military projects in Egypt and there were demands for the cessation of American aid to Egypt. Nasser rightly retorted that the US rocket programme had also been developed by a German scientist. (The Israelis did their best to disrupt the work of these scientists. Letter bombs were sent to a number of them and there was at least one assassination attempt and one attempt at kidnapping. The Israelis had exaggerated the threat that the scientists posed.) In November 1964 the US Information Service Library was set on fire by a crowd protesting against American policy in the Congo. Finally, through a misunderstanding, an American oil company plane was shot down in December near Alexandria. At the time discussions were due to open on Egypt's request for further aid in the form of wheat and the US Ambassador in Cairo, Lucius Battle, informed the Egyptian government that it would be inappropriate to open discussions in the tense atmosphere following the two above incidents. Nasser was once again incensed by what he interpreted as behaviour insulting Egypt's dignity and retaliated in a furious speech in which he invited the Americans to drink from the sea, that is, to jump in the lake.

The Americans replied by banning deliveries of wheat to Egypt for six months and implied that supplies of arms to Israel would be stepped up. Nasser was disillusioned with America and turned more to other possible allies. He signed a scientific agreement with Communist China and was even moving closer to France who had promised aid for development. Together with Tito and other leaders he called for a halt to US involvement in Vietnam. His statements during 1966 became more stridently anti-American and more aligned with those of the Soviet Union. He strongly criticised American arms deliveries to Israel as 'a policy antagonistic to the Arab nation'. In December he revealed that America had stopped sending wheat and accused the Americans of waging a 'war of starvation' against Egypt. Russia stepped in to replace the wheat supplies. Relations with the US deteriorated further during 1967 until the Arab–Israeli war when Nasser severed diplomatic relations and ordered the Americans out of Egypt as he believed the US had colluded with Israel in the war.

The Third Arab–Israeli War 1967

In December 1956 Israel began to withdraw troops from Sinai and a United Nations Emergency Force gradually replaced them. The Israelis delayed the evacuation of the area around Gaza (the Gaza Strip), which Egypt had administered although a part of Palestine, and the post at Sharm al-Shaikh which guarded the approach to the Israeli port of Eilat. Under pressure Israel finally left the two areas and UNEF troops moved in. In May 1957 Israel announced its acceptance of the Eisenhower Doctrine in an attempt to obtain American arms and restore the balance with the Arabs in face of Russian aid to Egypt. Egypt continued to bar the Suez Canal to Israeli ships and cargoes and defied Israel to challenge it. With growing boldness Nasser also challenged Israel to battle. In a speech in July 1959 to commemorate the third anniversary of the nationalisation of the Suez Canal he declared defiantly: 'If Ben-Gurion or Moshe Dayan is looking for the final battle, I am now announcing here in the name of the people, the people of the UAR, that we are awaiting the final battle in order to rid ourselves of Israel's crime'. He listed the weapons that Egypt would produce to strengthen the army: 'We are stronger today than in 1956, when we defeated Britain, France and Israel'. These were risky words as they strengthened the belief that the war in 1948 had been lost because of treachery, that the Suez war was really a victory, that Egypt would soon be militarily self-sufficient and that the next war would be the final battle. It was a dangerous illusion which had disastrous consequences.

During 1962 the arms race intensified with both sides acquiring rockets, planes and tanks. In January 1964 the states of the Arab League agreed to establish a unified military command for use against Israel and anounced measures to frustrate Israel's plan to divert the waters of the Jordan to irrigate the Negev desert. Fortunately for Israel these projects remained paper plans although the Israeli Prime Minister warned that his country would 'protect its vital rights'. Nasser intensified his criticism of the USA for delivering ever more sophisticated weapons to Israel such as Hawk missiles and Patton tanks. In February 1966 came mention of nuclear weapons on both sides although neither side admitted possession. Russia refused to give Egypt atomic weapons but offered a guarantee of nuclear protection if Israel developed or bought nuclear arms.

Looked at in retrospect the 1967 war was a tragedy in which each move was part of a chain leading inexorably to the final clash and in which the principal actor, Nasser, seemed to be dragged along by the tide of events. In November 1966 Egypt and Syria established a joint defence command and Israel immediately felt threatened, for what the Israelis feared most was a united Arab stand leading to a simultaneous attack on three fronts. There was a number of Israeli–Syrian clashes on the border and air battles in April 1967 followed by continuous fighting in May. The Russians warned the Egyptians that they had information that the Israelis had mobilised two brigades on the Syrian frontier. Kosygin, the Soviet leader, told the UN General Assembly on 19 June after the war: 'Information started to come to the Soviet Government and I think not only to us, that the Israeli Government planned to strike a swift blow against Syria at the end of May with the aim of smashing it and then to transfer hostilities to the territory of the UAR.'

The Prime Minister of Israel, Levi Eshkol, warned that Damascus could be occupied if necessary. Nasser reacted by sending troops to the Israeli border and Syria followed suit. The claim has been made that he believed that the presence of Egyptian troops would deter the Israelis from attacking Syria. It is fairly certain that the Russian information was not correct, at least in implying that the Israelis were going to carry out more than a punitive raid. The information might possibly have been fed to the Russians by the highly efficient Israeli intelligence service in order to provoke an Egyptian reaction. When Nasser was asked about this suggestion he replied 'I don't know; [it] may be right'. He then made the move which set the seal on the tragedy and there is more mystery about the true facts.

As Israel responded to Egypt's movement of troops by deploying its own forces, Nasser decided to increase pressure on 16 May by asking the United Nations to remove the Emergency Force from the Egyptian–Israeli frontier in Sinai. Nasser claimed later on several occasions that he had not asked UNEF to withdraw from the Sharm al-Shaikh post. According to the UN documents the Egyptian written request for withdrawal from the Sinai frontier had been accompanied by a verbal demand for withdrawal from Sharm al-Shaikh. On 18 May Egyptian forces appeared at the post and gave the UN commanding officer fifteen minutes before they took it over. Only later did Egypt formally request UNEF's withdrawal. The point is important as later the UN Secretary General, U Thant, was blamed for withdrawing all UN troops so precipitately and allowing Egypt to blockade the Straits of Tiran, thus causing war. The UN case is that Nasser forced their hand. If the UN version is correct it is difficult to believe that Nasser did not expect Israel to react. In fact Sadat reports that he said: 'If we close the Straits war will be a one hundred per cent certainty'.

On 23 May Egypt closed the Straits to Israeli shipping and both Egypt and Syria mobilised their armies. Israel likewise completed a partial mobilisation, criticised U Thant for his over-hasty actions and described the blockade as an act of aggression against Israel. Nasser in a speech at his air force headquarters retorted: 'The Jews have threatened war. We tell them: You are welcome, we are ready for war. Our armed forces and our people are ready ... this is a vital battle.' Those who met Nasser during this period reported that he looked strained and drawn. After the defeat he claimed that he had not wanted war, but many things he said before it demonstrated an attitude of defiance, even if he constantly stressed that Egypt would not strike first. It seemed that he felt impelled to utter threats while at the same time not believing in their implications. Field Marshal Amir and Shams Badran, the War Minister, both pushed Nasser to strike first, assuring him that the Egyptian army was strong enough to win. Badran was in Moscow on 25 May and was somewhat rudely surprised when the Russians urged restraint, saying in so many words – you have won a political victory, now is the time to compromise. Syrian sources also confirm that the consistent Russian advice was not to attack. The Americans likewise tried to restrain Nasser when the Israelis told them that Egypt was about to attack. A deadly game was apparently being played with much doublecrossing and deception. Sadat in return claimed that the Americans urged the Israelis to attack first and supplied them with information on Egyptian positions. The Russian Ambassador in Cairo woke Nasser at 3 a.m. on 27 May and begged Egypt to hold back. He brusquely rejected any advice and in a speech later that day denied that Egypt would fire the first shot in any war. He spoke of a negotiated peace if the Palestinian Arabs were allowed to return to their homeland. He even spoke of possible compromises over the Straits of Tiran. At the same time forces were dragging him in the other direction.

King Husain of Jordan landed in Cairo on 30 May and signed a defence agreement with Egypt. Even the leader of the Palestinian Liberation Organisation, Ahmad Shukairi, who had previously incited the people of Jordan to overthrow the King, sat by Husain's side. While the agreement spoke of 'repelling any attack', in public speeches Arab leaders were caught up in an atmosphere of extreme threats. Damascus proclaimed: 'The elimination of Israel is essential', and Baghdad: 'Our goal is clear — to wipe Israel off the face of the map', and Shukairi forecast that a war would leave few Jewish survivors. Many Arabs believed that the time had come for the final solution of the Jewish problem. The depth of resentment in the whole Arab world against what was universally considered the injustice of the establishment of the State of Israel welled up, and the public demand for revenge grew louder.

The Israelis took these threats seriously, observing the building up of Arab forces and recalling Nasser's long-range missiles and the use of gas in Yemen. There was great anxiety that there would be many Israeli casualties. There was also a political crisis over Prime Minister Eshkol's leadership. He was thought by many not to be decisive enough in the face of Arab threats. The cabinet was divided in its opinion over whether to attack or seek negotiation. Moshe Dayan, the determined and skilful commander of the Israeli army in 1956, was made defence minister to put some backbone into the government and he was convinced that Israel had to go to war. His influence prevailed.

Early on 5 June Israel struck. In three hours at least 300 of Egypt's 430 combat aircraft were destroyed, many on the ground as the pilots had not had time to take off. At the same time Israeli ground forces started a lightning strike into Sinai. Despite strong Egyptian resistance at many points, they had reached the Canal by 8 June, on which day both sides accepted a UN Security Council call for a cease fire. The pride of the Egyptian army, superior in numbers of men and equipment, supplied and trained by Russia, the representative of the new power of the Arab world, had been defeated in three days by a small nation facing enemies on three fronts. Why?

Many theories have been put forward. Nasser at first could not believe that the Israelis had done it themselves and suspected American and British help, but this time there was no collusion. Later he put all the blame on Abdel Hakim Amir who, he said, 'had caused the complete rout of the Egyptian forces in Sinai by trying to pull them back over the Canal in one day'. Haykal wrote that the 'Egyptian High Command was taken by surprise and it fell apart under the impact of the Israeli air strikes'. Both these accusations lay the blame on bad planning and execution and therefore on the whole structure of the Egyptian army. Military theorists have put forward several explanations for the Egyptian defeat. The chief one, and in a sense the only one that matters, is that Israel was basically a Western society based on Western technology and methods with a sophisticated industrial framework. It had a small literate population with relatively high living standards and high expectations and a fundamental determination to fight for its life. Egypt's situation was quite different: it had a large population, one of the lowest living standards in the world, and a developing society facing the problems of assimilating technological advances and socio-economic progress. Whereas weaker forces have been able to face and even defeat stronger armies of a colonial power in guerrilla battles, Egypt faced Israel in a total war which excluded the possibility of guerrilla tactics.

There was a number of failures in Egyptian military procedures. The troops were too hastily deployed in Sinai and this caused supply difficulties and administrative chaos. Once the retreat began there was evidence of a breakdown in communications and units were left to make their own way back across the Canal. Moreover, about one third of the army in Sinai were reservists called up urgently for the crisis. In the air force the lack of preparedness seemed total. Plans had been made to attack but few of these could be put into operation because of the early losses of aircraft. The maintenance and performance of the Israeli air force was also superior. Much was made of the fact that the Israeli aircraft, because of the efficiency of the ground staff, were able to make eight sorties a day with a ground turn round of ten minutes whereas the Egyptians were able to fly only two or three.

Commentators also noted in the Egyptian forces a lack of initiative. The Egyptian army fought courageously but found it difficult to improvise. Once defensive positions had been overrun or the set plan abandoned it soon disintegrated as an efficient organisation. A Russian commentator's opinion was:

> The truth is the USSR had overrated the ability of the commanding staff and logistics of the Egyptian military apparatus. Since 1956, the Egyptian army units up to battalion level had made great progress in terms of courage and manoeuvrability, but the shortcomings above this level turned out to be shocking.

The root cause was the social make-up of the army. The private soldiers and non-commissioned officers were drawn from the peasants and working classes of the towns — ill educated and poor, they did not bring high standards of efficiency and initiative from their backgrounds. The British somewhat improbably likened the *fellah* soldier to a bicycle 'which although incapable of standing up alone, is very useful while under the control of a skilful master'. There was a large gap between them and the higher officers who had often been trained abroad and felt somewhat distanced from the ordinary soldier. This gap, also there in civilian life, made efficient co-operation difficult to achieve. Despite these difficulties, where possible the Egyptian army put up fierce resistance and figures for casualties and losses tell their own story. Eighty per cent of military equipment was destroyed, 10,000 soldiers and 1,500 officers killed, 5,000 soldiers and 500 officers captured.

Politically, Nasser had put the nation in an impossible position. The blocking of the Gulf of Tiran ensured some kind of Israeli reply and yet he took no precautions. The Gulf was not mined nor were extra guns put there. Nasser took Soviet advice not to attack first so seriously that necessary preparations were not made, and he believed that both super-powers, the USA and USSR, were restraining their respective clients. Had he fallen victim to his own propaganda that Israel was merely a pawn of America and would not act alone? The Russians also made grave mistakes. They warned (inaccurately) of an impending Israeli attack and then hastily tried to cover up by preventing Egypt from striking first. In the event their ally was overwhelmed and Russian prestige greatly diminished. On the two other fronts Jordan lost east Jerusalem and the remaining Palestinian territory on the West Bank of the river Jordan and Syria lost part of the Golan Heights, the area overlooking the Sea of Galilee.

Setback 1967–70

Naksa (setback) had struck the Egyptians. There then followed one of the strangest events of Egypt's history. Nasser began to realise the magnitude of the defeat after at first refusing to believe the worst. He looked around for advice. Some in the army, notably those under Abdel Hakim Amir and Badran (whose advice to attack first had been ignored), advised him to go, others in the Arab Socialist Union to stay. On 9 June he spoke on television. A French correspondent described him:

His features drawn, his face tortured. He seemed thunderstruck. With a hesitant jolting diction, he read his text, stammering over the words... his voice choked. 'We have been accustomed... to speak with open hearts and to tell each other the facts... We cannot hide from ourselves the fact that we have met with a grave setback in the last few days...'

He went on to assert that Israel could not possibly have won alone, that it had had American and British military support in the air:

It can be said without fear of exaggeration that the enemy was operating with an airforce three times its normal strength.

Despite this refusal to accept 'facts', there were lessons to be drawn from defeat, especially the necessity to unite to destroy all traces of aggression. He continued:

> We now reach an important point in this soul searching by asking ourselves: Does this mean we do not assume responsibility for the consequences for this setback? I tell you truthfully that I am ready to assume the entire responsibility. I have decided to give up completely and finally every official post and every political role...I have asked my colleague...Zakariya Muhyidin, to take over the post of President of the Republic.

It is rare in history that absolute rulers have voluntarily given up power and it is not their habit to admit to making mistakes. It seems here, however, that Nasser is accepting full responsibility and finally resigning and the obvious question arises: was he sincere? Was it a contrived means of regaining the people's confidence and of reasserting his authority over his colleagues or did he subconsciously realise that he could not continue without the country's reaffirmation. It had been Nasser's habit to appeal directly to the people in times of crisis and change; as he wrote to President Lyndon Johnson: 'I have always been able to move the masses'. We shall never be certain of his innermost motives but even if he was entirely sincere in his wish to resign there was probably also a half-hidden hope that his resignation would not be accepted.

That hope, if it existed, was totally justified. On hearing his speech that Friday evening *his* masses erupted onto the streets of Cairo demanding that their leader remain. Thousands of citizens poured out, intoning their leader's name, rushing to the National Assembly to force deputies to reject the resignation, camping out overnight along the road from the presidential villa to the centre of Cairo to ensure that he went to the Assembly to withdraw his resignation. There were reports that the demonstrations had been organised by Nasser's supporters (and that his opponents had tried to suppress them) but in size and depth of emotion they went beyond perfunctory political demonstrations of support. It was a strange way to run a country – perhaps an example of total democracy – yet a dangerous identification of Egypt's future with one man. Nasser had led the country to defeat. Egypt without Nasser was unthinkable.

Tawfiq al-Hakim, Egypt's leading writer, summed up the situation not without some bitterness:

> No wonder that we clung to our leader after the defeat and that we made his personal existence a substitute for victory or a synonym for

it, because he had made us feel by all available means that there existed in Egypt and the whole Arab world only one intelligence, one power, one personality.

'I can do no other than obey the summons of our people' – thus the President withdrew his resignation on 10 June. 'I have decided to stay where the people want me to stay until all traces of aggression are erased'. He was, however, facing a paradox. He was incomparably the most powerful man in Egypt with the backing of the people. He was also the leader of a temporarily powerless country. He spoke fighting words, comparing himself to Winston Churchill and Egypt to Britain after the fall of France. It was an interesting comparison demonstrating once again his ambivalent attitude towards Britain: 'We all know what happened to Britain after Dunkirk. It did not accept surrender despite the fact that Nazi Germany with its armed forces was able to dominate all Europe.' Egypt would likewise stand against Israel until strength was regained to reconquer occupied territory.

Nasser had first to consolidate his position internally. He rounded on the army, on those he felt had pushed him to war, his closest friends Amir and Shams Badran, the Minister of War. They both resigned and eleven other senior commanders resigned or were retired. (Four hundred to five hundred officers were said to have been involved in a complete purge of the armed forces.) The break between Nasser and Amir was complete, Amir who had urged him to strike first and who had then encouraged him to resign. He felt strongly that the army had been betrayed by Nasser. He began plotting to regain his lost position and was even accused of planning the removal of Nasser. Sadat believes that Nasser had begun to suspect Amir's motives as early as 1962 when the two had disagreed over the command of the army and that Amir had been building up an independent power base. By February 1967 Nasser was complaining of him: 'The country is being run by a gang of thieves... I cannot continue to be President... while it is Amir who actually rules the country and does precisely what he wants'. Amir still retained a certain popularity in the army but before he could realise any of his plans he was arrested. The solidarity of the original Free Officers was broken irrevocably. A newspaper campaign was waged against him and he was finally driven to suicide on 14 September.

This break was a grievous blow to Nasser and it put him in an ever more solitary position. As Haykal described him: 'Alone now, he began to feel that there was a conspiracy against him. And, despite the support of the people, he felt humiliated. There was a deep scar on his soul.' He was the embodiment of Egypt and as such in an impossible position. Others were accused of plotting and sentenced to imprisonment and hard labour, including Shams Badran and the ex-director of the *mukhabarat* (intelligence services), Salah Nasr. Rather petty revenge was taken on the

Jews remaining in Egypt, who were harassed, imprisoned or expelled. By late 1968 most of them had emigrated.

Egypt suffered critical financial losses. Eighty per cent of military equipment had to be replaced. The Suez Canal was closed and produced no revenue. The development budget was severely curtailed and Egypt had to survive on large-scale aid from the Arab oil-exporting countries, Saudi Arabia, Libya and Kuwait. Nasser declared that the re-equipping of the armed forces was the first priority and he appealed to all Egyptians to participate in the struggle against Israel: 'The military struggle will have to be fought not only by the armed forces but by the whole nation'. But although the people had called Nasser back to lead them, they were not prepared to accept uncritically all he called on them to do.

During 1968 there was a strong reaction to the events of the previous year. In February a military tribunal convicted two air force commanders for negligence in the June war and acquitted two others. Popular reaction was immediate and widespread. There were demonstrations in Cairo, Alexandria and the industrial town of Helwan, in which thousands of workers and students took part, demanding severer sentences on the four air force officers. The demonstration, which had an anti-government tone, became threatening and numbers of policemen and· civilians were injured. (Some accounts reported that several demonstrators were killed.) Students staged a sit-in in Cairo University which was only ended when the government agreed to retry the officers and to release arrested demonstrators. The universities were subsequently closed. It was a brave confrontation after sixteen years of authoritarian government and a demonstration of popular frustration. During the unrest, pamphlets were circulated demanding a free parliament and condemning the sterility of the Arab Socialist Union and calling for its abolition.

Nasser decided to confront the situation by speaking as was his habit directly, and lengthily, to the people. He faced workers in a Helwan aircraft factory on 3 March. He summarised all the events from the defeat to the demonstrations which he ascribed to a misunderstanding:

> The misunderstanding began with the sentences issued in the airforce case...We all remember that the sentences were a shock to public sentiment...Everyone has reacted. I have already told you that we have been rather emotional since the June war...We are an emotional people and we think that the enemy is pressing heavily on us and that imperialism is plotting against us. Therefore anything disturbs us. I have also told you that our young people feel frustrated and confused.

Nasser blamed the ASU for participating in the demonstrations, the Helwan police for inefficiency, and the censorship of the press which prevented full news about the demonstrations from being published. 'So the issue was blown up beyond its true dimensions.' There were those who tried to exploit the demonstrations for their own purposes: 'enemies of the revolution and of the people, the imperialist lackeys'. Nasser admitted that the demonstrators had a case to be answered and it was

> obvious that it was impossible for us to suppress popular sentiment by force...We are a good people not inclined to bloody strife. But we must improve...Should reaction and imperialism decide to take advantage of our current situation and should they go to extremes, then the clash will be bloody.

So while warning objectors not to go too far, he was prepared to seek changes to satisfy popular demand, but 'I tell you frankly and clearly: there is no short cut to our objectives'. He concluded by promising to present a new plan of action to them in the immediate future. It was a speech which showed the strain he had felt during the previous ten months. He termed the confrontation with Amir a 'tiring side-battle'. It also showed Nasser's qualities and faults. He seemed as determined as ever to continue the struggle and to lead the people, but he offered no real political lead, only the clichés of 'sacrifice' and 'pure revolutionism', laying blame at the door of 'opportunists' and 'reactionaries'. As he himself admitted in his speech: 'Slogans devoid of real meaning cannot but be deceptive'.

The new plan of action, approved by a referendum in May, called for liberation of occupied land, and a new constitution which would reform the ASU, grant parliamentary control over the government and allow greater personal and press freedom. Popular elections would be held for the National Assembly. These promises did not satisfy all sections of the population and riots again broke out in November. Demonstrators protested against the authoritarian nature of the government and cries of 'Resign, Nasser' were even reported. There were clashes with the police and several demonstrators were killed or wounded. Universities and secondary schools were again closed. Although the referendum had confirmed the new programme, the people were clearly disappointed in its application, seeing no greater democracy or liberalisation. Nasser had made a few changes on paper but was still unwilling or unable to give the people a greater say in the running of the country.

He had been compelled to stay in office in order to try to eliminate all traces of occupation. Although he urged total mobilisation 'of the whole country to wage revolutionary war', in practice he had to urge the Russians to re-arm his country. Far from losing Soviet support he became the centre of their policy in the Middle East. He was regarded as moderate and realistic and an ally against extremists, typified by the Palestine Liberation Organisation and Arab conservatism. Inevitably, Egypt was at times a heavy liability but there was no reasonable alternative given Russian commitments in the area. The Russians continued to pour aid into Egypt, more than replacing lost military equipment with new and more advanced weapons. In 1971 Egypt was reported to have had 450 MIG fighters, 1,350 tanks, 100 naval vessels and SAM missiles. Of 20,000 Russian military personnel said to have been stationed in Egypt about three quarters were assigned to missile sites, with some 200 Soviet pilots flying MIG fighters. Russian funds were still committed to the completion of the Aswan Dam, the full operation of which began in January 1971.

The direct confrontation between Israel and Egypt continued across the Suez Canal and elsewhere. In the diplomatic field the dispute was bandied about in a series of discussions, missions, proposals and resolutions. The first move of the Arabs was to hold a summit conference in Khartoum in September 1967. The leaders were united in opposition to Israel and issued a declaration of complete rejection: no peace with Israel, no negotiations, no recognition, and the maintenance of the rights of the Palestinian people. Such defiance can be seen as totally unrealistic given the magnitude of the defeat and the state of the Arab armies, or it can be seen in terms of a magnificent Churchillian-type refusal to accept defeat. Naturally, the Israelis took a gloomy view of the resolutions. Clashes grew ever more serious. The towns of Suez and Ismailiya were shelled in retaliation for Egyptian fire across the Canal. Egyptian missiles sank the Israeli destroyer *Eilat* and the Israelis replied by destroying oil installations at Suez. Most of the population of the Canal towns was evacuated, causing severe overcrowding in other areas.

In the United Nations discussions went on. In November 1967 a resolution, number 242, was adopted which stated that the acquisition of territory by war was inadmissible. It required Israel to withdraw from 'territories of recent conflict' and demanded the acknowledgement of the sovereignty of all states in the area, freedom of navigation through international waterways and a just settlement of the refugee problem. The Security Council, including the USSR, approved the resolution, although it did not fully please anyone. Nasser called it unclear, the Israelis placed hope in the fact that it mentioned 'territories of recent conflict', not all of the territories, and the Palestinians rejected it outright. Gunnar Jarring, a Swedish diplomat at the UN, started a series of optimistic journeys in the Middle East in an attempt to bring the sides together, perhaps not altogether fruitless as gradually Egypt seemed to be taking a more conciliatory approach. In May 1968 it was reported that Egypt would accept resolution 242 if Israel agreed to evacuate all occupied areas. Israel rejected the approach as meaningless, insisting that negotiations should precede any evacuation. She was also alienated by Nasser's support for the PLO whose avowed objective was the establishment of a secular state in all 'liberated' Palestinian territory. Such support was to the Israelis inconsistent with any desire on Egypt's part for mutual recognition. Nasser replied that Israel refused to support resolution 242, while Egypt accepted it. 'So really what choice do I have but to support courageous resistance fighters who want to liberate their land', (refraining from defining exactly which 'land').

This mutual frustration led to the outbreak of the so-called 'war of attrition' from March 1969 until August 1970. In March 1969 a full-scale artillery duel took place, to be followed by commando raids by both sides, air fights and Israeli air raids deep into Egyptian territory. Many Egyptian targets were hit, both military and civilian. As the fighting increased the two superpowers promised to supply more weapons to their respective clients. In April 1970 Soviet pilots were detected flying missions over the Suez Canal and Soviet missiles were installed in the area. The Israelis made intensive efforts to destroy their sites.

During this long period of warfare diplomatic efforts to solve the dispute were continued. The US President Richard Nixon announced in February 1969 an initiative in support of Jarring's peace mission, but Israel rejected any solution which did not emanate directly from negotiations between Israel and the Arab states. Despite this the USA, USSR, Britain and France met at the United Nations to try to reach an agreement. Nothing resulted from these meetings, although the Soviet side did try to restrain the Egyptians from attempting too great provocations against Israel. The US Secretary of State, William Rogers, proposed in December 1969 an Israeli withdrawal in return for a binding peace agreement and at least had the dubious satisfaction of having his proposal rejected by both sides – Golda Meir, the Israeli Prime Minister, accusing him of 'moralising' and Nasser of 'attempting to destroy Arab unity'. Negotiations were deadlocked in the frozen immobility of the attitudes of the Arabs and the Israelis. From an Israeli point of view the only progress made was that Egypt's call for the evacuation of all occupied territories was no longer the pre-June 1967 call for the destruction of the state.

In June 1970 Nasser visited Moscow for talks on the Middle East. A joint communiqué after the talks stressed the importance of working within the framework of the UN resolution, which implied Egyptian recognition of Israel. Abba Eban, the Israeli Foreign Minister, said the communiqué only revealed that the USSR wanted no peace in the Middle East by insisting on withdrawal from all occupied areas. Nevertheless, Egypt and Israel heeded a US call for a three months' ceasefire on the Suez Canal on 7 August. The Palestinians refused to recognise the truce and continued to fight on other fronts denouncing Egypt in concert with Iraq and Syria for its acceptance. Nasser stated that he had observed the ceasefire on the understanding that America would exert pressure on Israel to accept the UN peace proposals. Otherwise, 'the situation will be grave ... We must not lose sight of the major fact ... What has been taken by force can only be recovered by force'. Israel had been persuaded to accept by promises of further American military aid.

Although there were violations of the ceasefire on the Suez front the greatest threat came from elsewhere. In Jordan the Palestinians had been attempting to show that they would break the truce. Moreover, they had become so powerful and ubiquitous in Jordan that they were acting as a state within a state. King Husain decided to end this situation. The Palestinians were devastatingly attacked by the Jordanian army in September (Black September) and destroyed as a threat to the regime. Nasser tried hard to bring the two sides together. Husain and Yasir Arafat, the chairman of the PLO, met under Nasser's aegis in Cairo on 27 September at an Arab summit meeting. Nasser wanted to avoid a split in the Arab world and worked devotedly as conciliator and mediator during the meeting. He succeeded in bringing about an unlikely reconciliation between the two bitter enemies.

The effort needed by Nasser was enormous. He was by then a tired and sick man. He had been suffering from diabetes since 1958 and from arterio-sclerosis of his leg. He had had treatment in Russia and his doctors had warned him to avoid physical and emotional strain. He had, of course, ignored their advice and suffered a heart attack in September 1969. The strain of the summit meeting was too much. He felt unwell at the airport on 28 September when saying farewell to Arab leaders and returned home to bed. He began to have another heart attack. At 5.00 p.m. he died.

As he had said some years earlier after escaping the 1954 assassination attempt: 'If I die, you are all Gamal Abdel Nassers'. The Egyptians were left to carry on the revolution without him.

5 Nasser's Ideology

Politics and Ideology

Nasser and the Free Officers carried out their coup in the name of the Egyptian people and once in power they had to justify their actions in order to gain legitimacy in the eyes of the people. The alternative would have been to establish a totalitarian dictatorship under which people's views counted for little.

This chapter attempts to explain the methods used to try to gain acceptance and the ideology propounded as a basis of the new order. There are two processes to be observed. Being in power, the officers took practical steps to govern the country, and they then attempted to formulate an ideology to justify those steps which would provide a framework for the future.

Any new regime whether imposed by military force or freely elected is a continuation of the previous one and has at least initially to use the existing framework of government. The political system in Egypt before the coup had been distorted by the presence of the British and by the desire above all of putting an end to the occupation. This overriding priority diverted attention from other problems. The weak figure of King Farouk had not provided inspiring leadership; political leaders had on the whole risen or fallen according to the favour they found with the King or to their ability to wring concessions out of the British. The predominantly poor and illiterate masses did not achieve a high voting rate, and much of the rural vote was controlled by large landowners. The industrial workers were not a large organised group. Egyptians were used to being governed by a central authority without their having much say in their own destiny. Parliamentary life was not deeply rooted in the political system and there was little tradition of government ministers being answerable before the people. As one Arab political thinker has written:

> The truth of the matter is that we the Arabs have inherited from the past a feeling that the state is separated from us; that it is imposed upon us; and that we have no influence upon it or interest in it ... The simple individual in our Arab society feels that the state is a powerful and distant thing and that he must accept its rulings without hesitation, pay taxes without argument and not ask anything in return ... that he has a duty toward it, but no rights forthcoming from it.

Egyptian society before 1952 had not developed a consensus on how a political system should be organised. There was a tendency for the masses to take to the streets or to violent action to express opposition or to force political changes and radical political movements which offered violent change or extreme solutions also attracted the adherence of considerable numbers of Egyptians. When elections were held there were usually accusations of corruption or manipulation. An acceptable formula for the orderly transfer of power from one group to another did not really exist. Non-democratic action seemed to many people, therefore, the only means for change available.

The lack of a consensus before 1952 meant that there was no immediate consensus for action available in the post-revolutionary period. Several ideological trends in the first half of the twentieth century had influenced political thought. The oldest of these trends was that propounded by a nineteenth-century thinker, Muhammad Abduh, who taught that society could be strengthened only if it accepted the need for change linked to Islamic principles. Islam should be the moral basis of a modern and progressive society. This moderate trend of Islamic reformism has had deep appeal in Egypt and has been at the root of the thought of those who wanted to modernise society without abandoning Islam. In practical terms, however, Abduh's vision of the ideal society submitting to God's commandments and living by them is difficult to realise given the constraints and demands of modern politics. The Muslim Brothers pressed this vision to its limit claiming that all worthwhile political ideas were already present in Islam, including social justice, democracy and equality.

Practical politics tended to push Islamic concepts into the background. The revolution of 1919 was an Egyptian national movement which sought full independence for Egypt. This was the motive dominating Egyptian politics from then until the British withdrawal in 1954. This type of nationalism was a potent force but it was not a coherent system of ideas for a political programme. The first constitution of the Wafd party authorised it to work for Egypt's independence by all possible means and the Wafd itself insisted that it was the Egyptian nation organised for political purposes. It adhered to certain general principles (which were not always put into practice): a democratic system of government, separation of politics and religion, a freely elected parliament with ministers responsible to it, the rights of the individual. It was a programme based on liberal democratic principles, deeply coloured by the nationalist struggle. In its concentration on freedom for Egypt it paid scant attention to the larger Arab world and there were indeed those associated with it who even denied that Egypt was part of the Arab world.

The trends of the extreme right were represented by Young Egypt (*Misr al-Fatah*) — the quasi fascist group — and of the left by the communists. The Free Officers had grown up amongst all these political ideas, but they launched their coup into the void without a coherent ideology of their own. They had not led a long liberation struggle, as the *Front de Libération Nationale* was to do in Algeria, gaining legitimacy and popular acceptance thereby. They were unknown soldiers who had secretly plotted a coup. An ideological framework was necessary for them within which to pursue their revolutionary goals. In a society without a political consensus an ideology must be provided to fill that need. This is particularly true in the case of developing countries which have recently thrown off a colonial regime. Nationalism or the anti-imperialist struggle is not sufficient in itself to provide the pattern for a future political programme. Especially when a new and inexperienced group has seized power is it necessary for them to legitimise their rule. An ideology must offer justification for their rule and the measures they wish to introduce, and provide a mechanism for giving the country a sense of order and identity. It should create a national link between the ruler and the ruled. Once the leaders have formulated their ideology they have to try to ensure that it is accepted by the whole country. All means of propaganda – rallies, speeches, slogans and education – are used, usually through the medium of a one-party system which through mass indoctrination attempts to develop a new revolutionary consciousness. In many states the personality of the leader is promoted as the embodiment of the new regime and as the source of the state's legitimacy. To achieve this he must be accepted by the mass of the people as their natural ruler, and not remain a remote dictator.

What is clear about the events of 1952 is that there was no mass revolutionary movement which swept the old regime from power. There was a clandestine, tightly knit army coup. The official version of the revolution published in 1962 in the National Charter imputed to the coup aspects it did not possess, that it was the work and the will of the whole Egyptian people. This interpretation was meant to be the basis of the revolutionary ideology that there had been a revolution which sprang from the people's will and irrevocably changed for the better all aspects of Egyptian life.

However, in 1952 the army, not the people, was the only organisation left to exercise strong leadership after the failures of the politicians. Contemporary accounts of the events of July 1952 express deep suspicion of the coup and an unwillingness to believe that anything had really changed after so many broken promises. The Free Officers' first political act was to force the abdication of King Farouk although it was not immediately accompanied by the proclamation of a republic. Otherwise their first announcement contained no precise plans or aims. They claimed that the army had acted on behalf of the people to 'clear the nation of its tyrants, and to reform the constitutional life of the country'. While searching around for a political programme they attempted to work with civilian politicians appointing Ali Mahir as prime minister and even invited members of the *Ikhwan* to serve in the government. Anwar Sadat makes a frank admission in his autobiography: 'We entrusted Ali Mahir with the formation of a new government instead of doing it ourselves – that is, instead of having a government of army officers – *because we had not prepared ourselves to take over power*' [italics added]. The Agrarian Reform Law of September 1952 limiting landownership to 200 feddans was a political measure to try to consolidate the Officers' power with the poorer people and to demonstrate the general direction of their policy.

As early as 31 July 1952 the Free Officers issued a demand that the political parties purge themselves of 'undesirable elements', which the parties did not take at all seriously. This refusal made the Officers suspect that the traditional politicians were incapable of reforming themselves. The Officers had, therefore, to try to appeal to the masses directly rather than through established political channels. They toured the country speaking to the people between September 1952 and June 1953. Leading members embarked on what they termed a programme of 'mobilisation of national sentiment'. They stressed that the army was part of the people and did not aspire to power for itself. Its aim was to cleanse the country and to bring in unity, order and work. The time of uncontrolled protest and demonstration was past. They particularly asked students and workers for their support. In so doing they were trying to weaken popular support for the Wafd and the *Ikhwan*. They sought to gain legitimacy by dissociating themselves from the previous regime and by identifying themselves with the moderate Islamic ethos. They preached from the pulpits of mosques stressing the Islamic character of their planned reforms. All these moves were an attempt to prepare the people for full submission to the new order.

By January 1953 it had become clear that the political parties were not prepared to co-operate with the Free Officers and they were formally dissolved, their property and funds confiscated and a three-year military dictatorship proclaimed. The Revolutionary Command Council (RCC) was now the sole source of authority, governing by decree and issuing legislation for the three-year transitional period, during which there would be no elections but preparations made for democratic government. General Neguib, the nominal leader subject to RCC control, was probably hoping at the time for an eventual return to a government system similar to that existing before the revolution, purged of corrupt elements.

In January 1953 a single legal political organisation was inaugurated, the Liberation Rally. It was not to be a party but a means of rallying the people round the new rulers, an organisation to mobilise popular support and to squeeze out potential opposition. Throughout his political life Nasser viewed such organisations only as a means of obtaining the *consent* of the people to his rule, not as a means of encouraging political discussion and participation. He was opposed to any groups other than the RCC seeking power and he wanted to encompass all aspects of political life within one organisation. He said: 'The Liberation Rally is not a political party ... Its creation was prompted by the desire to establish a body that would organize the people's forces and overhaul the social set-up'. Neguib conceived the Liberation Rally as a transitional phase on the way back to a multi-party system. Nasser never saw it in this way.

The programme of the Rally was announced in very general terms: the

withdrawal of British troops; a new constitution expressing the fundamental aspirations of the Egyptian people; an 'equitable' social system; a
'fair' economic system; a political system which was left undefined; and
friendly relations with all friendly powers. It was a programme which
promised everything to the Egyptian citizen, expressed in the vaguest
generalities, proving that the Free Officers had few definite political ideas.
However, the Egyptian people joined the Rally in their thousands until a
membership of some 2 million was claimed. Mass oaths of loyalty to the
regime were taken by civilians and soldiers when the Rally was inaugurated.
The organisation partially succeeded in its aims as it helped the regime to
clear the trade unions and federations and student organisations of opposition elements. When Neguib was making his bid for power in March 1954
Nasser and officers loyal to him were able to use the Rally to organise
demonstrations by students and trade union members against the proposed
return of constitutional life.

In June of the previous year the monarchy had been abolished and a
republic established. Although the monarchy had finally been unpopular,
its abolition did leave a gap which had to be filled. Nasser became deputy
prime minister, Abdel Hakim Amir commander-in-chief and other Free
Officers took key ministries. The army regime under Nasser was slowly
establishing itself without any supporting political framework. The
Egyptian people still had absolute rulers but these at least represented a
cross-section of native Egyptian society. The latest threat to the regime
came from the *Ikhwan* and their assassination attempt on Nasser in
October 1954. They were crushed and by the end of the year the RCC had
undisputed powers. Personal loyalty to Nasser became the key to obtaining
and retaining power. The army provided the 'legitimisation' of the regime
– Nasser was its personification. His popularity had grown after surviving
the assassination attempt and the 'revolution' began to acquire mystical
overtones. The very word took on a sacred quality whatever policies were
attached to it and this fact made any opponents of the RCC by definition
enemies of the revolution.

The next move in the political development of the regime was a new
constitution proclaimed in January 1956 and approved by a national
plebiscite in June. It marked the end of the transitional period of government between the fall of the old system and the establishment of the new,
and the end of any possibility of a return to the old. The document had
been drafted by Nasser and a group of his colleagues and it inaugurated a
presidential government system with a strong executive and ministers
responsible directly to the president. The six objectives of the revolution
were reaffirmed and a new political organisation, the National Union, was
announced through which 'the people would realize the aims of the
Revolution'. The Revolutionary Command Council was disbanded and
Nasser was elected Egypt's first six-year President with 99·9 per cent of
votes cast. He had established himself undisputed head of a regime which

had begun to legitimise itself in the eyes of the country. However, apart from the leadership, the political system of the country was far from being established and no firm ideology had been adopted. The events of the 1956 Suez invasion should have demonstrated the weakness of the political system but inexperience and a lack of ideological guidelines prevented the leaders from drawing the necessary conclusions. In fact, as it was taken as a victory for Egypt it became the beginning of a myth which was to have dangerous consequences.

The Liberation Rally did not foster any active political life and failed as an organisation by the autumn of 1956. Its offices were abandoned and its name was no longer mentioned in the government-controlled press. It had failed for several reasons — lack of leadership, of experienced cadres, of an efficient organisation and a comprehensive ideology. The RCC had not given it enough attention, nor any semblance of political power. It had neutralised the influence of the Wafd, the *Ikhwan* and the communists and had been able to 'create' demonstrations and once these objectives had been achieved the leadership felt able to terminate it.

The National Union, replacing all political parties, came into being in May 1957. It was to control all aspects of public activity and to be a focus for public loyalty to Nasser and the regime. An administrative structure was established which spread down to local level from the Higher Executive Committee appointed and headed by Nasser. All citizens were considered potential members of the NU with active members elected to its committees at village level or above. In theory the NU was to be the means of organising the masses behind the leadership. Nasser seemed to feel the need to establish this political framework even if he had no intention of giving it any real power. It was meant to exclude other groups from political power (such as the communists, or the *Ikhwan*) and to be a liaison between government and people. In fact Nasser was not seeking the participation of the people in politics but rather their approval of his policies and the assurance that political criticism could be stifled within the National Union. Control was its main function — of opposition, of the students, of the unions. Its subsidiary task was to awaken and develop the national consciousness and a sense of collective and public responsibility. But it again lacked a clear ideology and a comprehensive programme for change and consequently failed. Nasser himself eventually admitted its shortcomings, which were highlighted by the difficulties of the three-year Egyptian–Syrian union.

Ideologically, the United Arab Republic added problems to the development of Egypt when Egyptian political society was still unformed. The National Union was stretched to breaking point by its expansion to Syria and Nasser's charismatic authority was not enough by itself to keep the UAR intact.

To help the development of political consciousness the Constitution provided for the establishment of a National Assembly. Candidates for the 350 seats had to be screened by the National Union Executive Committee. Voting in the election was compulsory. A £E50 deposit for filing a candidacy was required by law which meant only relatively well-to-do citizens could stand for election. Workers accounted for some 3 per cent of the seats and peasants won practically none. The Assembly was little more than a rubber stamp with no clear functions. Potential opposition candidates had obviously been eliminated and it merely provided a forum in which Nasser and his colleagues could make lengthy statements and announce policy decisions. There was little debate and less opposition. Although Nasser had condemned fake democracy and sham parliament, the National Assembly had as little power as has the Soviet People's Congress. He viewed it as a mirror in which approval for his policies was reflected.

The Charter

The break-up of the United Arab Republic was a severe blow to Nasser. It caused him difficult self-questioning and re-assessment. He admitted that he had made mistakes in his plans and policies, although his general ideas had been sound. The socialist solution was correct but had been inadequately applied. He had been too kind to reaction and opportunism which would have to be ruthlessly rooted out. 'It is inevitable', he said in October 1961, 'that we should now carry out a complete reform operation that will re-draft the ideals and morals of society.'

In November he issued a statement which charted the new path for Egypt. The Egyptian 'people themselves...must now lead the development and show the way with their national ideology to the future they seek and the happy times for which they are struggling'. A National Congress of Popular Powers would debate a charter which Nasser would place before it. 'The main responsibility of the Congress will be to discuss the President's report in which he will present the draft national covenant ...which will profoundly express the masses' needs, problems and aspirations.' These proposals once more demonstrate Nasser's reluctance to share power. He would summon a Congress, but only to debate (and in practice approve) the charter which he had already prepared. Brave or foolhardy would be the Egyptian who would stand up to criticise his President's proposals.

The draft Charter for National Action was published in May 1962. It proclaimed that Egypt was to embark on a course based on the principles of scientific socialism and it was the first serious attempt to define an ideology of the revolution. Egypt was the vanguard of revolution in the whole Arab world, the objectives of which were freedom, socialism and unity. Egyptian history had led up to this moment and had imposed on the country the socialist solution which was, according to Nasser, the solution favoured by the masses. To put into operation a large number of socialist measures the Charter decreed the setting up of a third mass political organisation − the Arab Socialist Union (ASU). The debate on the Charter was held in the Congress and closed without the adoption of a single modification.

Arab Socialist Union

The ASU was a much more serious undertaking than its two predecessors, the Liberation Rally and the National Union. It was more seriously organised and had a visible ideology yet its development was hindered by two factors −− the presence of army officers and the lack of trained officials. In this way it was unlike the one-party systems in communist countries on which it was modelled.

The base of the ASU was units in schools, factories, villages and city districts. Above these were groups of several units, which in turn were combined at the level of government. At the top were the National Congress, the General Central Committee and the real power − the Supreme Executive Committee which included some of the regime's leading personalities with Nasser as chairman. Membership of the ASU was open to all citizens except feudal and capitalist elements and by 1968 it was said to have 5 million members. Nasser wanted it to be a union of the army, peasants and workers, organised so that citizens could join as individuals but not as members of groups which were forbidden. It was a highly centralised body and its top committee was closely interlocked with the government, closely paralleling the system in the Soviet Union. It was a body by which policies and directives could be passed down from the top to the local levels. Nasser did not intend it to be a body whereby suggestions passed in the opposite direction.

Within the total membership some half a million were considered activists who would lead and influence the rest, while a further 20,000 or so were to be trained as a politically active vanguard. An Institute of Socialist Studies was opened in 1965 to execute this task. It is doubtful whether the total number to be trained was ever achieved. This large structure was to mobilise the country and eliminate passivity and prevent reactionary (feudalist, capitalist, *Ikhwan*) and deviationist (communist) elements from gaining power. In practice some communists were eventually allowed to join the ASU to strengthen it ideologically. At all levels the principles of self-criticism, criticism of others, sacrifice and example were to be encouraged.

At the top level there was no very clear distinction between the government and the ASU − the same army officers were members of both − and gradually the ASU began to assume administrative functions, as was almost inevitable. The leader of both was Nasser. At the lower levels the

ASU had a substantial impact on political and social life. It offered an alternative to the traditional centres of power, especially in the villages. The local ASU Bureaus attempted to influence many aspects of life such as education, production, prices and sports. Membership of the ASU became a means of gaining influence and of easing professional and personal success. There could, of course, be abuse as with all one-party systems. Conformity could be enforced and non-members persecuted or discriminated against. The local ASU leaders were encouraged to counteract deviation and to spread the new political culture. Too enthusiastic an interpretation of these functions could lead to the denunciation, persecution and even imprisonment of unco-operative persons. Another danger was that political conformity could lead to promotion without efficiency. In all, the ASU encouraged political participation within carefully controlled and prescribed limits. The Secretary-General of the ASU, Ali Sabry, outlined the aim of the leadership when he said in 1966 that he organised the country's political structure so that it could provide 'the proper guidance of the masses'. From such an approach, proper guidance, it is but a short step to a police state which enforces conformity. The worst aspect of this was the setting up of the Committee for the Liquidation of Feudalism to root out opposition and non-conformity. Sadat bitterly accused this body of practising terror, humiliation and repression, of midnight arrests, the invasion of property and torture.

A provision of the constitution of 1962 was the election of a National Assembly to exercise control over the activities of the executive authority. The Assembly could withdraw its confidence from the government or any minister in which case they would have to resign. The president had the right to dissolve the Assembly — for reasons which were not stated. The Assembly was elected in March 1964 and had a rather different membership from the earlier body. It was claimed that at least 60 per cent was composed of farmers and workers. As a body, despite the above provisions, it was expected to be another rubber stamp. However, on occasion the deputies did question government policies in such areas as housing, higher education and land reform. Ministers were willing to defend their policies and answer questions but none was ever forced to resign and debates usually ended with unanimous approval for government policy. Nasser used the Assembly as a forum for the airing of grievances, not allowing it any great influence. One critic claimed rightly that it never had any real power. (It is interesting that for several years Nasser used Anwar Sadat as speaker of the Assembly.) Nasser often criticised sham democracy as such yet the Assembly seemed important to him as a symbol of the wider participation of the Egyptian people in the affairs of government.

The short period between the establishment of the ASU and the defeat of 1967 showed at least two things — that the socialist system was not yet strong enough successfully to oppose the Israelis; and that Nasser's

personal system of government *was* strong enough to overcome a catas-
trophic defeat. This system survived, despite strong criticism, until his
death. Its achievement was that the Free Officers had a great stability
and internal cohesion, which depended totally on Nasser's leadership
and not on an accepted political system and ideology throughout the
country. Moreover, the acceptance that Nasser had gained did not always
extend to all the other leaders. As long as Nasser retained great popularity there was less pressure on him to 'routinise his charisma', that is
to transform his personal popularity into a less personal system of government. Nasser delayed this process because of his dislike of sharing power
and his mistrust of others, and because he was happy appealing directly
to the people.

Egypt experienced some internal troubles during 1965–7. The *Ikhwan*
had been active once more, the fight in Yemen had gone badly, and there
were food shortages especially in 1966 when the United States stopped
wheat shipments. The climax of trouble came with the defeat of June
1967. Nasser immediately broadcast to the people his offer to resign but,
as described earlier, then submitted to the popular will to remain in
office. He accepted responsibility for the defeat and admitted that mistakes had been made, with some at least of the blame laid on others, and
he proposed yet another programme for action. He allowed public criticism of the regime and debate and inquiry. The central problem was how
to organise society so that the Israeli occupation could be ended and
further defeat avoided.

The ASU was active in criticising the army's tendency to keep separate
from the rest of society and demanded that it become more politicised
to ensure victory in future. The disclosures that Amir had tried to build
the army as a separate centre of power and that he had plotted against
Nasser came as a great shock to the public. After the former's death,
attempts were made to reform the army by introducing tighter discipline
and by recognising the importance of a better trained and educated and
more committed force. The successful campaign under Sadat in 1973
showed that some of the reforms had had an effect. Nasser also tried to
reform the unpopular police and intelligence systems (*mukhabarat*) by
attempting to moderate their more extreme behaviour. His dilemma was
that he relied greatly on them to keep his regime in power.

In March 1968 he announced a new programme of social and political
reform. Once again it was very much his own. He began by increasing the
sentences on the generals held responsible for the defeat and promised
to liberate all occupied territory. He brought new civilian members into
the cabinet to balance the proportion of army officers. He wanted to
rebuild the ASU by bringing in new members and proposed a permanent
constitution which would maintain the socialist progress already made and
give greater rights to workers and peasants. Other provisions were entirely
laudable – the establishment of a modern state, the definition of the

powers of the president, the protection of property, the authority of the National Assembly, the right to seek justice – the problem was to put them into practice. But it did seem that Nasser at last wanted some limitation and sharing of his power and a more open society.

There was more public criticism, especially by Mohammed Haykal, the editor of the newspaper *al-Ahram* and Nasser's 'unofficial' spokesman. He began to float ideas (coming from Nasser?) of a multi-faceted society under the aegis of the one party, the ASU. The students led bold demonstrations in favour of automatic admission to universities which the police put down with considerable loss of life. Others in Egypt backed a hard line against all forms of protest which they saw as counter-revolutionary. To student demands were added demands for the lifting of censorship, criticism of military rule and attitudes, and pleas for a freer society in general. The defeat of 1967 had opened a Pandora's box of complaints which had been latent and suppressed because of fear of persecution.

Nasser reacted to the new mood by appealing directly to the people and explaining his proposed reforms to all sections of the population. In May 1968 he asked them for their support by voting in a referendum in favour of his programme, and they overwhelmingly (99·98 per cent) obliged. Once again he had demonstrated that 'l'état c'est moi' – that all legitimacy stemmed from him and Egyptians relied on him to provide a pattern and leadership for their life.

Practical action was taken to reorganise the ASU which resulted in elections being held for membership of the basic units which were to elect a new National Congress. The election in July 1968 resulted in a wide cross-section of members, both socially, occupationally and politically. Nasser was elected President of the Congress and a Committee of 100 was chosen to prepare an agenda. It submitted a programme in September which called for the mobilisation of all resources to expel the Israelis. At the top of the pyramid of power of the ASU was a ten-man Supreme Executive Committee elected by the Central Committee from twenty officially (that is, by Nasser) approved candidates. In fact only eight candidates received enough votes. Half of these eight were ex-officers, half civilians. The state now had a strong and complex political organisation which seemed to represent a wide spectrum of political views, although all within the ASU.

It was not as strong as it seemed. Firstly the whole political structure depended on one man; and the ASU still had to gain political credibility. It had been carefully organised as a result of 1967, but it had not yet achieved very much. It still had to prove itself, and in a difficult situation. It could not found a state as had the Soviet Communist Party, nor lead a victorious struggle against colonisers as had the FLN in Algeria. Its legitimisation would have to come through expelling the Israelis from Egyptian soil. There also existed some potential struggles, between the ASU and the army, between left and centre within the ASU and between the ASU and the National Assembly. One interesting fact to emerge from the elections to the Assembly in January 1969 was the election of twenty-three candidates who had stood (who had had the courage to stand) independently of the ASU. This was somewhat surprising given Nasser's insistence on a one-party state.

By the time of Nasser's death in September 1970 the ASU in its strengthened role, the system in the broader atmosphere of criticism and freedom, and the President in his perhaps greater willingness to share responsibility had not had time to prove themselves. Nasser had himself clearly gained the adherence of the majority of the population. The political system he bequeathed had still to prove itself.

Islam and Politics

The course of any revolution is influenced by the traditions of the country in which it takes place. A revolution is by definition a turning point in a country's history, but while some aim to restore, others wish to establish a totally new system by destroying the old. The Russian revolution tried to destroy religion, that in Iran in 1979 to restore religion to a central place in politics. The Free Officers had no precise plans and what ideas they had certainly did not include the elimination of Islam. Nasser was no Ataturk with the concept of a secular state. He valued Islam as an essential part of Egyptian life which could further the ends of the revolution. There were several strands to Egyptian Islam – the popular Islam rooted deep in society; the firmly held religious traditions of the Azhar university; the radical appeal of the Muslim Brothers, with whom the Free Officers were to a large extent in competition. Nothing the latter proposed must be seen to conflict with Islamic principles and yet these same principles should not hinder the development of a progressive, modernised society. At each step due weight had to be given to Islamic feelings and Islamic principles utilised to reinforce the legitimacy of the regime.

To appeal to the masses, the Free Officers made their adherence to Islam clear. From the early days some preached the Friday sermon in the mosques to attract mass acceptance of their movement. They stressed the Islamic character of their planned reforms, founded on the principles of justice and equality. They continued to use the mosque as a forum for spreading information about government policies. This use of a religious institution as a means of spreading information on secular policies was a natural consequence of the fact that Islam embraces all aspects of life – sacred and secular. Nasser made the pilgrimage to Mecca in August 1954 during the struggle with the *Ikhwan* as a clear indication that, although he had had to suppress opponents who based their message on Islamic principles, he was no less a Muslim than they.

In September the RCC founded the Islamic Congress with Anwar Sadat as Secretary-General. It was an agency of the presidency and thus under the control of Nasser. It was founded when the struggle with the *Ikhwan* was in its last stages as a demonstration that army officers too were defenders of the faith. The Congress established relations with the conservative religious leaders as a first step in bringing them into line. The attitude of the *ulama* (teachers) of the Azhar was crucial to the Officers. As the most venerable religious institution in Egypt it embodied Muslim orthodoxy and legitimacy. It could not be tolerated as an alternative centre of power. If the *ulama* did not willingly support the regime they had to be made to conform. They were by tradition conservative in the sense of preserving age-old values and of maintaining their position of influence. Nasser decided that the best method of ensuring their compliance was to end the semi-independent position of the Azhar itself, a move opposed by some *ulama* who protested against government interference in religious affairs, and there followed a period of passive resistance and non-co-operation. Some *ulama* resigned in protest and the regime took the opportunity to appoint more compliant replacements and to seek co-operation with the more progressive ones. Eventually in 1961 the Azhar was compelled to submit to pressure from within and without when the government announced a law to reorganise the ancient university. It added new 'secular' faculties to the existing theological ones to enable students to gain access to 'modern' fields of knowledge – that is to break the hold of the conservative teachers. It was also to enable the Azhar to bring about harmony between the teachings of Islam and Muslim life in each generation; in other words the Azhar must be relevant to the new socialist society in Egypt.

There could be no overt opposition to Nasser at the height of his power. In fact some of the *ulama* went to the other extreme, to sycophancy and a total acceptance of the new order. In the journal of the Azhar, the Shaikh (rector) wrote in 1961: 'The new law includes a solution for every problem ... It wants Islam to be revived, *ulama* to be of strong faith, living for the sake and not by means of it ...' Another writer, the editor of the journal, saw Nasser and his regime as the fourth golden age of the Arabs in which the principles of Islam were being applied. The capitulation of the Azhar to Nasser was complete. In fact there was no choice. The government had 'nationalised' the university and a council was appointed to run its affairs. The Shaikh of the Azhar, still a respected figure and important to the regime as the symbol of religious orthodoxy, no longer had any independent power.

No attempt was made to tamper with the teachings of Islam and indeed a number of Azhar *ulama* were useful when Nasser promulgated his Charter with its call to socialism. The Charter itself makes only a few brief references to Islam and does not give it a central role in the creation of the new society. It stressed the 'eternal moral values' of *religions*. The *ulama*, however, were eager to prove that the values of Islam and socialism were precisely similar — social justice, equality, brotherhood, freedom (in all fields) dignity and the elimination of want. And one of the Free Officers, Ali Sabry, claimed that 'the charter has established religion as the foundation of our surge forward to secure social justice ... as the substance of social revolution'. (He meant not only Islam but all revealed religion.) Islamic scholars set out to discover religious sanction for the ideas of socialism, for class solidarity, nationalisation and for the power of the state and especially of its leader. For example, a tradition from the prophet Muhammad that 'People own three things in common, water, grass and fire' was interpreted as a justification for common state ownership of essential industries. Nasser was depicted in terms of the just leader who was foreseen in Islam to come to eliminate tyranny and corruption, to fit Islamic values to the demands of the modern world.

The appeal to Islam was intensified somewhat after 1965 for two reasons: the resurgence of the *Ikhwan* and the defeat of 1967. The appeal of the *Ikhwan* had not evaporated even though their organisation had been suppressed. They even attempted an abortive conspiracy and many of the leading conspirators were relatively young members of the new middle class, significantly showing that Nasser had failed to integrate them into his system. Immediately a campaign was undertaken to 'convince' the population of the benefits of the regime and of the destructive nature of the *Ikhwan*. The Shaikh of the Azhar preached against their beliefs and in favour of the regime's programme. The government was more severely tested by the defeat of 1967 and had painfully to try to regain its plausibility. One of the ways it attempted to do this was to appeal more than ever to Islamic values. In a time of deep stress religion was used as a buttress for social and national life. Traditional Islamic themes and symbols were revived and Nasser made frequent references to Allah in his speeches. The leaders of the regime together attended a mosque service soon after the June defeat and even more significantly a large number of *Ikhwan* were released as a gesture of Islamic goodwill.

In a speech in July 1967 marking the anniversary of the revolution Nasser noticeably tried to shift the blame for the defeat away from himself. Perhaps, he said,

Allah was trying to teach Egypt a lesson, to purify it in order to build the new society. The nation had to accept this testing as its destiny. It had known the Israeli attack was coming but had been unable to prevent defeat.

Nasser resorted to quoting a popular saying: 'Precaution is pointless in face of fate'.

Arab Nationalism and Egyptianism

The Egyptian national identity is composed of a number of factors. A long history of civilisation in the Nile valley gave it its 'pharaonic' Egyptian character. The Muslim conquest gave it its deeply Islamic aspect. The same conquest brought the Arabic language and Arab culture and made it a part of the wider Arab world. More than most countries in the area Egypt has had a continuous identity, but at different times different aspects of this identity have been stressed. As a leading Egyptian writer has commented:

> There is no question that Egypt has had an identity for centuries. The difficulty is to place it in a wider context. This is only necessary with regard to the outside world.

After the revolution it was the Arab aspect which came to the fore. In a sense Nasser's greatest popularity was achieved outside Egypt where it has been said Arab nationalism invented him and made him its hero. There is no doubt that he was the greatest modern leader in the eyes of the Arab masses. He was for them the symbol of dignity regained and the fighter against imperialism, the epitome of Arab nationalism. Yet he took Egypt into a number of pan-Arab ventures which ended in failure and rebuff – union with Syria, war in Yemen, war against Israel.

A noted Egyptian intellectual has written that 'Arabism never truly struck roots in Egypt even at the height of Nasser's popular appeal except as a political expedient'. Many Egyptians would agree with this statement although others would claim that Egypt is first and foremost part of the Arab world and that its destiny is indissolubly linked with it. Nasser himself made Arab nationalism his personal message, especially in the sense that he was its natural leader and Egypt the nucleus state of the Arab world.

What was the Arab nationalism to which Nasser appealed? It is the belief that all those who are Arab by language, history and culture form a natural unity and that political unity in the face of the rest of the world is a necessity. All Arab leaders paid homage to this feeling but in practical terms little was achieved. The unity of language, of religion of the majority, and therefore of a cultural heritage has given to most Arabs a feeling of brotherhood: but political, economic or a customs union has not been achieved for more than a brief period and among two or three countries. Nevertheless, Nasser became champion of and spokesman for the ideal of unity. He was forced into this role by his confrontation with Israel, Britain and France and by appearing on the world stage as a leader of the non-aligned powers. This gave him great popularity with the Arab general public. It did not necessarily help Egypt, perhaps only in the sense that it diverted attention for a time away from internal problems.

It also caused heart-searching among Egyptians. It has already been pointed out that the disappearance of the very name of Egypt during the United Arab Republic caused some resentment and the question was consequently asked — what is an Egyptian? Nasser said: 'I am Egyptian. And I feel Arab because I am deeply affected by the fortunes and misfortunes of the Arabs, wherever they may occur.' Others would probably say something similar. Yet after the defeat of 1967, in a war undertaken by Egypt, Syria and Jordan on behalf of the Arab world, there was some feeling that Egypt had suffered enough for the Arabs, and that Egyptians should rely primarily on themselves for their salvation. Several writers in print stressed the Egyptian-ness of Egypt and Haykal, in trying to ascertain the causes of defeat, wrote that the leadership had been too slow in identifying the Egyptian personality. There could be no doubt that Egypt had proved its devotion to the Arab cause, yet had only suffered thereby. There emerged from the self-questionings after 1967 not a consensus but a more balanced view of the Egyptian commitment to the Arab world which gave Egyptian interests at least equal weight.

Arab Socialism

Arab socialism is socialism adapted to the needs of Egypt. There is little that distinguishes it from socialism as practised in other parts of the world, although some of its proponents would deny this. Nasser finally came to socialism in the Charter of 1962. He decided that his dedication to the socialist path had until then been inadequate and that a firmer ideology was necessary to enable Egypt to modernise itself. Rather late in the day he came to believe that socialism was the only solution. The Charter includes a section entitled 'The inevitability of the socialist solution', which claims that this solution was a historical inevitability imposed by reality, the broad aspirations of the masses and the changing nature of the world. 'Scientific socialism' was the chosen path. The capitalist system had been discredited by its exploitation of the country and by its association with imperialism. It is interesting, though, that Nasser made it clear that his type of socialism was to be different from Marxist communism. There were principles in Islam and in Egyptian society which forbade the introduction of a thoroughgoing godless communist system. He had earlier (in 1958) said that Egypt would benefit from the experience of other nations while blindly copying none. His approach was empirical, adapting political systems to Egyptian needs rather than forcing Egyptian society into a rigid pattern:

The broad lines of this pattern are socialism, co-operation and democracy, and our task is to adapt these principles to our circumstances and to proceed with the work of building a growing, integrated society.

Socialism had to choose the most humanitarian path. The Islamic ideals of equality, social justice and brotherhood were more relevant to Arab socialism, which would grow out of the masses rather than be imposed from above.

It was to be a balance between the capitalistic stress on individual interests and the communist emphasis on class conflict and would be derived from the revelation through Muhammad of the ideal Islamic society, interpreted by Arab–Muslim thinkers throughout history, and by the present leaders' knowledge of the practical demands of economic and social development. The Islamic ideal meant a society without injustice, which meant freedom from hunger, want and exploitation, which in its turn implied common ownership of the means of production and a planned society. Within the framework of national unity all would be encouraged to co-operate for the national good – farmers, workers, small businessmen, intellectuals, professionals, non-exploiting proprietors and soldiers would unite against exploitation. The planned society was the best method of marshalling Egypt's human and economic resources.

The principles of Islam were appealed to in many ways to support socialist policies and to gain wider acceptance in society. This 'woolly' approach did not satisfy Egypt's Marxist intellectuals who called for the adoption of a stricter scientific and secular socialism. The former head of the Socialist Institute, a Marxist called by Nasser to establish this Institute, once described four attitudes amongst the Egyptian masses which he believed were in contradiction to the basic values of the socialist transformation and which had to be changed: fatalism; absence of faith in science and its findings; slovenliness and a refusal to submit to the requirements of life; rejection of any planning or regulation of life. Only by adopting a rigorous scientific socialism could these attitudes be overcome and new ones instilled. Because of a shortage of ideologues Nasser used a number of Marxists as theorists of Arab socialism who had to compromise their beliefs in a secular society and be content with calling for new moral and social patterns.

Obviously, too, Nasser's version of socialism did not satisfy Soviet leaders and ideologues. They wanted a whole-hearted adoption of Marxism and had little patience with the Egyptian compromise. Apart from lengthy critiques by Soviet commentators, the Communist Party Secretary Brezhnev is reported to have said: 'Nasser is a bit mad in matters of ideology ... When the Arab masses realize their real interests, we will no longer have need of any Nasser'.

Ideological Influences on Nasser

Nasser throughout his life was subject to a series of political influences which helped to shape his eventual ideology. His point of view was modified as the external circumstances which shaped it changed. The main influence in his youth was the fact of the British presence, which he considered humiliated Egypt and distorted Egyptian politics and society. He consequently embraced the philosophies of those he thought best suited to end the occupation – the militant *Misr al-Fatah*. Like many Egyptians he had an ambivalent attitude towards the British, especially seeming to admire Churchill and his stand against Nazi Germany after Dunkirk. It was, however, the attitude of Churchill as a leader that he admired rather than the fact that he was British. In his early reading he had studied the lives of a number of heroes who provided a pattern of leadership, of resistance and success. The careers of Alexander the Great, Napoleon and Gandhi particularly interested him and, as we have seen, from an early age Nasser felt personally involved in politics and probably foresaw for himself a leading role.

His childhood in the Egyptian countryside and city and his acquaintance with poverty brought to him the unshakeable belief in the need to obtain social justice for the people who were the victims of political and economic exploitation. Coming from the people he had a strong fellow feeling with them and the key word in his view of them was 'dignity': they had the right to hold their heads up as the foundation of the Egyptian nation.

Nasser was also part of the Islamic tradition of the country and the various strands of thought, from the popular religion of the people, through the liberalising and modernising ideas of thinkers such as Muhammad Abduh with his emphasis on an Islamic social programme, to the fundamentalist appeal of the Muslim Brothers. All these currents influenced Nasser's thought. He assimilated them and they coloured his future ideology, while remaining a very pragmatic man. He had a strong confidence in his own ability to chart the correct path for Egypt without relying exclusively on a pre-formulated framework.

When the Free Officers took power many shades of political opinion were represented – the fascist, communist, Islamic fundamentalist and radical socialist. Nasser had to pick his way among these conflicting views while embracing none. As he continued in power he came under other non-Egyptian political influences, those of leaders from the Third and communist worlds. His closest relationship was with President Tito of Yugoslavia who taught him the concept of a socialism not subservient to Soviet communism and worked out in the closest possible conformity with local conditions. Because of Tito's independent stance *vis-à-vis* Russia, 'independent' socialism assumed a certain respectability and Nasser took many ideas from the Yugoslav experiment. According to Sadat:

All [socialist] formulas had been borrowed from Yugoslavia, due to Nasser's close personal relationship with President Tito. Nasser had interminable conversations with him and always showed admiration for his views.

Nasser's relationship with other communists was less close and more difficult. He and Khrushchev fought a running battle over ideology and Nasser was not deeply influenced by him. Any attempt to push him further along the road of Soviet communism was strongly resisted. He had a see-saw relationship with Egyptian communists, at times imprisoning them, and at others releasing them and using them to help to develop his socialist doctrines.

How Nasser Ruled

The final point to consider in discussing the political system of Egypt is the manner in which Nasser built up and maintained his authority. His was a personalised leadership and the legitimacy of the regime stemmed from him. This gave him an enormous personal power which he utilised to strengthen his own position. In many ways he felt that all that mattered in the Egyptian political system was the bond between himself and the Egyptian masses. Although he was motivated by a deep concern for their welfare he wanted them as a support for his policies and did not encourage political participation or overt criticism. His regime had to weather a number of crises and at such times he used the classical tactic of diverting the people's attention to something else, usually in a heart-to-heart speech. He liked to address the people directly to maintain a direct link, and he enjoyed the influence he could exert over large audiences, who felt themselves the recipients of his confidences and ideas. This direct method – 'government by monologue' according to one critic – could, however, have its drawbacks. A shrewd observer, the leading Egyptian writer Tawfiq al-Hakim, expressed his doubts in *The Return of Consciousness*, an influential book published after Nasser's death:

The country began to get used to the rule of an individual and trusted and loved him. The masses, when loving do not criticize. One by one, the voices used to criticize were lowered and the beloved leader himself began to be accustomed to a rule in which there was no criticism. The iron curtain began slowly to fall between the people and the actions of the absolute ruler. We loved him but did not know the inside of his thoughts or the real motives for his actions. We only knew of internal or external affairs what he told us, speaking at festival times or other occasions from his high platform. From his isolated position he would make speeches without any trouble lasting for hours in which he made us into heroes under his leadership and made the great states around us into dwarves. We applauded with wonder and pride.

In this way a link between ruler and people – which was almost entirely one way – was maintained, and he was not averse to adding an element of organisation (and coercion?). Hakim relates an interesting sidelight:

> I once met a peasant I knew and asked why he was in Cairo. He said it was connected with the Committee of the ASU in his village. They had brought him and colleagues by train with travel documents to gather together to welcome Nasser on his return to Egypt on some occasion... They were lodged and fed at state expense. They had to shout to him certain slogans printed and distributed to them... for example: '*General shout* – Nasir, Nasir, Nasir; *group shout* – Long live Nasser of Arabism; then *general shout* – hero of the revolution, hero-leader...'.

Nasser told the people what he thought they should hear. He hardly heard what they were saying – for at least two reasons. The conjunction of his position of power and his natural inclinations led him to become more autocratic. Several observers have noted this tendency. One wrote that 'The Council of Ministers under his chairmanship became an audience. Nasser was the only speaker'. Government ministers were there to listen and to receive instructions. Sadat considered him to be a conspirator by nature who suspected intrigues and listened to gossip. Such a man could easily confuse these with honest dissent and comment. 'Anxiety gnawed continually at his heart, as he regarded everyone with suspicion.' This meant that those who surrounded him were unlikely to oppose him. His mistrust was justified in that the man he trusted most, Amir, was the one who eventually betrayed him. 'Egyptian rulers are doomed, however good their intentions... if their rule is of long duration... to end up as tyrants', wrote one Egyptian observer of Nasser. He had obtained his position of supreme authority by being accepted as absolute ruler by his people and by imposing himself as leader of the Free Officers. To maintain this and due to his suspicious nature he established a system of cross-checking institutions. He controlled the security apparatus (*mukhabarat*), the army, the administration and the Arab Socialist Union. The army was the basis of his power and he used his position as arbiter among the various institutions to ensure that none of them became too powerful. He shuffled his ministers and officials, listened continually to reports from the *mukhabarat*, and was not averse to imprisoning and torturing suspected opponents to ensure conformity and eliminate opposition. Nasser became the prisoner of the authoritarian system he had been instrumental in establishing. He did not wish to hear criticism. Therefore no one raised his voice. He ignored what he had himself written in the Charter: 'Real leadership consists in being sensitive to the demands of the people, in expressing these demands, and in finding means to answer them'.

Sadat expressed the extreme view of this attitude: 'Nasser looked on any protests, any objection or criticism, any attempt at fact-finding or the least expression of resentment, as a counter-revolutionary reaction that must be ruthlessly crushed'. He cultivated among the Egyptians 'a regime of fear'. He stood at the top of the pyramid of power he had established, yet he had to rely on others to put into practice the policies he wished to introduce. This he did by keeping near to him a handful of the Free Officers as the ruling élite and giving them key posts in the government. Even these fluctuated and only Amir remained in the close inner circle all his political life. Of course this close relationship could be abused. Sadat observed that Nasser's policies were much influenced by his own emotional reactions and that his associates realised this: 'They would provide him with a certain piece of information ... calculated to produce in him a strong reaction ... and make him do exactly what *they* wanted'. In turn each Officer built up his own system of client—patron relationship which gave him relative freedom of action but prevented the establishment of either a totalitarian government or a government based on checks and balances between institutions. Personal relationships in government were all-important, and these stemmed from the President himself.

6 Sadat's Revolution of Rectification

President Nasser's death left an apparently unfillable gap in Egyptian political life. For eighteen years he had been the central figure of the revolution and the Arab world. No one in the government seemed remotely fitted to follow him. Great leaders are unique figures who cannot be replicated and have to be followed by successors in a different mould with their own style. Anwar Sadat was a Free Officer who had worked modestly in Nasser's shade, some say a trimmer. He had been secretary of the rather ineffective Islamic Congress and of the National Union, and speaker of the somewhat powerless National Assembly. He had been appointed vice-president in December 1969 and therefore took over on Nasser's death, a virtually unknown quantity. It is not clear why Nasser had chosen him and Sadat expressed an initial reluctance to take over. He soon, however, slipped into the role and began positively to enjoy the exercise of power.[9] He believed that 'Nasser's legacy was, to put it mildly, unclear' and that his predecessor had reduced 'the revolution to a huge, dark and terrible pit, inspiring fear and hatred, but allowing no escape'. As the political and economic situation became clearer to him he began to formulate his own policies. He found that his position with regard to foreign policy was diametrically opposed to that of Nasser, and that Nasser's economic legacy was 'in even poorer shape than the political'. Sadat's avowed aim was to build a society 'of dignity, serenity, tranquillity and affluence' — brave words in the face of such formidable problems.

He soon showed unexpected strength and cunning in establishing himself. His fellow members in government had at first thought him to be a figurehead behind whom they could direct policy and were very surprised when he began to take independent initiatives, including new approaches to the United States, and his backing of yet another attempt at Arab unity — a proposed federation of Egypt, Libya and Syria. The proposal was approved by President Assad of Syria and pushed by the mercurial Colonel Qaddafi of Libya who had recently taken power after an army coup. Sadat rather hesitantly believed he was following Nasser's unionist policies. The federation was used as a pretext for his opponents to come into the open; they were led by Ali Sabry, Vice Premier and former Secretary of the Arab Socialist Union. At a meeting of the Executive Committee of the ASU in spring 1971 Sabry and his supporters resigned in protest against the federation and tried to organise mass opposition to Sadat in the ASU and amongst the police. They failed because they could not appeal to any mass support and did not have much unity of purpose amongst themselves. In any case Sadat moved too quickly for them and arrested all the conspirators in May 1971, thereby terminating what he called 'the nightmare of the central struggle for power'. At a subsequent trial ninety-one of them were sentenced. At the same time Sadat strengthened his support within the army, promising it a strong and honourable future role in the state. In return it assured him that it was not involved in this 'childsplay'. He was slowly establishing himself in power as his own man, shaking off any allegiance to or reliance on the heritage of the previous regime.

Sadat especially chafed under three of Nasser's bequests – the close ties with the Soviet Union, what he called the 'inane socialist slogans' which distorted social justice, and the Israeli occupation of Sinai and all that it meant. He quickly showed how his mind was working on all three points when he announced in May a second revolution, known as 'the revolution of rectification', to correct the course of the 1952 revolution which had been distorted by numerous errors. As early as December 1970 he had lifted the sequestration order on private property, a pointer to further 'liberalisation' to come in the political and economic fields. His relationship with Russia was uneasy from the first. He was largely trapped, however, as Nasser had equipped the armed forces with Soviet arms and any change in equipment would necessarily be very long term, Sadat had more immediate plans. His course of action was, therefore, rather zigzag and tried Soviet patience to its limits. In May 1971, after arresting his opponents whom he accused of being Moscow's agents, he signed a Treaty of Friendship with the Soviet Union. This did not prevent bitter disagreement between the two countries over the supply of weapons. Sadat accused the Russians of continual prevarication and of never delivering the most up-to-date equipment. (He complained that Israel always had a much easier time with the United States.) His frustration reached a peak in July 1972 when promised weapons had not arrived. Sadat, much to the surprise of the West, ordered all Soviet military experts (some 15,000) to leave the country and insisted that only Egyptians should man and own the military equipment in the country. Sadat's private reason for the expulsion was that in the coming war he wanted only Egyptians to be involved. In public he blamed Soviet arrogance which he said was comparable to that of the British under the High Commissioner. This move did not lead to a complete break and eight months later the largest arms deal ever between the two countries was concluded. Evidently, the Russians had swallowed their pride.

As relations with Russia worsened Sadat turned to the West for aid, especially to the United States which he believed to be the only country able to put pressure on Israel. Nasser had bequeathed to Sadat the urgent priority of expelling the Israelis from occupied Sinai. Following the war of attrition a ceasefire had been signed in August 1970 and to follow this up Sadat launched in February 1971 what he termed a peace initiative. He was willing to sign a peace treaty with Israel and open the Suez Canal in return for a partial Israeli withdrawal and the recrossing of Egyptian troops into Sinai. Recognition of Israel was a tremendous step and one that needed great courage. The other shock to public opinion was the invitation to the American Secretary of State, William Rogers, to visit Cairo, which he did in May. He seemed to reach an agreement with Sadat but he was unable to persuade the Israelis that Egypt was serious. Sadat was understandably disillusioned by this setback, dismissed the Rogers Plan (see page 82) and the ceasefire and named 1971 the year of decision, the year in which he would put an end to Israeli occupation. Few believed he would achieve anything and he was openly mocked in Cairo when December 1971 came and went. He lamely explained that an unexpected fog on the battle front had frustrated his plans and the joke in Egypt was that by decree he was going to extend 1971 by several months![10]

In May 1972 President Nixon met Brezhnev, and Sadat was convinced that the two superpowers would try to prevent a new war in the Middle East, that a position of stalemate had been reached (no peace, no war) and that he would never be able to negotiate successfully from his position of weakness. He therefore decided on a war which would administer a shock to entrenched attitudes. Soviet weapons began to arrive, he was free of Soviet advisers who had counselled caution, and meticulous planning for war began.

On the morning of 6 October 1973, Egyptian troops crossed the Suez Canal and stormed the Israeli fortifications on the east bank – the so-called Bar Lev line. It proved surprisingly vulnerable and the Israeli troops were completely overwhelmed. More troops and tanks crossed and began the push into Sinai. As the Israelis recovered from the initial shock fierce battles took place and Israeli troops because of a disastrous failure in Egyptian communication crossed the Canal in some force and began to encircle the Egyptian Third Army Corps. In the north another initial advance by Syrian troops into Israel was halted and pushed back towards Damascus. The Israelis had come, however, dangerously near to defeat and were saved by a massive American airlift of war equipment. Egypt received Soviet arms to make good her losses. By 20 October the Israelis were threatening to starve out the trapped Third Army, although the Egyptians claim that the situation was never serious and that the Israelis themselves were being encircled. A United Nations-sponsored ceasefire was finally accepted by both sides on 22 October and by Syria on 29 October when Israeli troops were only twenty miles from Damascus.

Ever since arguments have raged over who 'won' the war. To Egypt it was an unqualified victory with Israel saved only by American help – for Sadat 'the myth ... of [Israel's] invincible airforce, armory, and soldiers was finally shattered'. Certainly Israel had been taken disastrously unawares by the well-planned Egyptian assault, yet recovered well enough to strike back. Both sides suffered serious losses in men and material – human losses which could be ill afforded (Israel lost 2,552 killed and missing, Egypt some 9,000 killed and 11,000 wounded), and material losses which Russia and America made good (the Arabs 450 planes and 1,900 tanks, the Israelis 120 planes and more than 800 tanks and armoured vehicles). Sadat had been prepared for losses. He wanted to shock Israel (which he did) and to prove to the world that Arab soldiers could plan and fight on equal terms. It was a war to regain self respect, to shake the superpowers and in the words of Tawfiq al-Hakim, a 'spiritual crossing to a new stage in our history'. It gave Sadat an entirely fresh basis from which to negotiate. It also brought the world economy a new factor – the oil weapon. Cuts in production were effected by members of OAPEC (the Organisation of Arab Petroleum Exporting Countries) and most placed an embargo on deliveries to the USA in the hope that it would cause America to modify its pro-Israeli policy. Gradually the embargo broke down in face of little change in American policy although the disruption of supplies did result in permanent large price rises.

In Egypt Sadat was hailed as the 'hero of the crossing' and became a popular leader in his own right. It was a more real 'victory' than Nasser's repulsion of the tripartite aggresssion in 1956 though unfortunately it only haltingly and partially brought the desired results. But it did bring the United States more fully into the search for peace which was one of Sadat's main objectives. Henry Kissinger, the US Secretary of State, had worked hard to bring about the ceasefire and he and Sadat developed a close working relationship. He helped to arrange a conference in Geneva in December between Egypt, Jordan and Israel, with the USA and USSR attending, to discuss disengagement on the Suez and Syrian fronts on which sporadic fighting had continued after the ceasefire. The conference achieved little of substance and a disengagement on the Suez front was achieved in January 1974 only through the personal efforts of Kissinger who had 'shuttled' between Aswan and Jerusalem for negotiations. By 21 February the Israelis had moved back across the Canal to a prescribed zone in the Sinai Desert. These moves led to a resumption of US–Egyptian diplomatic relations broken since 1967 and to the clearance of the Canal, blocked also since 1967.

Sadat placed his faith almost entirely in the USA, believing that they held '99 per cent of the cards in this game'. Nevertheless Kissinger was unable to achieve miracles and anyway his attention was diverted by Watergate, the affair which eventually led to President Nixon's resignation. He started a second shuttle in March 1975 which foundered on Israeli intransigence in April that year. Eventually, a second disengagement was agreed in September 1975 by which Israel undertook to withdraw further in Sinai and to return the oilfields there in return for an Egyptian pledge not to use force again.

At the same time as Sadat was facing his major international problem, he was also wrestling with internal economic affairs. He sought and received considerable US aid and some arms and tried to postpone repayment of the Soviet debts. The two aspects of his policy were closely intertwined. He wanted peace with Israel in order to pursue economic development at home in an atmosphere of stability and security which would encourage foreign investment. A big drain on the budget were the large government subsidies on basic foodstuffs and other items. If food prices had risen in line with inflation the urban poor would soon have found many items beyond their reach. As long as their income did not rise (in fact per capita incomes were dropping as population increased) the government had to tread extremely warily in the area of subsidies. In late 1976 Egypt was seeking loans from the World Bank which august body has certain ideas on national finance, among them a dislike of subsidisation. To satisfy the Bank the government announced in January 1977 the ending of several subsidies — including those on flour, sugar, rice and cooking oil — together with the cancellation of bonuses and pay increases.

The result was immediate and shocking. On 18 and 19 January there was heavy rioting in towns from Aswan to Alexandria, variously described as the biggest upheaval since the rising against the British in 1919, a second Black Saturday, or as the first time that the army had been brought into the streets since 1952. There was apparently little animosity towards foreigners: targets were institutions such as ASU offices and police stations and signs of wealth and corruption such as large cars and nightclubs. It was an uprising of the ruled against the rulers. The government was caught napping and the army had to be used to quell the disturbances. In Cairo alone seventy-seven people were killed. The price rises were immediately rescinded, the bonuses and pay increases retained. The rioters had won. One slogan shouted during the riots was 'Hero of the crossing where is our breakfast?'. Another was 'Nasser, Nasser!'. Sadat was stunned, and while realising that the subsidies were the main cause he looked around for scapegoats, blaming the left and the Marxists and arresting hundreds of them. It was the beginning of a gradual yet noticeable decline in his popularity. Sadat overreacted in the apparent belief that all his policies were being threatened. A stricter press censorship was introduced and a state of emergency proclaimed. It did seem, however, that the people were asking for full stomachs rather than changes in policy.

Sadat continued to pursue his external goals, promising the poor that their problems would be eased once peace was achieved. He looked to the Geneva conference for further progress with Israel and encountered numerous obstacles. Menachem Begin became the new Israeli prime minister, a hardliner and supporter of Israeli expansion. He approved the development of settlements on the occupied West Bank of Jordan and massive raids into Southern Lebanon, and refused to countenance any approach to or negotiation with the Palestine Liberation Organisation. Sadat was consequently driven to another dramatic gesture — he went to Jerusalem in November 1977 to present his case in person to the enemy. Arab opinion was shocked and the rest of the world watched in amazement.

The hero had made another crossing, this time the difficult psychological one of recognising the foe on his own ground.

In a speech to the Israeli Parliament on 20 November he presented himself very much as the man upon whom history had laid the burden of bringing peace to the area:

> There are moments in the lives of nations and peoples when it is incumbent upon those known for their wisdom and clarity of vision to survey the problem with all its complexities and vain memories in a bold drive toward new horizons.

The goal of his visit was to 'achieve a durable peace based on justice' – peace between all the Arabs and Israel together with a 'just solution of the Palestinian problem'. He was very frank in his speech, detailing all the difficulties that had arisen between Israel and the Arabs and demanding in return for peace and secure frontiers, the evacuation of territories occupied in 1967 (including Jerusalem) and the right of the Palestinians to self-determination and the establishment of a state.

Mr Begin in his reply made no commitments, and in fact moved the peace process forward hardly at all. The intervention of President Carter was necessary. He visited Egypt and Israel in January 1978 to initiate the moves which led to a meeting of the three countries at Camp David outside Washington in September. Talks proceeded slowly, foundering on disagreement over Israeli settlements on the West Bank[11] and Palestinian statehood. Begin was particularly opposed to any concessions to the PLO. He seemed to be going out of his way to alienate the Egyptians when he approved further settlements in February 1979. A second meeting was held at Camp David in the same month and a breakthrough was certainly made, although only in certain limited areas. In March a peace treaty was signed between Egypt and Israel with a great show of cordiality between Sadat, Begin and Carter. Israel agreed to withdraw from Sinai within three years of the treaty, normal diplomatic and trade relations were to be established, and Israeli ships would pass unhindered through the Suez Canal. The USA would monitor Sinai and Egypt would be unable to act entirely freely in the area. So much Egypt achieved, but at the same time Begin was saying unpalatable things which went rather unregarded. Settlements would continue (after a moratorium of only three months), Jerusalem would remain undivided, there would be no Palestinian state, merely a strictly limited autonomy. It is not clear whether Sadat did not take these words entirely seriously or whether he took them as a negotiating position. Other Arab states saw them as the substance of the negotiations and accused him of making a separate treaty with Israel and of abandoning the Palestinian cause. Egypt was expelled from the Arab camp, the Arab League headquarters were moved to Tunis, and diplomatic relations broken. Sadat was branded by the Arab world as a traitor and his peace treaty was 'rejected'.

In April 1979 the first Israeli ship passed through the Suez Canal and Egypt returned to the occupied town of al-Arish in Sinai. In February 1980 an Israeli Embassy was opened in Cairo.

Sadat had a difficult time after signing the treaty and although the Egyptian people approved it in a referendum in May 1979 by 99·9 per cent of the votes cast in a 90 per cent turnout, opposition to it was widespread. In the People's Assembly thirteen deputies had the courage to vote against it and other groups and parties − from Muslim Brothers to Marxists − expressed disapproval. Sadat achieved peace at the price of isolation and an almost total dependence on the USA. Relations with the USSR were delicate with neither side wanting a complete break. Soviet arms were thought to have arrived in 1980 although Russian commentators complained bitterly that Egypt had undergone 'a surprising metamorphosis' from a fighter against imperialism to 'a traitor to the interest of the Arab people', and they asked whether Sadat had forgotten Soviet help in 1956, aid in building the Aswan Dam, and the airlift of arms in 1973. In return for withdrawal from Sinai Israel obtained many of her major aims − peace with the most powerful Arab state, right of passage through Suez and the right to trade with and invest in Egypt. Sadat got back some territory, US aid and arms but little else. A May 1980 deadline for talks on Palestinian autonomy passed without action and Israel refused to contemplate real Palestinian autonomy or negotiation with the PLO. Settlements have multiplied on the West Bank. Jerusalem was proclaimed the indivisible and eternal capital of the state.

This lack of progress, Egypt's isolation and no real material improvements for the poor combined to increase Sadat's unpopularity. He reacted to criticism by imprisoning his opponents and strengthening censorship. In 1981 he made a mass arrest of people he believed to be working against him. It seemed that all his promises and policies were falling in ruins about him and while he remained a popular figure to the West, he became more and more isolated in Egypt. The world was taken aback by his assassination in October 1981. The Arabs rejoiced. The West mourned a great leader. The Egyptians remained rather indifferent and did not pour out to his funeral as they had done to Nasser's. The assassins were Islamic extremists, alienated by his rapprochement with the West and Israel and they shot him as an individual punishment. They did not seem to be part of a wider plot.

Once again Egypt was left leaderless. Vice-President Husni Mubarak took over in an orderly succession and was approved overwhelmingly in a referendum. An airforceman by profession, he had commanded the Egypt air forces in 1973. On assuming power he promised to carry on Sadat's policies towards Israel. At the same time he stamped on all opposition and trouble from the Islamic fundamentalists. He took over an Egypt vastly different from that of Nasser. His problems were no less grave.

Politics under Sadat

In the first eleven years after Nasser's death Egyptian politics underwent a radical realignment. Sadat's foreign and economic policies needed a more flexible, liberal and democratic political system, and although by 1981 a new political life had not taken root, some efforts had been made to encourage less dogmatic political trends and to further constructive political debate. Sadat himself admitted that he was not clear about the nature of Nasser's legacy and that in several respects his position was diametrically opposed to that of his predecessor. He had to move warily as he tested the water. His more liberal attitude had been demonstrated early by his restoration of sequestrated property, and the struggle against Ali Sabry led to the immediate dismantling of parts of Nasser's apparatus. Sadat was particularly opposed to what he termed 'centres of powers' – the clique of top army officers, the élite of the ASU, the intelligence service and police force. In his 'corrective revolution' of May 1971 he weakened the power of these rival bodies by purges of personnel and he introduced his plan for national action. He claimed that true democracy would be introduced under a just legal system which respected the rights of the individual. A new constitution approved in September by a referendum (Sadat's method of gaining national approval) enshrined these concepts. A National (People's) Assembly was elected which began to criticise and debate more openly; the ASU was placed under civilian leadership in an attempt to make it a more effective organisation divorced from government. The new first secretary began several weeks of discussion late in 1972 with ASU leaders in order to work out its future organisation. It was generally admitted that it had failed in its task of politicising the people and of creating institutions which would propagate a coherent ideology. Nothing was done immediately to change the situation although the ASU was slowly losing ground as a body for action.

Little more was done in the political sphere until after the October 1973 war. In the interim mention was made of a 'democratic dialogue' in which the nation would discuss its political future. It was becoming apparent that whatever happened the legacy bequeathed by Nasser would not remain unmodified for long. Sadat's attitude towards a rigid socialism was clear:

> We had, with crass stupidity, copied the Soviet pattern of socialism, although we lacked the necessary resources, technical capabilities and capital ... our socialism began to be tinged in practice with Marxism. Any free enterprise system came to be regarded as odious capitalism

and the private sector as synonymous with exploitation and robbery. Individual effort came to a standstill, and from this stemmed the terrible passivity of the people that I still suffer from.

The Nasser period of socialism had been 'an utter failure'.

Once the war was over in April 1974, Sadat issued a document, known as the October Paper, the aim of which was to provide the guidelines for Egypt's development. He stressed that there was to be a continuation of Nasser's revolution while attempting to eliminate its negative aspects. The Paper's terms were very general, almost so general as to be meaningless — rapid economic development, social and cultural progress, an open and secure society, and Egypt's entry into the age of science. Apart from these pious hopes, there seemed to be no precise political philosophy, except that the promise of an open society implied more political freedom. The Paper was unanimously approved by the People's Assembly and in a referendum in May the people voted 99·95 per cent in favour.

A second paper presented to the Assembly in September discussed the role of the ASU which Sadat had described as a 'house of contradiction'. He said that its main mistakes had been that membership had been seen as compulsory, that the centres of power had imposed their own ideas and that it was too close to the government in any way to censure policy. He asked a Committee to collect views on its and the country's political future. All shades of opinion were made known. The peasants and workers insisted that the 'gains of the revolution' had to be preserved at all costs — such things as land reform, free medicine and education, nationalised industries and worker management. They were on the whole loyal to the ASU and the one-party system. Students' and women's organisations also were against any tampering with revolutionary gains. The right wing called for freedom of the press, a parliamentary and multi-party system, and a strong private sector. The left wanted to defend the revolution and claimed that Nasser's policies were basically correct and imperfectly carried out; more thorough-going socialism was necessary. The centre cautiously agreed that Nasserism had its points but that its policies had not been effectively controlled by the people.

Sadat listened and presumably pondered. By May 1975 it was reported that 4 million people had re-registered as members of the ASU prior to new elections for officers, a demonstration that it had not been ineffective in gaining the loyalty of a considerable section of the population. Those who did not join must have been indifferent or have wanted a different forum in which to express their political opinions. For Sadat, as for Nasser, the ASU was a useful body in which to contain political conflict until he came up with other ideas. He was trying to build up institutions which would be clearly different from the 'centres of power' that he so much disliked under Nasser. The institutions recognised as legal bodies were to be the government under the president, the People's Assembly, the press and, temporarily, the ASU.

The pressure for a multi-party system did not disappear. It started as a call for different platforms (*minbars* – the preaching pulpits in mosques) within the ASU, and in March 1976 three such platforms were authorised: on the left the National Progressive Union Organisation of Marxist orientation, led by Khalid Muhyidin, a Free Officer and colleague of Nasser, which called for more public ownership and the right to strike; on the right the Socialist Liberal Organisation which advocated free enterprise; in the 'centre' the Arab Socialist Organisation which supported the government and promised to safeguard the 'heritage of Nasser'. Elections were held in October (Sadat had already been re-elected president in September) with 1,600 candidates for 350 seats. As expected the ASU won an overwhelming majority, 280 seats, with the SLO winning twelve and the NPUO only four.[12] The remainder went to independent candidates. Sadat in his speech at the opening of the new Assembly announced that the platforms would become political parties under the financial control and supervision of the ASU but otherwise 'absolutely free... within the limits of the law'. The pre-revolutionary parties had been 'decadent' and should not be revived. No parties founded on a 'religious or racial basis would be countenanced'. The three parties were named: centre: Arab Socialist Party; left: National Progressive Union Party, and right: Free Socialist Party. The ASU would retain control over the press.

The opposition on both sides began to criticise sharply Sadat's policies much to his annoyance. He seemed to want a party system with a tame opposition which would muffle its criticism. Gradually he tightened his control over the left and right and tried to gain legitimacy through referenda. As has been noted, Sadat blamed the January 1977 food riots on leftist instigation and 105 members of the NPUP were arrested. He introduced emergency measures (approved by a referendum!) which severely curtailed political activity and made demonstrations, strikes and sit-ins illegal.

There was strong criticism of these measures from left and right for being 'unconstitutional' and 'unjustified'. One member of the Assembly described the day on which they were introduced as a 'fatal date in Egypt's history' comparable to the 'ignominy of February 1942' when Lampson confronted King Farouk. The students especially resented any retreat from democracy. However, more arrests of leftists were made and restrictions placed on others. Some editors of journals, known leftists, were dismissed. A bill was passed in the Assembly in June 1977 which stipulated that no party would be allowed to function unless it had twenty parliamentary members, an obvious move to silence the opposition. The law did allow, however, the formation of new parties if their programme did not conflict with Islamic law and they were not based on a class, sectarian or geographical basis. Sadat claimed that the left disqualified itself by being 'stooges of the Soviet Union' and not a real Egyptian opposition.

A political crisis was caused by Sadat's visit to Jerusalem in November. The opposition was taken unaware. Some independents welcomed the move, the right wing supported the initiative but blamed the government for weakness, while the NPUP eventually condemned the visit and some of its members were arrested. (An interesting and almost irrelevant development during this period was the short-lived revival of the pre-revolutionary Wafd party in January 1978. It had really outlived its usefulness, was an anachronism and soon disbanded in June.) By May Sadat was clearly irritated by any criticism of his 'peace process'. He denounced those who had instigated 'a campaign of doubt' against his policies and once again asked for support in a referendum. He obtained it and immediately began to hunt out his leftist opponents. A member of the NPUP was arrested and Khalid Muhyidin himself was accused of 'defaming' the government. Numerous journalists were dismissed or restricted from travelling. In June Muhyidin said that he was suspending his party's activity in protest against a new law which purged critics of the government from public life.

In July Sadat announced that to strengthen his political position he would form his own party, The National Democratic Party, with the admirable motto: 'Food for every mouth, a house for every individual and prosperity for all'. Basically socialist and democratic it would be an example of revolutionary purity. Said Sadat: 'In all history I cannot find an example of such totally democratic action as we have taken in establishing the NDP'. It signalled the final demise of the Arab Socialist Union which merged with the NDP. It also meant the 'twilight' of the National Progressive Unionist Party — 'there is no place for it among us'. A new, more pliable left-wing opposition party was founded, the Socialist Labour Party, under, according to Sadat, an 'honest, patriotic leadership', its vice-president being Sadat's brother-in-law.

By-passing parliament, Sadat's peace with Israel was ratified by the people in April 1979. They also approved the dissolution of the People's Assembly, for which new elections were held in June. They resulted in another overwhelming victory for Sadat's party. No members of the NPUP were elected and they complained that the election had been rigged. Twenty-eight SLP members did gain seats and they were not afraid to criticise quite openly aspects of Sadat's policy, reminding him that the Camp David accords were nothing if they did not solve the Palestinian problem. They claimed, moreover, that despite their membership of the Assembly Egypt was still a one-party state.

A somewhat strange development took place early in 1980. Sadat introduced a new draft law — the law of *aib*, which means shame or vice. It was a law to forbid in practice criticism of the regime, branding it as unethical and against the well-being of the state. A socialist prosecutor had power to arraign anyone before a special court for political offences and if thought necessary to send him for trial before a 'Court of Value'. It was a strange and slightly sinister method of political thought control. Fortunately, it aroused immediate controversy and lawyers were united against it, their leader admitting that he had ransacked the laws of dictatorships and democracies alike and had found no equivalent. The law was finally modified when passed by the People's Assembly, although still making it a crime to advocate any doctrine which implied a negation of divine teaching or urged disloyalty to the nation. If used to full effect, such a law was not far removed from those of a police state.

In a sense Sadat was trying to put himself and his policies above criticism, seeing himself as the embodiment or father of the state (he spoke of Egyptian soldiers as his 'sons'). But at the same time he seemed unwilling to be a dictator, retaining an elected Assembly and a freer society. Both aspects of his attitude were demonstrated in 1980. In May an amended constitution was approved which allowed him an unlimited number of terms as president; later, in October, a *shura* – a senate of wise men – was proposed to offer advice and guidance on the future of the country. The same constitution declared that Egypt was a democratic, socialist state with a mixed economy and an independent press.

Sadat unfolded in October 1980 his political philosophy which newspapers at once dubbed Sadatism – a combination of ethics at home and abroad, correct behaviour in every sphere, national loyalty before loyalty to any political faith, a liberal economy under socialist management and the preservation of Islamic guidance: the sum total of individual happiness creates the common welfare. It was thus that Sadat proclaimed his vision of the ideal society. Like Nasser his vision was constrained by the demands of politics and economics and his path littered with good intentions. Like many men with supreme power he was eventually unable to tolerate any criticism and Egypt became a tense and unhappy country under his rule. He was unable to put into practice what he preached.

Islam's Increasing Politicisation

Under Sadat there were interesting developments in the political aspects of Islam. Sadat called the Nasser era a period of materialism and unbelief and professed himself to be a sincere, believing Muslim motivated in all his actions by love of his fellow men. He did not, however, follow consistently Islamic policies although there were slightly hesitant moves in that direction from time to time. In fact his approaches to the West and Israel aroused resentment amongst fundamentalist Islamic groups. To some extent he was caught in a dilemma. When he relied on aid from Saudi Arabia he felt under pressure to prove that Egypt was a strict Muslim country. There were proposals to ban alcohol, to punish apostasy by death and to introduce Islamic criminal penalties such as amputation of the hand for theft. Nothing was done in this direction and most Egyptians would probably have been opposed to them and, for example, to any regression in the progress achieved in women's equality. When Sadat was ostracised by the Arabs after Camp David he was relieved to some extent of the pressure and was, in the pursuit of liberalisation and equality, able to introduce measures which moved Egypt in a different direction, not to becoming a non-Muslim society, but one which interpreted Islam in a less rigid manner.

Sadat made a distinction which strictly speaking is not valid in Islam – that of a separation between religion and politics. He said in 1979: 'Those who wish to practise Islam can go to the mosques, and those who wish to engage in politics may do so through legal institutions'. He was driven to this attitude by a series of developments whereby Muslims engaged in more and more extreme politics. He first encouraged Islamic movements as an ally against the leftist opposition and by so doing opened a Pandora's box which proved difficult to control. After 1967 the irrepressible Muslim Brothers had resumed some of their activities, especially among students. Nasser released some of the detained *Ikhwan* and Sadat completed the process. Others returned from exile and by the late 1970s their propaganda and recruitment had noticeably increased. At least one Cairo mosque was in 1980 openly filled to overflowing with Brothers praying, and at the end of Ramadan a large public square (outside the ex-royal palace) was covered with carpets on which thousands of Brothers prayed. The journal propagating their philosophy, *al-Dawa*, reappeared in 1976 after being banned since 1954. Sadat allowed them this freedom of 'religious' action while withholding political status. This was resented and there were calls for recognition as a political party able to participate in elections. They did not, however, resort to the kind of violence for which they were notorious in earlier years. For this reason, perhaps, more extreme groups emerged.

The programme of the *Ikhwan* did not change. It deplored the moral deterioration in Egypt and called for the introduction of thoroughgoing Islamic principles based entirely on the *sharia* (Islamic law). Only thus would Egypt avoid the dangers of corruption and contamination from the West. They criticised Sadat for opening the country to too much Western influence. They criticised the socialist economy of Nasser because it failed to introduce a society of equality and justice and denied people their liberty. Nationalised industries actually transferred ownership of plants to the government and not the people. Under Sadat they aimed for the abolition of the left-wing parties, the banning of communism as an atheist creed, and the purging of the government and bureaucracy. They opposed the accommodation with Israel, a country which had usurped Islamic territory and against which the *jihad* had to continue. They were deeply disturbed by Egypt's isolation from the Islamic Arab world.

The *Ikhwan* tried to recruit new members especially amongst students and civil servants. Their propaganda was carried out on university campuses by Islamic 'groups' whose activities were very obvious. Women students wore 'modest' dress and head coverings; meetings, conferences, sales of literature and lectures were regularly and openly held. They tried to exert pressure on the universities to segregate teaching and lectures. The struggle for influence among students caused the government some disquiet and the authorities kept a wary eye on them as their activities could easily have slipped into the political sphere. Sadat was implacably opposed to universities becoming, as he said, 'arenas of political rowdiness'.

More immediately damaging were the activities of more extreme groups, notably the group of 'Penitence and Withdrawal' (*Jamaat al-takfir wa-al-hijra* – the title implies those who accuse society of unbelief and therefore withdraw from it. This is the age-old Islamic custom, beginning with the prophet Muhammad, of migrating away from a corrupt society). The group's existence had been known from 1973 and it had been implicated in an alleged plot to overthrow the government. The group's ideology was a total rejection of society as it existed and a call for a return to a state of 'pure' Islam. Its leader, Ahmad Shukri Mustafa, a young ex-agricultural student, declared:

> I reject the Egyptian regime and the Egyptian reality in all its aspects since everything in it is in contradiction to the *sharia* and belongs to heresy ... we demand a return to natural simplicity and reject the so-called modern progress.

Mustafa declared himself to be God's representative on earth, who would found a new community which would conquer the whole world; the world would then come to an end. Such movements and leaders have been common in Islam and are a symptom of the utter despair felt by Muslims when faced by what they consider total corruption and delusion.

In July 1977 the group shocked the public by kidnapping and murdering an ex-government minister when its demands were not met. Bombings and killings occurred in Cairo and 400 members of the group were arrested and accused of trying to overthrow the regime. Five were executed for the minister's death and others sentenced to imprisonment. The government faced with such Muslim extremism reacted by trying to divert public criticism with its proposal to reintroduce the traditional Islamic laws of death for apostasy and adultery and the whipping of drunkards. This was a panicky overreaction which caused considerable public concern. In September the government announced that the law on apostasy at least would be shelved.

Other similar groups appeared in Egypt. In November 1979 over one hundred members of a group called *Jihad* were arrested and charged with forming an anti-government party. In January 1980 the same group carried out bomb attacks against churches in Alexandria. It and other bodies were accused of receiving arms and aid from foreign governments (mainly Libya) in order to carry out sabotage. It was members of these or similar groups which carried their hatred of Sadat and his policies to the limit of assassinating him.

In the midst of this religious ferment Sadat forbade any political party being formed by a religious sect, and at the same time he sought Islamic legitimacy for his policies. He used the Azhar to support his détente with Israel, much as Nasser had used it at various times. In May 1979 the *ulama* issued a ruling on the peace treaty, which showed that the tradition of religious leaders supporting state policy was very much alive. They said:

> Egypt is an Islamic country, and it is the duty of its guardian to ensure its protection. If he considers that the interest of the Muslims lies in being gentle towards their enemies, this is permissible because he is responsible in matters of peace and war... and more knowledgeable about the affairs of his subjects... The existence of treaties between Muslims and their enemies is governed by clear regulations established by Islam... The al-Azhar *ulama* are of the opinion that the Egyptian–Israeli treaty was concluded within the context of Islamic judgement. It springs from a position of strength following the waging of the *jihad* battle and the victory [of October 1973].

The statement ended with an appeal (warning?) from the Koran to other Muslims to follow Egypt's lead 'lest ye lose heart and your power depart'. Perhaps as a reward, and certainly as a sop to Muslim feeling, Sadat's amended constitution approved by referendum made the *sharia* the main source of legislation in Egypt.

Sadat and Arabism

Sadat's course towards Arabism, as towards most things, veered. He ran the gamut from Arab hero to Arab pariah. His first move was to approve the abortive federation with Libya and Syria in 1971, largely under the prompting of Colonel Qaddafi. It was an ill-planned and clumsy attempt at union which fell apart in bitterness and recrimination. Sadat always found relations with Qaddafi difficult and even went to war with his country for a short period in 1977.

The war of 1973 was in some ways a peak of Arab unity – a practical demonstration of the Arab will. Led by Egypt and Syria in a joint command, several other Arab states joined the battle – Jordan, Iraq, Saudi Arabia, Morocco, Sudan and Algeria. The initial victory was an Arab achievement which was brought to a halt by the total American support

for Israel. The Arab states approved the following Geneva conference as
an attempt to end the stalemate but they soon began to suspect Egypt
of wanting to go it alone. Sadat's approaches to America, while a logical
move given his political philosophy, alienated other Arabs who assumed
that too close a connection would eventually lead to Egyptian isolation
from the Arab world. Several Arab states formed a 'northern front' against
Israel on the assumption that Egypt was then *hors de combat*. Sadat did
his best to counter these moves. In America in 1975 he on several occasions stressed his devotion to the Palestinian cause, claiming 'We do
not hold any part of Arab territory to be less dear to us than occupied
Egyptian territory'. In 1976 there was an attempt to patch things up in a
short-lived united political leadership between Syria ₐnd Egypt which
Jordan joined in 1977. Nevertheless, after the peace treaty with Israel,
Egypt became isolated from most other Arab states, who formed a
'rejectionist' front, rejecting any negotiations with or recognition of
Israel, although not all states were equally eager to join. Arab airlines
stopped flying to Cairo, embassies were closed and the Arab League
expelled Egypt and moved its headquarters from Cairo. The leftist opposition accused Sadat of taking Egypt from its natural position at the head
of the Arab world. Sadat did not take this criticism lightly and strongly
counter-attacked his Arab so-called friends:

> Our Arab brothers, led by the rejectionist front and our Saudi brothers,
> are squandering whatever assets they have had with us ... We know the
> rejectionist front. The attitude of Syria ... is one of hatred, bitterness,
> inability and ignorance. The attitude of the Iraqis is worse. All of you
> know the foolish child of Libya ... I am not including South Yemen
> because it is not worth wasting time on it.

Although such words betrayed a deep concern over Egypt's isolation,
there was also a certain feeling in the country that it had done enough
for the Arabs. The ironic comment was that the Arabs were determined
to fight on against Israel to the last Egyptian! There was discussion after
Camp David of 'neutrality' (*hiyad*), of whether Egypt's interests should be
put first even at the risk of continuing isolation. Sadat emphasised his pride
in Egypt and her history, especially since 1978. As early as September
1970 he abandoned the name United Arab Republic in favour of the
Arab Republic of Egypt. In speeches he went out of his way to stress the
continuity and length of Egyptian civilisation. To a conference on shipping
in Cairo he said that Egypt was the logical host for it, 'having been the
first nation ever to build ships, and probably the site of the invention of
the "wheel"'. In his memoirs he wrote:

> The Egyptian people differ from many other peoples, even within the
> Arab world ... Our cultural depths are there; our cultural roots are

alive, as vigorous as ever after more than 7,000 years...Our Egyptian civilization...has always been inspired by man's love of, and attachment to the land.

He even called for the reburial of the royal mummies on display in the Egyptian Museum, as their exposure to public gaze did not befit Egypt's historical dignity.

The debate has continued. Egypt has remained quintessentially Egyptian and yet Arab, the natural leader of the Arab world.

Sadat's Rule

Sadat had observed the manner in which Nasser had ruled for nearly eighteen years before he took power. He knew intimately and claimed to hate the power centres and structures that had grown up and the atmosphere of suspicion and mistrust. He set about destroying these, gradually dismantling the whole Nasserist apparatus. One left-wing critic wrote that after Nasser, Sadat changed most things except the presidency. In place of power centres he tried to establish less personal institutions, the People's Assembly, the press and the multi-party system, although Egypt remained basically a one-party state -- that of the centre party which was very much an extension of Sadat's personality. He was the master, in some ways more than Nasser was. The ASU went, and the army, although favoured by Sadat, had a less political role. The vice-president was, however, a military man and it seemed that Sadat's policies must at the very least not have been opposed by the armed forces.

Sadat was in some ways more open than Nasser, claiming to keep no secrets from the people and to allow them a greater share in government, although his more ebullient declarations, if not exactly doubletalk, should at least be taken guardedly: 'It is not a question of ruler and ruled... because whoever lives in the land of Egypt...today has the right to shape the Egyptian decision'. He enjoyed addressing the people directly, as did Nasser, and projected himself as the nation's father. His favourite method of gaining approval was through the near unanimous referendum. His openness and sincerity often appeared misguided to other politicians as, for example, when he allowed the ex-Shah of Iran to return to Egypt to die.

Egypt's liberalisation was far from being institutionally rooted on his death and, while initially allowing some opposition and criticism, Sadat never allowed it to go too far. He eventually resorted to arresting any critics he disapproved of.

The Search for Economic Progress

All developing countries have the same general economic goals – elimination of poverty, raising of living standards, industrialisation, agricultural efficiency and technological progress. Not all countries approach these goals in the same way, nor are all countries equally endowed with natural resources. Egypt has the Nile at the centre of her development, but few other resources and the handicap of a rapidly expanding population. All economic planning has to take account of these factors and to deal with the problems they pose – poverty, urban overcrowding, unemployment and low national income. These are in addition to the problems of modernising the country in the human field, accustoming workers to new techniques and modes of life, encouraging the acceptance of birth control and ensuring general efficiency. Egypt does possess, however, the advantage of a long period of development and a basic infrastructure of railways, harbours and roads.

Population and Manpower

Any proposed economic growth development may be vitiated by rapid population growth. It can be a case of running to stand still. Egypt has a population growth rate which rose to 2·5 or 2·6 per cent in the 1980s. This is a high percentage compared to the less than 1·0 per cent rate of Western Europe. The world average in 1975 was 2·0 per cent. In the period 1964–72 it seems that the growth rate for Egypt dropped to this average but unaccountably rose after 1972. In 1971 the population was put at 34 million giving Egypt about the twentieth largest population in the world. In 1986 it was 50 million. The rapid increase is accounted for by a fairly static birth rate and a sharply declining death rate resulting from improving health facilities. There is some difference between the birth rate in town and country and in the urban professional classes (5 per cent of the total) there has been a noticeable drop in the size of families. The large population means that Egypt's habitable areas are densely populated, and great pressure is put on the large urban complexes of Cairo and Alexandria. The density more than doubled between 1927 (410 inhabitants per square kilometre) and 1970 (1000). Another notable feature of the population is the large proportion of children under the age of 15 and the correspondingly smaller number of people over 45. In Egypt 43 per cent of the population in 1970 was under 15 and 17 per cent over 45. In Britain these percentages were 23 per cent and 35 per cent respectively.

All these figures have implications for Egypt — the provision of educ. tional facilities for the young, the growing numbers of school leavers to be found employment and university and higher education. Without expansion of education there is bound to be a large number of illiterates — as much as 70 per cent in 1960. A larger rural population means increased pressure on available land and lower living standards if there is no increase in agricultural productivity, and the pressure to migrate to the cities is greater. The whole tenor of life is affected by overpopulation, from finding available land to cultivate to large classes in school and university, competition for jobs and health and social facilities, and the daily struggle for transport across Cairo. Overcrowding in the capital is particularly acute where some facilities such as telephones, sewers, taxis and buses are barely able to cope with the demands put upon them.

The government has officially encouraged birth control but progress is limited by several factors. The larger families tend to be in rural areas where children are a source of labour, income and prestige and a proof of virility; and where illiteracy is greatest the use of family planning is the least likely to find acceptance. It is usually with a change of life style — brought about by education, a wife working, the influence of television, a move from the land — that families decrease in size. These changes come slowly or affect only a small section of the population and it is likely that the size of Egypt's population will hinder economic development for a long time to come.

The country's economy is affected both by the size of the population and by its movement. Internal migration between country and town began in the 1930s and greatly increased in the 1960s and 1970s causing the severe overcrowding of Cairo and elsewhere. Emigration abroad had begun in the 1940s and 1950s but rose sharply after 1973. There are more than 3 million Egyptians working abroad who benefit the economy with remittances but whose absence deprives the country of certain skills. In addition the high wages earned abroad contribute to inflation at home. The large population does not ensure an excess of labour in all fields, and emigration means that the skills in short supply often have to be imported from abroad at high cost. There has not only been a brain drain but also a muscle drain. In the construction sector, for example, many workers emigrated and consequently costs and wages in that sector have risen.

Natural Resources

Egypt's economic problems caused by a large population are worsened by a lack of natural resources. The deserts provide certain amounts of mineral deposits for building and for fertilisers, and iron ore which is processed mainly by the iron and steel complex at Helwan outside Cairo. Oil has

significant quantities south of Suez on the Red Sea and in
t. These latter wells were lost to Israel after the 1967 war
utput was expropriated. The wells were returned in 1975
med that Israel had taken the equivalent of $2000 million
.. in 1970 discoveries were made in the Western Desert and large-scale
oil exploration was continued in the deserts and offshore. Egypt is now a
substantial producer of oil — in 1980 some 32 million tonnes (only around
one-twentieth of Saudi Arabia's annual production). The long-term target
is set at 50 million tonnes annually. Local consumption in 1980 was some
12 million tonnes, leaving a substantial surplus for export. Britain, India
and the USA all bought oil from Egypt. In 1980 the hoped-for income
from oil was over $2000 million. This welcome income can be a tempo-
rary benefit only as it is forecast that by the year 2000 Egypt's petroleum
needs will exceed production by some 15 million tonnes. In addition to
oil, large reserves of natural gas have been found on the Mediterranean
coast, enough to meet the needs of Cairo and Alexandria for several
decades. Production rose from 40,000 tons in 1975 to 400,000 in 1980.

Although the deserts provide some help to the economy it is still the
Nile which is the centre of Egyptian life and which irrigates the narrow
strip of land from the Sudan to Cairo where it broadens out into the
Delta. The river created the soil from which for centuries Egyptians
have drawn their sustenance. With fertilisers, proper drainage and requisite
amounts of water the soil can be among the most productive in the world.
It is, however, hard to work and needs continuous cultivation and irrigation. It is cultivated to the limit of productiveness and to the very edge
of the desert. It is estimated that better drainage would increase the
productiveness of the land by some 25–30 per cent. (The great changes
brought about by the opening of the High Dam will be discussed in a
following section.) Because of the abundance of manpower much work
in Egyptian agriculture is carried out by hand — sowing, irrigating, some
water raising and digging channels. Animals such as camels, donkeys
and buffaloes are used to help in tasks like ploughing, and raising and
distributing water. The fertility of the soil allows a number of fruit trees
(citrus, vines, dates, figs, pomegranates and so on) and crops to be grown.
Among the latter are, in winter, wheat and barley, onions, lentils and
clover; in autumn, maize; and in summer, cotton, rice, maize, millet
and sugar-cane. Cotton has since the nineteenth century been the most
important crop for providing agricultural income and for export. Egyptian
long-staple cotton is particularly valued and of high quality. Despite a
gradual decrease in the percentage of exports, cotton in 1970 still represented about half the total. In 1979 there was a record crop after the
price had been raised by 30 per cent. Several vegetables are grown throughout the year, sometimes now for export.

The government, in an attempt to regulate agricultural production,
introduced quotas for crops and state control of marketing. The peasant

felt cramped by these measures and was reluctant to grow crops for whici. he was not receiving the market price. Sadat promised to pay higher prices to encourage the production of crops such as cotton, rice and wheat. But on the whole the peasant has been neglected and as a result Egypt has had to import much of its food. In 1980 it was estimated that the agricultural deficit was $2000 million and in 1978 Egypt produced a mere 28 per cent of its wheat needs. On the other hand there has been a surplus of fruit and vegetables which the peasant grows as cash crops, and an increase in the production of barsim (clover for animal feed) which he sells to cattle raisers. Although Sadat promised agricultural self-sufficiency this is still a long way off. Eight per cent of the investment budget in the five-year plan 1979–83 was devoted to agricultural development and the government has claimed that agricultural production just keeps ahead of the population growth.

Among other natural resources livestock has a certain importance although the lack of meadows and grazing land hinders the development of a large cattle and sheep industry. Milk is usually provided by goats or the water buffalo and, apart from home-grown chickens, much meat has to be imported. President Sadat criticised farmers for slaughtering their cattle when too young (about 60 kg) because of lack of fodder, when Austrian cows, he said, grew to a weight of 500 kg.

Land Reform

A new revolutionary government must destroy the bases of power of the *ancien régime*. These are represented partly by large landowners, often a symbol of a corrupt 'feudal' system, exploiters of poor peasants and absentee landlords. Some regimes come into power with plans for a root and branch reform of landholding such as the total nationalisation of land in Russia and China and the collectivisation of farms and peasant holdings. The Free Officers did not have such sweeping plans but were nevertheless dedicated to some kind of land reform and to improving the welfare of the peasant whom they saw as the basis of Egyptian society. A prosperous productive peasantry would mean a prosperous productive country. The inequality in landholding in Egypt before the revolution was obvious. The large owners included the State, the royal family, local notables and an urban class including foreigners. In 1952 some 2,000 owners held 20 per cent of the land; at the other end of the scale more than 2 million owners held 13 per cent of the land. This meant that these latter had tiny plots of land which they did not always cultivate themselves but leased to others. At the very bottom of the scale were the millions of landless agricultural labourers. The Islamic laws of inheritance which divide land in a fixed proportion amongst the heirs meant that even the smallest plots were continually being fragmented. In some cases

d own strips of land in different parts of his village. Some-
lease or sell his plot and go off to work in the town.

new Land Reform Law limited the maximum individual
feddans (1 feddan = 1·038 acres). Land held above this
.... by an individual was expropriated and gradually redistributed to
landless tenants in plots of two to five feddans. Land subject to expropriation represented, however, some 10 per cent of the total area and only
a minority of agricultural families gained or lost. The redistributed land
was to be paid for over thirty years and the recipients had to join one
of the agricultural co-operative societies which were to be established.
These plots were not to be sold or sublet, or divided through inheritance
(a contravention of Islamic law).

Later laws modified the 1952 provisions. The financial burden on the
peasants was lessened and in 1961 the maximum for individual holdings
was reduced to 100 feddans. As Nasser increased his socialist and nationalisation measures more land was acquired by the confiscation of certain
properties and in 1963 foreign landholders were expropriated. In 1969
the maximum holding was again lowered – this time to fifty feddans.
During this period as more action was taken against the large owners, the
interest on the repayments of the peasants was gradually reduced to nil
and the conditions of tenants were eased. Yet as can be seen no attempt
was made completely to nationalise the land, to abolish private ownership
and establish total collectivisation. Despite the ever present possibilities
of slips 'twixt cup and lip' the intentions of the redistribution were to
some extent realised. There were lags between appropriation and redistribution, caused by the machinery of the Agrarian Reform Authority, but
by 1971 nearly 1 million feddans had been distributed to almost 350,000
families. This still left inequality, however. In 1978 it was reported that
95 per cent of landowners who possessed fewer than five feddans held
less than half the agricultural land, leaving 5 per cent of medium and big
landowners with over 50 per cent. Since 1970 ways round the landholding
limitation have been found and some large farmers have become very
prosperous, although without a reversion to the pre-revolutionary situation. The reforms did not give land to all and it is important to stress that
land reform has not noticeably affected landless peasants since the redistribution was mostly confined to previous tenants and small farmers. The
position of the landless labourers has remained deplorable. In 1972 they
represented half the rural population and at the middle of the decade 44
per cent of rural households were below the poverty line. Capitalist–
feudal inequality had been replaced by socialist inequality.

Co-operatives

The first agricultural co-operatives were established in 1910 in an attempt to ease the lot of the peasant, but they ended as little more than credit institutions favouring the larger owners to the disadvantage of the small landholders who often had to depend on the none too tender mercies of the moneylender. The revolution removed the large landowners who had nevertheless provided certain benefits to the agriculture of Egypt. The establishment of new co-operatives was meant to replace their role in providing credit, marketing and organisation. The First Reform Law in 1952 decreed that all peasants who received land were to form co-operatives in their villages. The government gradually extended the co-operative system to cover most of rural Egypt by the mid-1960s. In 1970 some 5,000 co-operatives had 3 million members. The local co-operative was created in the village with a minimum membership of twenty and run by an elected council under the direction of a supervisor, usually an agricultural specialist. They were to be an important instrument of change which would influence the remotest parts of the country. The co-operatives themselves were to organise and improve agricultural production, establish marketing and pricing systems and provide credit, but they were not to be models of Soviet collectives or Chinese communes.

On the whole the co-operatives do not seem to have achieved their aims. The two main stumbling blocks were the unequal distribution of land and the weight of the Egyptian bureaucracy. Not all the agronomists sent to rural areas were efficient or dedicated and peasants tended to resent advice proferred by younger technologists. Although government direction of crop rotation has led to increases in production, the obligation to plant a certain crop a year on all their land has had a deleterious effect on small and poor peasants who have had to depend on the open market for their needs. Improved credit supplies helped agricultural production but one observer, Dr Samir Radwan, found that it was the larger owners who mainly benefited from this, while the indebtedness of small peasants grew worse. The same writer concluded that, although the whole package of reforms introduced by the government had been more successful than schemes in other countries, the impetus slowed in the 1970s and many problems remained — the unequal distribution of land and income, the bias towards the richer farmer, the continuing plight of the small peasant and the landless. The move away from the socialist solution under Sadat meant that less attention was paid to co-operatives. He was willing to import food in order to satisfy Egypt rather than aim for a dramatic increase in production. He was also temperamentally opposed to a large-scale coercion of the peasants or of any other section of the population.

The High Dam

The Nile has been an unreliable fairy godmother to Egypt. The concept of controlling and exploiting its power had long been attractive. One method of attempting to do this was to dam the river near the town of Aswan. British engineers built a dam in 1902 designed to trap the summer flood water and allow its flow through later in the year to irrigate land for second or even third crops during the low water season. The project was successful but its usefulness was outstripped by the growth of the population so the dam was heightened in 1912 and again in 1933. From this dam a system of irrigation was developed. The flood water was released in the low season into a carefully laid out series of irrigation canals and ditches and water regularly reached the land which produced at different times of the year the various crops already mentioned. This carefully controlled system kept Egypt alive but at a level barely above subsistence for a larger part of the population. In addition, despite the efficiency of the system, the reservoir at Aswan could not store enough water in plentiful years to eliminate shortages in lean times.

British, Greek and Egyptian engineers puzzled over various schemes to solve this problem to irrigate more land and perhaps also provide hydro-electric power. A Greek engineer living in Egypt, Adrian Daninos, proposed in 1948 a scheme to build a High Dam at Aswan which would retain the flood waters of two consecutive years and provide electricity. The proposal aroused considerable interest but it came at an inauspicious time for the Egyptian government, then facing war in Palestine and unrest at home. The plan lay dormant until it was shown to Nasser who saw it as an attractive scheme which would both solve Egypt's problems and bring the achievements of the revolution to world attention.

Outside financial and technical help was essential for the completion of such an enormous undertaking. The World Bank and the American and British governments were first approached and agreed to finance the project. As has been mentioned in Chapter 2, the blunt renunciation of this agreement was the direct cause of the nationalisation of the Suez Canal, the Suez invasion and the entry of the Soviet Union on a large scale into Egyptian affairs. After some hesitation Russia agreed in October 1958 to help build and finance the dam if the work were executed with Russian equipment and by Russian engineers. Nasser accepted these proposals and almost immediately Russian equipment and men arrived in Egypt. Construction of the dam began in January 1960 and it was officially inaugurated in May 1964 by President Nasser and Mr Khrushchev, who set off an explosion which blew away the sand dam holding back the waters in the Aswan gorge. Work on the dam and the connected power station was completed in 1970. The dam was officially opened by President Sadat and President Podgorny of the USSR in January 1971. The dam now stands massively upstream from the town surmounted by a monument to Soviet–Egyptian friendship. Behind it stretches the new Lake Nasser for an aston-ishing 500 kilometres. Large areas of territory in Egyptian and Sudanese Nubia were flooded, necessitating the removal of population and the re-siting of several Pharaonic statues and temples. It seems that the lake has even changed the climate over Aswan, as clouds and rain are now experienced. The total project is estimated to have cost some £E300 million plus £E25 million in interest on the Soviet loan. Repayment was completed in 1978.

It is perhaps too early to establish positively all the benefits and problems brought about by the construction of the dam, although some results are already obvious. Firstly, the clear water that flows from the dam no longer carries the fertilising silt, some of which used to be deposited on irrigated land, while most flowed into the sea. This will have to be replaced with other fertilisers. The water also flows more quickly and tends to erode the bed of the river and reduce the water level. The dam may affect fish life both in the reservoir and in the Mediterranean. The nutrients trapped in the lake should encourage fish to breed there, but the fact that they no longer reach the sea may damage the fishing industry. In addition the dam has affected the chemical make-up of the river encouraging the growth of the Nile hyacinth which chokes the irrigation canals.

The dam has, however, brought a number of benefits, including 650,000 feddans of reclaimed land, the conversion of 700,000 feddans of basin-irrigated land (that is, gathering flood water in specially prepared large basins) in Upper Egypt to perennial irrigation, the provision of water to bring 1 million feddans under rice cultivation, the provision of electricity (with plans for further hydro-electric stations), improved drainage, flood control and navigation. It is, however, apparent that the High Dam cannot fulfil all that was expected of it. The Nile cannot supply all the water that Egypt (and Sudan) will need and the future growth of cultivated land must depend on other projects, but the dam proved its value in 1972 when a low flood without the dam could have meant the loss of a third of the cotton and rice crops.

Land Reclamation

This is the, perhaps misleading, term for the attempt to increase the cultivated area by using land of all kinds not previously cultivated. The Dutch example of damming the sea to produce the polders is the most famous example. The pressure of population has driven Egyptian planners to produce schemes for making more land available. Great hopes were placed in these schemes which have unfortunately failed to live up to their promise. About half a million feddans of new land were being cultivated in 1972 (and reclamation started on a further 400,000), but the poor quality of the soils has militated against very profitable reclamation. Great expenditure is needed to make the soil fertile and some eight years are needed before it becomes marginally productive. The new land has been administered by state bodies and a centralised bureaucracy has hindered efficient development. Not many peasants have been attracted to areas of reclaimed land. By 1975 it was reported that only 35,000 families had been resettled. More people had preferred to migrate to the large urban areas.

Although cultivated land is continuously being lost to urban sprawl it is expensive to reclaim land, build and maintain canals, install electrical and pumping equipment, resettle peasants and train them in new techniques. In 1976 it was recognised that reclaimed land had been a net economic loss. Despite all these problems, conquest of infertile areas is still seen as a partial solution to Egypt's land hunger if suitable areas can be found and the financial obstacles overcome. Several areas have been developed, notably Tahrir (liberation) province to the north west of the Delta and others are planned. One very expensive scheme that is being investigated is the filling of the Qattara depression in the Western Desert with sea water from the Mediterranean to generate electricity and to irrigate new land. The reclaimed areas have usually been managed as state farms which if efficiently run can make savings through mechanisation and large-scale operations. The disadvantage is that such farms do not absorb much labour or many settlers. If successful, new crops can be produced such as grapes, citrus, sugar beet and soya beans, which can be exported to earn foreign currency.

From Planning and Nationalisation to the 'Opening-up'

Agricultural development and the High Dam were aspects of the Free Officers' overall vision of the modernisation and economic progress of Egypt. To try to achieve this vision the regime early adopted a system of planning. A Permanent Council for National Production was established which had within its responsibility agriculture, the High Dam, transport, electricity and industrialisation. Gradually, under socialist influence, the state undertook comprehensive planning for most aspects of the national economy and followed this up with its wholesale measures of nationalisation.

Political considerations influenced many of Nasser's economic moves. The High Dam and take-over of the Suez Canal are examples of this and he introduced more socialist measures into Egypt as a result of the split in the United Arab Republic in 1961. By 1963 public ownership had been extended to all banks, public utilities, transport, larger industries, construction and haulage firms, department stores and hotels. The export–import trade and the selling of major crops were also taken over by the state. Small businesses, most retail trade, residential property (except where sequestrated or confiscated), and much agricultural land were left in private hands. The motive for nationalisation was certainly ideological, but Egyptian moderation, and a certain realism, forestalled the introduction of a total Soviet-type system.

Most developing countries consider the nationalisation of important industrial undertakings necessary for ideological, nationalistic and economic reasons. It is, therefore, fruitless to ask whether these undertakings could have better been left to private enterprise. In Egypt's case many of them were in foreign hands, for example, banks and the Suez Canal, and in post-revolutionary Egypt such a situation was impossible. Also, few countries can avoid the pressure to undertake prestige projects, such as steel factories, car industries, aircraft and missile production, which have small relevance to the country's economic welfare but which contribute to its image of progress and power. Egypt in particular was compelled to try to adopt an efficient military posture *vis-à-vis* Israel. The above reasons aside, economists looking at Egypt's progress since nationalisation and overall planning are reluctant to give a firm answer to the question: has public ownership hindered or helped Egypt's economy? Certainly, as Britain's case has proved, nationalised industries can be inefficient, but in small countries there is often no alternative to state enterprise if foreign investment is prohibited.

President Sadat brought quite a different philosophy to the economy of Egypt. While not wanting to lose the gains of socialism and the revolution he attempted to liberalise the economy, to 'open' it to outside investment and to encourage the private sector. This was clearly a political issue in which he was opposed by the left who wanted more nationalisation, and pushed by the right who wanted more private enterprise. The great slogan of Sadat's regime was *infitah* – the 'opening-up' (of the economy), the liberalisation of trade and the removal of exchange controls. The economic committee of the National Democratic Party carefully walked a tightrope. Its report in 1980 stated:

> Concerning the open-door policy, it is neither a return to capitalism and the principles of economic freedom held prior to the revolution nor a shift from the social democratic direction emphasized by the public sector's control of the basic sources of production.

It stressed the need for an *effective* public sector, and the importance of a private sector working within the framework of the national development plan. In May 1980 the nation in a referendum approved the formula that 'Egypt is a democratic socialist state with a mixed economy'.

Sadat on taking power was faced with severe economic problems, not least of which was the protected public sector. His belief that too much socialism killed initiative and effort has already been alluded to and as early as 1971 a new law was announced to encourage foreign investment. This was not too successful as there was at the time a lack of confidence in Egypt's economy and future and foreign businessmen were haunted by the fear of nationalisation. The better prospect of peace and stability

ter the 1973 war brought forth a further law which in practice permitted foreign investment in most parts of the economy. Assurances
were given that money invested would be safe from nationalisation or
expropriation. The government hoped that the most fruitful field for
investment would be joint undertakings with public sector enterprises.
In fact, investors have preferred to put money into tourist ventures,
hotels and other developments, office and apartment buildings, and
banking. In 1981 some fifty-five foreign banks were active in the country.
The public sector, previously protected under Nasser, has suffered both
from a lack of commitment on the part of the government and from
competition from imports. Those which cannot compete have, according
to an economic minister, 'no hope of survival'. Holding companies were
to be set up to take over public sector firms and to find a foreign partner
'to get things done more efficiently'. Once the ideological commitment
to a total state economy has weakened, nationalised industries have
either to become efficient and profit-making or they disappear completely
or are absorbed into the private sector. By 1981 it was estimated that
the public sector was providing only one-tenth of the output of the
private.

Industrialisation

Industrial development in Egypt can be traced back to the period of
Muhammad Ali in the early nineteenth century. The Free Officers found
a small industrial sector in existence when they took power, and they
took the lead in encouraging further industrial development. Textiles
based on cotton provided the major share of industrial production, followed by food and beverages and with much smaller shares for coal,
chemicals, metals, transport, machinery, clothing, paper, wood and
leather. Egypt now produces a range of products, including chemicals for
fertilisers, refrigerators, radio and television sets, clothing and textiles,
tinned food and building materials. Plans were in hand in 1980 for
numerous joint foreign-Egyptian undertakings in various industries.

Priority was given to the establishment of an iron and steel industry,
which was specifically seen as symbolising, in Nasser's words, 'the national
independence of the country and the starting of the route to economic
development'. It was a prestige project, bolstered by economic arguments
such as the stimulation of other industrial projects and the saving of
foreign currency. Moreover, iron ore was known to exist in Egypt. But
political factors did weigh heavily in the decision of the National Production
Council to establish a steel works in Helwan outside Cairo. As Nasser said
in 1955 when inaugurating the project: 'I am happy to see the steel
industry in Egypt contrary to what had been said that Egypt is an agrarian
country and could never become an industrial one'. The Egyptian Iron

and Steel Company was established with the help of the German firm Demag. Its initial production was below capacity and ran at a loss but later with Russian help larger production units and more modern techniques were introduced which increased capacity. Production went entirely to meet the needs of the home market and there was no surplus capacity. In 1980 plans were announced for the building of two further factories to produce aluminium and scaffolding.

In addition to the largely fictitious production of missiles and aircraft an attempt was made in co-operation with European manufacturers to produce cars. One astonishing looking vehicle, the Ramses, appeared with a German engine and a local body. It was not very successful. More successful has been the assembly of foreign cars and other vehicles, mainly Fiats, but with a capacity that has never caught up with demand. Transport is in fact a major problem in the economic development of Egypt. The country is fortunate in having a fairly extensive railway system (over 4,000 kilometres) which closely follows the Nile from Alexandria to Aswan, with lesser lines to Suez and westwards. The track, rolling stock and equipment deteriorated through lack of maintenance and is in need of replacement and repair. The line to Aswan is important for transporting goods, although much material, especially locally, is carried by road.

Suez Canal

The Canal since its construction has never been isolated from politics. It gave the British the excuse for staying on until 1955 and for attempting to return in 1956. It was the barrier the Israelis reached in 1956 and 1967 and the waterway across which the war of attrition was fought in 1969. With so much disruption it is difficult to look clearly at its long-term effects on Egypt's economy. In 1952 the Canal was operated by the Suez Maritime Canal Company essentially as a non-Egyptian undertaking. The headquarters of the Company were in Paris and it had a board of thirty-two directors on which only five Egyptians sat. Most officials and pilots were non-Egyptian. By the 1949 agreement between the Company and the Egyptian government Egypt was to receive a mere 7 per cent of the gross annual profits. In 1952 over 14,500 transits were made through the Canal providing a total revenue of £E35 million. Economically such a situation could not be tolerated, and politically the whole Canal issue was a constant reminder of the colonial past. On nationalising the Canal in 1956 Nasser declared that Egypt would henceforth receive all transit dues and would use the money to finance the building of the High Dam. The Suez Canal Authority was established and, despite foreign disbelief, when the Canal was cleared after the 1956 invasion, ran operations efficiently until the 1967 war forced its second closure. The decade 1957–67 was one of steady progress under the guidance of Mahmud Yunis, the director of the Authority. Facilities were improved and the number of transits rose to 21,250 in 1966, increasing revenue from £E51 million in 1961 to £E95 million in 1966. The majority of the pilots was by 1965 Egyptian, and even *The Times* was moved to comment in 1966 that 'the record of Egyptian management in the Suez Canal has been excellent', thereby eating its words of March 1957 that prospective Canal users 'viewed with dismay a situation in which the Suez Canal might be re-opened for navigation with, as yet, no international guarantee of its use at a reasonable level of dues, without discrimination, and no assurance that there will be carried out the urgent improvement work required'. In 1966 plans were announced to deepen the Canal to allow larger ships to pass through, especially the larger oil tankers then in service. Work began in February 1967. In June the Israelis reached the east bank and the Canal was blocked. It was still closed to shipping when Nasser died, and was one of the many problems he left unsolved. As long as it remained closed Egypt was losing some £E100 million in annual revenues.

Sadat took its reopening as a top priority. The 1973 war was once again fought across it and the recapture of the east bank enabled him to set about clearing it of sunken ships, mines and unexploded ammunition. With great courage it was reopened to shipping in June 1975 as a symbol of Egypt's determined search for peace and prosperity. Since then it has been widened and improved to cut down passage time and to take larger tankers. An oil pipeline (SUMED) runs alongside it and a road tunnel to Sinai has been built underneath it. There are plans for even more expansion. The Canal towns are being rebuilt and developed and large 'free zones' opened at Suez and Port Said. In 1980 revenue from the Canal was estimated at some $1,000 million, thus at last providing the Egyptian economy with a substantial income. All Sadat's plans depended on the Canal area never again being a battlefield.

Balance of Trade and Economic Growth

Every country is a part of the world economic system and, whether developed or not, has to export goods to earn the currency needed to import material for industrial and military purposes and to purchase consumer goods. Egypt moved from being a tightly controlled economy under Nasser to a more open one under Sadat who had a number of advantages not available to his predecessor. During the period 1956–64 there was a rapid growth in the economy which then slowed down when aid from the United States ceased and because of the disastrous consequences of the 1967 war.

On taking over Sadat found the Suez Canal closed, oil fields under Israeli occupation, massive foreign debts, failing industry and a falling per capita income. Since then oil and Canal revenues have increased substantially, the many Egyptians working abroad send home large remittances, tourism has increased, and from having a chronic balance of trade deficit, in 1980 there was a projected $1,200 million overall surplus. In 1981 this surplus disappeared and was replaced by a deficit made up by US and European aid. The value of exports rose from £E234 million in 1952 to £E385 million in the *five* months June–October 1980. At the same time there was an enormous rise in imports after 1973, especially in food and consumer goods, while the traditional exports did not increase very much. However, experts stress that economic recovery may be fragile as oil and the Canal account for one third of all government revenue and little new oil has been found, as the Suez income depends on the state of world trade, as the number of emigrants appears to be static, and as tourists are very easily discouraged by political uncertainty. Inflation is severe and the majority of the population still desperately poor. The government is committed to massive food subsidies, estimated at $1,500 million in 1979, is in debt abroad ($8,000 million to Russia) and must depend on foreign aid (in 1980 $2,200 million from the United States and $1,000 million from the European Community).

Nasser promised Egypt a bright future economically, when political independence freed the country from foreign exploitation. He faced problems, however, which seemed almost insuperable. An increasing population together with a lack of resources tended to negate all economic progress. Despite the achievements of the High Dam, the running of the Suez Canal, some industrialisation and land reclamation, he left Egypt a country struggling with chronic poverty and under-development. Nasser's dearest wish was to improve the lot of the poor peasant and the urban dweller. In any country economic development is essentially long term and in his eighteen years he could see only initial steps taken towards this goal, but, as in political life, he put Egypt on to a new economic road. Sadat, with the same aims and wishes, chose a different path and changed the economy radically during the period 1974–81.

8 Education and the Growth of Culture

Education provides the soil from which all other aspects of a country's development grow. In school are formed attitudes which influence the child throughout the rest of his life. In a developing country at least two basic problems have to be faced — the inheritance of an education system inadequate for the country's needs, and the lack of teachers at all levels who possess the necessary qualifications to 'guide' children into an understanding and acceptance of new standards, aims and ideologies. In the early stages of independence, or in a post-revolutionary situation, when all society's energies need to be employed to pursue new policies, children have to be taught by teachers from under the old regime. Techniques, attitudes, curricula and physical conditions can be modified only slowly.

Education in Egypt has a long and varied history in which two main trends are distinguishable. The more ancient of these is the Islamic. In the centre of Islamic culture in Egypt has stood for a thousand years the Azhar mosque, providing an education in the Islamic sciences of tradition, theology, law and Koranic interpretation. This traditional type of education fulfilled the task of instilling into the student the principles of Islam and of maintaining them in Egyptian society. Side by side there developed a more secular type of education in elementary, primary (middle) and secondary schools and, eventually, in universities. Only a minority of children attended those institutions in which the traditional methods of rote learning were still followed. An Egyptian educationalist pointed to the weaknesses produced by these methods — a lack of initiative and adventure, of social intelligence and vision, of independent thinking and of knowledge (differentiating between true knowledge and rote information).

Education under Socialism

The aim of the revolution was to transform society. Education in the broadest sense was the fundamental means of achieving this. The goals of education were expressed most strongly in the Charter of 1962 and in the writings of ideologists in the early 1960s when Nasser was most deeply committed to an overall socialist approach. In the long term the transformation would begin with the youngest child in the elementary school who would be educated in the principles of socialism, Arabism and national consciousness. The student would be taught (the word used was 'directed') to co-operate with the state in achieving its goals, it was hoped without question. In return for the benefits the state provided, such as free education and medical facilities, the citizen was expected to work to build socialism. Deviation was frowned on. In fact those who chose not to co-operate would have to be re-educated until their 'habits, customs and thinking' were reformed. It was an authoritarian approach, with the state the fountain of all goodness and wisdom, and although the Charter frequently mentioned 'freedom' for the individual it was a freedom within strictly prescribed limits.

The Free Officers soon after the revolution turned their attention towards educational reform and gradually attempted to bring education within an overall plan for the country's development. Stress was laid on the introduction of technical and vocational education and on the improvement of teacher training and administration. With the introduction of ideological programmes more attention was paid to politicising education and to relating it to planned changes in society in general. In 1960 Nasser created a Committee on National Education whose task was 'to form a new generation of youth, who understand the stage through which their nation is at present passing'. Compulsory lessons in socialist principles were introduced along with textbooks written stressing the correctness of government policies and giving the official version of Egyptian history.

Often these lessons do not seem to have been very profound. One observer of village schools reported in 1966–7 that 'nearly all the school headmasters interviewed denied that the secondary and primary schools were openly or directly teaching any political ideology to the village children'. It was observed, however, that the children were undergoing a certain amount of political indoctrination.

> Usually when entering the classroom, the teacher would ask the students to stand. Rising to their feet they would shout 'Nasser' or 'freedom' or perhaps 'independence', and when asked to sit down they again would shout, usually a word symbolizing some aspect of the regime's ideology. I made it a practice to question students as to their preference for future employment and the three most popular vocations mentioned were military officer, engineer and schoolteacher, in that order. The children would repeat rhythmically at morning assembly, Nasser, Nasser, Nasser, or shout out G–A–M–A–L Gamal! A song popular among elementary students was 'Nasser, all of us love you, we will remain by your side, Nasser, leader of all, oh Nasser'.

A French scholar, Olivier Carré, has made an interesting analysis of some of those school textbooks which emphasise the close links between socialism, Islamic teaching and obedience to the leader and government. The introduction to one of the books states that its purpose is 'to induce in the students a sincere faith which will help to mould society on the strong foundations of true democracy and authentic socialism'. 'Young people should be trained to believe in God and in their homeland, and to work for their society on the bases of socialism, democracy and co-operative action'. The textbooks throughout stress that the state must be founded on social justice, the dignity of the individual and of work, equality and responsibility. Capitalism is rejected entirely and imperialism is shown as an injustice to human personality. Obedience is required of the citizen to the law and to the head of state. In return, the leader must show concern and respect for his citizens and be a model of good conduct. The government must concern itself with all aspects of the citizen's life.

While President Sadat would have endorsed most of these principles, as in other spheres of life he tried to bring to education a more open approach not rigidly based on a socialist ideology. It is impossible to change course immediately and all plans are essentially long term. The search was being made for a 'uniquely Egyptian solution, rather than waiting for others to present a ready-made educational pattern to be implemented'. Sadat believed that the preservation of Egyptian national characteristics through education was just as important as innovation. It was yet another aspect of his idea of continuity with change, of a liberal outlook while searching for a suitable solution for the problems of society. No one educational solution would be dismissed out of hand and none followed uncritically. As under Nasser, suitable education open to all was seen as the foundation on which any future progress could be built.

These were the recommended principles of good education, and while it was easy to prepare textbooks it was not so simple to solve the other problems. Primary and elementary education was dealt with first and the distinction between the two abolished in 1953. The length of stay in these schools was extended from four to six years. Promotion within the school was made automatic (instead of by examination) if the pupil attended regularly. The attempt to provide universal primary education, which was planned for 1965, has not succeeded and has been postponed at least twice. Nevertheless, the numbers of children at school did increase from 1·3 million in 1953 to 3·6 million in 1970, and an estimated 4·5 million in 1980 out of 8 million eligible. It was still much more difficult for children in the countryside to obtain a primary education than for those in towns. Such a steep increase also brought problems such as overcrowding in inadequate buildings and a lack of trained teachers. Classes had to become larger with the resultant strains upon the teachers and an inability to give adequate individual attention. It is well known that even in highly developed educational systems pupils in large classes can finish their education virtually illiterate, and in Egypt it is believed that many of those who do graduate from rural schools fall back into illiteracy within a few years.

The reliance on rote learning can accelerate this tendency. One visitor to a village school observed:

As we entered the school yard, three teachers were observed talking together while their students were in the classrooms shouting their daily recitations. When we entered the classrooms and asked for a demonstration of their reading skills, many of the students were able to 'read' their primer without even looking at the pages.

One major problem in Egypt – and all Arab countries – is that there exist in practice two languages. In the villages children speak the Egyptian dialect form of Arabic which is not written. In school they learn written, literary, grammatical Arabic which they would not use in conversation. Thus, after leaving school, unless there is constant practice in reading and writing the facility can easily slip away. They would also have difficulty in understanding certain radio and television programmes such as news broadcasts which are given in literary Arabic. Concern was expressed at the enormous cost of attempting to provide universal elementary education when so many students revert to illiteracy. Given the predominantly rural and populous urban nature of Egyptian society this will remain a problem for years to come, and literacy can be maintained only when habits change encouraged by the spread of such aids as mobile public libraries, cinema units, television programmes and 'culture caravans' – all of which have been attempted by the Ministry of Culture.

At about the age of 12 students enter preparatory school (which is the middle school) if they pass a stiff competitive examination. Many students fall at this hurdle and in 1966 only about 20 per cent of children of age 12–15 were attending preparatory schools. It was originally intended that these schools should provide both academic and vocational training but it was soon obvious that vocational training was best given later in school life at the secondary stage (15–18 years). Competition for entrance to preparatory schools is great as this is the path to higher education. The government has moved to expand this level until it becomes compulsory in the future. The increase has already affected standards and in its turn puts further pressure on places in institutes of higher education.

The secondary stage is entered after another examination and the government planned that only about 43 per cent would be accepted for promotion. At this level a substantial proportion of students enter vocational and technical schools – industrial, commercial and agricultural. In 1970 293,000 students were at academic schools and 241,000 at technical. There is a great demand in Egypt, as in all developing countries, for skilled manpower in most fields. There equally seems to be no catching up with this demand, not least because of a marked reluctance among students to go into technical occupations. A government report stated that 'occupations of the "white-collar type" are always preferred to the "blue-collar type"', even though the latter type of occupation provided more opportunities, better pay and promotion. Egypt has for many years been struggling to overcome this aversion, which is by no means unique or unknown elsewhere. Secondary education also left many students dissatisfied, whether it had been academic or vocational. The same report stated that in 1968 only 18 per cent of secondary school leavers were happy in the positions they occupied. There were other criticisms of the educational system and educationalists realised that it was not achieving the aims set for it. One Egyptian expert wrote in 1964 that 'our educational system at all its levels is not meeting the requirements of our society. It needs a radical overhauling both in structure and in content'. Education was still confused with the ability to absorb and memorise facts in order to regurgitate them for examination. Planners had been too concerned with quantity rather than quality, and the curricula did not reflect the problems of Egyptian society. One leading critic claimed that the stress on politicisation in schools had led to a lowering of standards, and that education had been blinkered by it.

Higher Education

Great attention has been paid to higher education and the difficulties encountered at lower levels are also found at the top. Numbers are one of the chief problems. Reforms and improvements are often vitiated by sheer weight of numbers. In 1951 35,000 students were studying at university; in 1969 the total was 140,000 with another 53,000 in the Azhar and higher institutes. The reform of the Azhar, already mentioned, changed the religious institution into a university with additional 'secular' faculties. While still training religious scholars, its graduates now can compete equally with those of the other universities. University education has a great attraction in Egypt and is seen as the passport to secure and prestigious employment. The government has encouraged this trend by making higher education free, planning several new universities, opening the doors of universities and permitting non-university students to take external degrees. These latter are not an unmixed blessing as they have to teach themselves and impose extra strain on the overworked examiners. In addition a number of institutes of higher education, originally intended to give specialised training, have gradually become ordinary universities in all but name – in fact a parallel, but inferior system.

The large numbers of students impose severe burdens on facilities and teachers, especially in arts faculties. Lectures have to be given to audiences of hundreds of students who crowd the lecture theatres, sitting on the stairs and window sills, or outside the room in corridors listening to loud-speakers. Lecture notes are memorised (teachers sometimes distribute duplicated synopses) and reproduced for examination. It has been estimated that in the Faculty of Letters in Cairo 180,000 examination papers have to be marked by 100 teachers. In other faculties pressures on libraries, laboratories and equipment are equally great. The larg graduates in 'non-productive' subjects produce pressure engineers, technologists and others are in short supply. Such conditions do not encourage university teachers leave the country, either permanently for Europe or Amei periods in other Arab countries. It has been a common experience to visit a faculty in Egypt to discover that up to half the teachers are teaching abroad. While such educational co-operation has been essential to the Arab world it may lower the standards of Egyptian education. These conditions also produce frustrated graduates and it is no coincidence that university students have been to the forefront of political discontent, following the pre-revolutionary tradition. It has been mentioned that students challenged Nasser after the 1967 defeat and they were also active in demonstrations after his death, in 1971, 1972, 1974 and later.

Culture

Education is part and parcel of the general culture of a country and culture is at the root of a country's character and life. While the uneducated may to some extent appreciate music and art, the growth of literature depends on an educated reading public.

Literature is not, nor should it be, a means to an end. (Taha Husain)
Art without politics is not art. (Ahmad Salih)

These two quotations express two opposed points of view about the place of art, literature and culture in society. In a developing country committed to a socialist programme the view can be held that everything in society should contribute to that programme and that nothing should be allowed to hinder or criticise it. This view can lead to the Zhdanov approach in the Soviet Union by which all art and artists have to conform to rigid supervision and strict censorship. Egypt did not adopt such a system yet her artists probably feel that it is their duty to make a positive contribution to the development of the country and that they have a responsibility as intellectuals to foster an understanding of its problems and to encourage education in the broadest sense. Most would also probably accept what an Egyptian critic, Abdel Azim Anis, has written: 'Unless a writer accepts his responsibility towards himself, his community, his country and nationality his freedom may turn into anarchy'. This responsibility has been termed 'commitment'. What has been said by an Egyptian scholar of Arab writers in general applies to Egyptian authors in particular:

Writers in the Arab countries are faced with the problem of commitment in an acute form ... The Arab writer ... has been growing more keenly and painfully aware of the need to harness all human activities, including intellectual and literary ones, to the overriding aims of realizing social and material progress, and of creating a more rational, just and equitable distribution of the available resources and opportunities.

This kind of commitment did not mean that one ideology had to be strictly followed, and since Nasser in fact formulated his ideas only slowly, writers could themselves contribute to the process of formulation and use their art to criticise certain aspects of policy and life. There has been endless discussion in print about the role of the artist in Egypt and no real consensus has emerged. In its turn the state has made a deliberate effort to encourage art and to promote culture. Yet the artist by his very nature and his calling stands apart from society, often feeling alienated and unable to do very much. He works in the realm of ideas and launches these ideas into society, and can only stand back and wait to see whether they are accepted and have any effect. In Egypt (as in other countries) writers have been imprisoned, persecuted or exiled for their ideas and therefore have to face very acutely the consequences of their writings. In the end, however, literature stands or falls on its own intrinsic merit, and not on whether it purveys certain political ideas.

As part of its efforts to control all aspects of public life the revolutionary regime in Egypt established in 1956 a Higher Council for the Promotion of Literature and Arts with the object of encouraging and patronising artistic activities within the prescribed goals of the revolution, which if carried too far could have meant state control and censorship. But in Egypt the lack of a will (or desire) for extreme measures meant that literature flourished with reasonable freedom even if its message had sometimes to be veiled. A former official in the Ministry of Culture described government policy towards art as the attempt 'to ensure the patronage of the arts without creating a sense of totalitarian oppressiveness, to create intelligible links between cultural and socio-economic development'. Moreover, as almost no writers could support themselves on their literary earnings alone they had other posts, often in the government, which they did not want to jeopardise.

The state encouraged literary creation by establishing a publishing house and offering various awards and prizes. The house's aim was 'to contribute to the accomplishment of the cultural revolution' and publish some four books a day. Such a policy could all too easily encourage the party hacks. In 1962 the Institute of Theatre and Music announced a competition for a one-act play which would 'glorify positive, fruitful work for the public's welfare under socialism'. The competition turned out to be a failure, the entries consisting largely of speeches, propaganda and 'endless political debates'.

Prose Writing

All forms of art and literature have flourished since the revolution. The novel and short story have in particular seen a remarkable development under the leadership of a number of outstanding writers. On the whole they are little known outside the Arab world although in recent years the number of translations into European languages has been increasing. It seems that none has as yet made an impression similar to, for example, the great novels translated from Russian, but the tradition of the Arab novel is much shorter. The first modern Egyptian novel appeared in 1914. From then until the Second World War five or six novels worthy of mention appeared. In the 1940s novel writing seems to have taken off and by the time of the revolution there were several established names who continued to write in the years following. As the novel was not an established form in Arabic literature a tradition had slowly to be built up from the first pale imitations and adaptations of European works to the original works being written today. The reading public for the novel in Egypt is not very large and an average edition totals 4,000 copies although there are popular titles which far exceed this number. In addition, some 60 per cent of the total Egyptian book production is exported to the Arab world and elsewhere, and some controversial books by Egyptian writers have first been published outside Egypt, usually in Beirut.

Nagib Mahfouz is Egypt's leading novelist. He was born in a district of old Cairo in 1912, went to Cairo University to study philosophy and in 1939 became a civil servant. In 1954 he joined the Ministry of Culture. He is a prolific writer, having published some thirty novels and collections of short stories since his first novel appeared in 1939. In his work are represented the stages of the development of the Egyptian novel itself. His first works were historical novels, modelled on Scott and Dumas, using an ancient Egyptian background in which to set themes of contemporary relevance. In one, a young pharoah (Farouk?) begins to disappoint his people who rebel against him; in another the ancient Egyptians are busy fighting invaders from the north (the British?)

Although Mahfouz did not become a militant Marxist he was greatly influenced by socialist thought early in his career and in his works published between 1945 and 1956 he abandoned the historical setting for contemporary Cairo which he portrays with unremitting realism. In five novels and in a trilogy of connected works he has drawn the best imaginative record of the impact of economic, political and social forces on the life of the lower middle class in the 1930s and 1940s. The five novels, according to one Egyptian critic,

> paint a ruthless picture of the life of the lower middle class of Cairo ... The poverty, the frustrations and confined lives of petty government officials and small tradesmen are laid bare. The picture is so convincingly depressing that the heart sinks with the weight of it all.

Novels of social protest, bitterly critical of an unjust social and political order, they are pervaded by Mahfouz's overall feeling of pessimism and gloom. Death is the finale of most of them. In *Midaqq Alley* (a street in old Cairo), probably his most popular, the effect of the Second World War and of the British occupation on the inhabitants of the alley is shown. While some find profitable jobs with the British army, others find their lives disrupted. The heroine, the beauty of the alley, becomes discontented and is drawn to seek the money the soldiers have in their pockets. The novel ends in tragedy. Her fiancé eventually discovers her in a tavern in the middle of a group of British soldiers. He assaults her and is beaten to death by the drunken soldiers.

The trilogy likewise portrays life in old Cairo from 1917–44, the chronicle of a family of poorer merchants and the effects on it of Egyptian history and politics during a difficult and frustrating period. The author is particularly concerned with the process of change, and its influence in Egyptian society on the life of the members of the family. Politics are a part of this process of change. The characters participate in or are affected by demonstrations against the British and by the nationalist movement. It is interesting that the end of the book shows the leading characters, two brothers, having different hopes for the political future of Egypt – those of the Muslim Brothers, and those of socialism. It is clear that Mahfouz favoured the socialist solution, and that he was dissatisfied with the monarchist regime. The trilogy was completed before the revolution, but published only in 1956–7 and in a sense the 'political' aim of the work was by then superfluous.

His next work, *The Children of our Quarter*, appeared in 1959 and was radically different in tone from his previous novels. Several explanations have been offered for this ten-year silence. Mahfouz himself claimed that the revolution had brought the answer to his questionings about life and its purpose and that it would change those aspects of life he had criticised in his novels. This seems a naive explanation, yet it may be no coincidence that his silence lasted through the early years of the revolution. Perhaps his hopes for a radical socialist transformation of Egypt were disillusioned and he therefore turned away from the social criticism of his earlier work to a more metaphysical, spiritual approach using allegory and allusion. *The Children of our Quarter* is an allegory in which humanity makes repeated attempts under various prophets to save itself from cruel rulers, poverty and misery. The prophets are modelled on Moses, Jesus and Muhammad. The creator stands back while these attempts are defeated until he is finally killed on the emergence of the scientist who realises too late that the creator was at least a symbol for the people in their life. The basic meaning of the allegory is clear. When the novel first appeared in serial form in a newspaper it caused a great uproar and was denounced in the pulpits of mosques for its godlessness and profanity. The novel had other messages, including the preaching of a gentle type of socialism.

Mahfouz was apparently undeterred by the storm of criticism and continued to write novels which have gradually become more spiritual and psychological. His attention to social forces and political issues remains but he has become more concerned with the deeper meaning of the plight of the individual in a period of great change. His outstanding novel of the period is *Miramar Pension* which appeared just before, and to some seemed a prediction of, the disaster of 1967. It reflected the disillusion of many intellectuals with the political excesses and mistakes of the previous decade. He courageously paints a gloomy picture of the moral failure of the revolution and seems to despair of solving the problems of Egypt. (It is interesting that Nasser accused Mahfouz of attacking him for many years, to which he replied that he had only been producing literature.) *Miramar* moves the setting from Cairo to Alexandria where, in a small pension, there meets a group of people, each representing a different aspect of Egyptian social and political life, who express their criticism of past and present policies. One makes an open attack on the Arab Socialist Union. The book made a very popular film.

Mahfouz's later works plunge into the absurd and abstruse, symbolic, almost obscurantist writing, which reflects the hopelessness felt after the 1967 defeat. The work depicts insoluble dilemmas; suffering and fear are the lot of the characters. He believes that politics have been used to mislead the people, who are in any case easily misled. In *Heart of the Night* (1975) one of the characters declares:

Reason retains its own language only in the field of scientific research. The language to which the millions respond is still the language of the emotions and the instincts, the songs of nation, homeland and racialism, and mad dreams and delusions. This is the universal tragedy.

In *Mirrors* (1972) Mahfouz speaks through a character saying 'I used to have faith but everything collapsed after June fifth 1967 ... The whole world is a futile vacuous nothing'. One novel published in 1974, *Karnak* (a café in Cairo), is a damning review of the situation under Nasser. The three protagonists are arrested at various times, imprisoned, tortured and even killed, on the accusation that they are communists or Muslim Brothers. The chief torturer − who is dismissed after 1967 − attempts to justify his action by claiming that all Egyptians are criminals and victims. The novel is a political document and a frank exposé of torture. It was also made into a very popular film.

Yusuf Idris (1927−), Egypt's leading short story writer, has also written novels and plays (some twenty-five published volumes). He brings to his work a breadth of vision and a deep concern with the plight of man in the world. He sets his stories in contemporary Egypt and is interested in the social and political background but regards the human being as more important than any political question. He sees many threats to the quality of humanity in his characters in their daily lives – politics, corruption, harsh social conventions. They come from all kinds of background and he is especially interested in that area of social behaviour where rules are the strictest – sex and the relationship between men and women. Idris's training as a doctor and his work in a large government hospital have made him particularly sympathetic to the problems of the misfit, the persecuted and the sick. His work is influenced by the various political and social circumstances through which he has lived, the British occupation, the disaster in Palestine and the various hopes, plans, frustrations and catastrophes of the Nasser era. He joined the guerrilla organisations fighting the British, supported Nasser initially but soon became disillusioned. He clashed with the regime and was arrested and imprisoned. For a short while he was a member of the communist party until he became disillusioned with its ideology.

Despite the hopes that were raised during this period it is the frustration and the disappointed ideals that are the salient feature of many of his stories. He is trying to answer the question why his characters, despite their human potential, fall into misery and frustration. It is a universal question set in an Egyptian context. In one short story, *A Summer Night*, a group of village lads go in search of a woman in the neighbouring town who they think will fulfil all their lusts. When they find she does not exist, they vent their rage on the companion who fabricated her, and return to their village frustrated, hopes shattered, to face an inexorable fate:

> After a while we the village boys found ourselves retracing our foot-steps, returning to our village along the same road. An overwhelming power was pushing us along. We were returning limping and leaning on one another, flagging, and thinking of the coming day, which would catch up with us, give shape to the ground in front of us, bringing in the cares of the world. The hot, dry, harsh day we could see rising before us like a giant larger than the sun. There was no pity in his heart, no shred of cloth above his body. In his hand there was a large club, raised up, awaiting us. As we approached him his eyes were sparking with fire. We were fearful and submissive, knowing full well that we could not escape his hand.

In another work, *The Shame*, Idris shows the effect of corruption on a young woman who goes to work as the first female in an office of men. Despite her struggles she eventually succumbs to the temptations of gaining a little illegal extra money to help to keep her brother at school. Seemingly helpless she gradually collapses morally, unable to stand alone against the pressure of her colleagues.

In his stories and novels dealing with village life Idris is concerned to show the influence of various taboos on the villagers' lives and the unhappiness they can cause. The villagers *en masse* form a disapproving background against which the individual cannot fight. This hopeless struggle is most movingly depicted in the story *Shaikh Shaikha* whose anti-hero is a literal misfit, a misshapen almost inhuman creature, deaf and dumb, who is tolerated in his village as he is considered totally harmless. He is allowed to witness as an unnoticed observer all the people's secrets and their intimate lives. Slowly they begin to suspect that he may after all be able to appreciate what is going on, and in a growing atmosphere of mistrust and hate the villagers turn on him and beat his head in with a stone. Even such a helpless and inoffensive creature does not escape suffering and catastrophe.

Of the many other novels and stories written during the revolution only one or two more can be mentioned. Many were written by party hacks who used their characters, especially the peasants, as mere tools to put over the message of the regime. An outstanding exception is the novel *The Earth* by Abdel Rahman Sharqawi (1920–) which deals sympathetically with the life of Egyptian peasants. Published in 1953, the concern he shows for the *fellah* was probably encouraged by the attitude of the revolution towards the peasants. The novel relates the story of a village's fight against an unjust government during the 1930s. Sharqawi portrays in great detail the life of the village, its traditions, quarrels and customs. As a social realist writer he is concerned to demonstrate his strong political commitment. He had been a socialist before the revolution, and joined a Marxist study group while at university. His later work became more openly committed and perhaps less in literary value. *The Peasant* (1967) relates a village's struggle against members of the old exploiting classes, this time with the government on its side rather than against it.

Drama

Drama is another literary form not native to Arabic culture which was introduced to Egypt under Western influence. After the revolution it developed strongly and had a great impact, primarily because of the immediate effect a play can have on a large group of people gathered together at one time with a shared knowledge of political and social conditions. One critic has written that, if the short story had a predominant role in Egyptian literature in the 1950s, drama was the major genre for self-expression and for the assertion of the public's preoccupations in the 1960s. The audiences came to expect that the theatre would reflect their own problems and give them some kind of moral leadership.

Much of the drama produced has been the theatre of criticism, satirising such things as a hidebound bureaucracy, opportunism and the dangers of dehumanising society to which ideologies and authoritarian regimes are liable. It is somewhat ironic that the flowering of the theatre in Cairo was partly due to government encouragement where small theatres were opened, plays televised and texts published. Many types of play have been attempted from poetic drama to the theatre of the absurd and although some surreal plays have been popular, at least one dramatist claimed that social realism as opposed to the absurd or philosophical approach was the most important trend of the 1960s. In more recent plays themes have been taken from the social and public (political) fields, notably that of the weak individual ground down by more powerful outside forces and by the seeming whims of the impersonal world. This is an aspect of life faced by all but perhaps more forcibly by a society in the grip of change. Plays have also been set in the countryside where the clash between the *fellah* mentality and officialdom and between modernisation and custom looms large.

Out of the many plays written since the revolution, three may be singled out as representing particular themes. Tawfiq al-Hakim (1898–1987) was Egypt's grand old man of letters, a prolific playwright, short story writer, essayist and novelist. He wrote over thirty longer plays together with collections of much shorter ones. They cover a multitude of themes from the philosophical, based on classical subjects, to the contemporary, ostensibly criticising Nasser and the revolution. He also wrote a number of plays on social themes and ventured into the theatre of the absurd. In 1959 he wrote what some have taken to be his most important and successful play, *Al-Sultan al-ha'ir*, the perplexed sultan, translated as *The Sultan's Dilemma*. It has a universal theme relevant to contemporary Egypt but set several centuries earlier. It is the conflict between the application of the principle of law in government and its cynical disregard. Although Hakim had earlier written that the artist should keep aloof from party politics, he did not intend to isolate himself from life and society and *The Sultan's Dilemma* is a clear demonstration of his concern with morality in society. A sultan in the middle ages discovers that by mischance he is still a slave and that according to law he can only be freed by an owner after being publicly auctioned. The Chief Justice upholds the law ('The sword really can cut off tongues and heads . . . but it's not so decisive where questions and problems are concerned'). After some heartsearching ('What does it matter if we shed a little blood for the sake of good government?'), and despite contrary advice from the Prime Minister, the Sultan agrees. He is bought by a rich widow with the reputation of being a courtesan whose only condition before freeing him at dawn is to spend a (virtuous) night in his company. The Prime Minister suspects the intentions of the widow and commands the muezzin unlawfully to announce the dawn prayer at about midnight. The Sultan obviously sees through the trick and scolds the Minister ('Put an end at once to this mockery and meanness . . . aren't you ashamed of playing about with the law like this?'). He wishes to carry out the bargain with his purchaser, but she agrees to release him. He rewards her.

The play is written humorously and with a deft touch and the message is clear, both specifically – that rulers (in Egypt) should not be above the law – and more generally and cynically – that those who at one time uphold the law can also break it when it suits their convenience. The author himself wrote that

> the play was inspired by the question that now puzzles the world: is the solution to its problems to be sought... by resorting to force or by upholding principles? Those who have the power and are in a position to determine the fate of mankind... are frightened and perplexed, not knowing what to do... The author has put this problem of choice and the present attitude to it in a historical oriental setting.

The play was produced to popular acclaim in Cairo in the days before Hakim became disillusioned with the revolution. It could be that the Sultan is both a flattering portrait of Nasser and a pointed hint to him for the future. And beneath the politics is the deeper human problem of putting honesty, love and justice above self interest.

Mikhail Roman was quite a different man from Hakim. Trained as a scientist he taught at the Institute of Industry and died aged only about 50. He was an 'amateur' dramatist who turned late to playwriting, yet he is considered to be an outstanding figure. His work aroused strong reactions amongst public and critics and he represents anger at its most violent in the Egyptian theatre. His work is controversial and caused months of verbal fighting when it was produced. (In fact the censor banned several of his plays or a theatre company, anticipating a ban, did not accept a text.) Although he wrote twelve plays, only five have been performed. It is again ironic that some of these were published by the Ministry of Culture. *Al-wafid (The New Arrival)* was first performed in 1965 after the censor had granted permission for one night's performance before a special audience. It is a one-act play which takes place in a Kafkaesque atmosphere. The new arrival comes to a big impersonal 'hotel' which has a large complex of buttons and button pushers. Through various encounters he slowly loses all sense of security and is overtaken by the feeling that he is facing a mindless and soulless technological organisation. His insecurity is increased by techniques of interrogation, by the promising of food and withholding it, and by the authorities' refusing to recognise him unless he produces a discarded train ticket. Without it to them he does not exist. Even his former friends cannot break regulations to acknowledge him. He says to his erstwhile friend:

> But I'm like a brother to you. We were brought up together.
> *Friend:*   I'm very sorry. The machine has to be told everything – your job and the work you do, everything.
> *New arrival:* And without all this information, my very existence becomes doubtful. Do I become non-existent?
> *Friend:*   Here, at any rate.

The new arrival slowly reaches the edge of insanity as he feels totally helpless and isolated: 'What a strange feeling of insignificance, what a frightening feeling of loneliness', he shouts despairingly: 'I do exist ... I can't ever become non-existent. It's impossible, I exist, I do. I'm here!'

This short but effective play refers to the universal condition of men threatened and made to feel insecure by 'progress', whose roots are shaken by the onward march of technology in society — the man who is deemed not to exist if he is not recorded in the computer file and who has no one to appeal to. The nightmarish atmosphere of the situation is brilliantly evoked in this play.

Yusuf Idris, mentioned as a short story writer, also writes plays. In 1964 he wrote a series of articles calling for a specifically Egyptian theatre which would grow from the heart of society, no longer a pale model of the European stage. He claimed that this theatre already existed in Egyptian life and that dramatists had 'to take a fresh look at [themselves] and [their] life, so as to distinguish between the authentic and the acquired there'. Idris also distinguished between the Greek version of tragedy (of man struggling against blind fate) and the Egyptian in which the hero is 'master of his own density and conducts his own life ... Man himself makes his life and his destiny ... is boundlessly free, and at the same time equally responsible for his choice'. Many critics rushed to attack Idris for his views, accusing him of cultural chauvinism although in fact the play he wrote to put his views into practice had nothing in it that had not already been used in European drama and little even specifically Egyptian. It is, nevertheless, an outstanding play, a tour de force, produced in 1964 amid great acclaim — entitled *Al-farafir*, a name Idris manufactured to mean servants, stooges or puppets. Idris wrote later (in 1971) that 'the problems of modern man are so deep that they reach a metaphysical level' and he tried to illustrate this theme in his play, a play of ideas, owing much to the theatre of the absurd. There is no plot, only a series of encounters between characters representing different ideas or points of view. Several of the cast sit amongst the audience who are often addressed directly. The anti-hero is Farfur (the singular of *Farafir*) who is servant to the 'Master' and who throughout the play struggles to escape from his subordinate status. He is quite a sympathetic character who has ideas above his station and yet cannot alter things — rather different from Idris's model of the Egyptian who is 'master of his own destiny'. Various ruses are attempted, changing roles, founding a state, enlisting the help of members of the audience and of the author who becomes younger and smaller during the action and eventually totally irresponsible for anything that happens. Finally he dies and Farfur ends his life endlessly circling around the Master who has become a system. The subject is treated with wit and the opportunity is taken to satirise different aspects of Egyptian life and of universal behaviour. For example, the possibilities of employment are being discussed.

Master:	Don't you have any job where one can earn one's keep by the sweat of his brow?
Farfur:	Yes...work as a thief.
Master:	O.K. I'm ready.
Farfur:	Do you want to work as a big thief or a medium one or small?
Master:	That doesn't need an answer...big of course.
Farfur:	Good, then work in the government Export Import Department.
Master:	And the medium thief?
Farfur:	Then you open a Co-operative Society.

On government hospitals:

Farfur:	Is Kasr al-Ainy in Cairo hospital any better?
Master:	No it isn't. The sick are dead before they can even get in there!

If the play has a message it is not one of hope but that life is unfair in most of its aspects and that death is not much better.

Farfur:	Whoever tries to reorganize this mixed-up world is mad and who leaves it alone in its confusion is sensible. There is no system which puts us equal side by side. Resignation is the only possible solution.
Master:	Life without a solution is a million times better than death with one. Life itself is some sort of solution. Even though it has its faults the smart thing is to complete it, not abolish it.

Poetry

Poetry amongst Arabic speakers is a flourishing art with origins dating back to well before the beginning of Islam when the public recital of odes was a feature of Bedouin life. A tradition of metre and rhyme was later established which lasted virtually unchanged until the twentieth century. This stultification often meant that language and form were more important than content. Poetry was a public art with applause and appreciation given for repetitious rhyme and verbal juggling. In the present century Arabic poetry has passed through most of the stages of European poetry — neoclassicism, romanticism, symbolism, surrealism, social realism, and even mysticism. It has also become a much more private art although it can still be used on public occasions in honour of public figures and events.

Many of the Arab poets who led innovating trends in the pre-revolutionary period were Egyptian. In later years the lead passed to Iraqis, Lebanese, Syrians and Palestinians. For the latter especially poetry has been used to express their deep sense of loss and longing for their homeland. Lebanon has been a centre of the avant-garde and the experimental and its effect has spread throughout the Arabic-speaking world. One Syrian poet, Ali Ahmad Said (known as Adunis) has had a widespread influence. He sees poetry as a means of inducing revolutionary change and of creating a new society. The poet is a revolutionary hero who will lead his people into the new world, no longer a passive romantic sufferer but the active redeemer. (It is interesting that such Christian imagery is not uncommon in poetry written by Muslims.) Perhaps no Egyptian poet shares exactly the views of Adunis, although like most artists they feel acutely the ills of society and the anxieties of modern man, and believe that the poet's 'commitment' must be obvious in his writing.

Salah Abdel Sabur (1931–81) was Egypt's leading poet. He was educated at Cairo University where he became acquainted with Western writers, especially T. S. Eliot. Under the revolution he edited a leading literary journal and was director of a state publishing house. He then became Director of the National Library. His earlier poetry demonstrates his commitment and social realism. In 1954 he wrote a poem entitled 'People in My Country', a harsh vision of life and death and fate in Egypt which begins:

> The people in my country are hawk-like, rapacious.
> Their singing is like winter shivering in wisps of rain.
> Their laughter sizzles like a flame in the wood.
> Their footsteps try to sink in the earth.
> They kill, steal, drink and belch
> But they are human
> And good hearted when they possess a handful of coins
> And believe in Fate.

The poet returns to his village, where his uncle is telling the villagers the story of a rich man who built castles and yet the angel of death finally summoned him. They cry out:

> What is the purpose of man's toiling, of life, oh God?
> How harsh and desolate you are, Oh God!

The poet's poor uncle dies (like the rich man) and is buried, yet the mourners now do not mention God for it was a year of hunger. The uncle's grandson stands by the grave:

> And when he stretched to the heavens his sturdy arm
> There swelled in his eyes a look of scorn
> For the year was a year of hunger.

The villagers are confounded by a fate which treats rich and poor alike and rewards toil with death. Bitterly and helplessly they shake their fist at an indifferent God.

As Abdel Sabur writes in another poem:

> Oh our great Lord, Oh my torturer
> How often you have afflicted me.

This gloomy vision was reinforced in a poem in the same collection entitled 'The Tatars have Attacked', which paints a horrific picture of a ravaged city (Baghdad after the Mongol invasion in 1258). It is a depressing view of a world after any disastrous war and is complete in itself although, if we believe poets are visionaries, it could be taken to portray Egypt after the 1967 defeat. In vivid language he depicts the defeated army:

> Our battalions returned ripped apart when the day was burning.
> The black flag, the wounded, the dead caravan,
> The hollow drum, the abject heedless footsteps
> A soldier's hands pounds on the wood.
> The tune of hunger.

Amid the ruin and destruction, the mothers and children terrified, the poet swears vengeance and sees some hope for the future:

> And I and all our comrades, mother, when the day faded
> Swore by hatred that we would cry in the morning for the Tatar's blood.
> Mother, say to the young
> 'My little ones
> We will search among our dark homes when day breaks
> And we shall build what the Tatars have destroyed'.

However pessimistic the poet's vision may seem it is somewhat redeemed by these final lines. In his later work Abdel Sabur expresses a more personal view tinged with melancholy and even mysticism. In one collection entitled *Dreams of an Ancient Knight*, he expounds themes of suffering and disillusionment. In the poem 'A Song to God' he cries out in his loneliness:

> God, O my loneliness behind closed doors
> God, would that you grant me serenity.

In language reminiscent of mediaeval mysticism he lays his suffering at his Lord's door:

> My sadness is heavy and burdensome this evening
> As tho' it were the torture of those shackled in hell.

> Our great Lord, my torturer
> Weaver of dreams in our eyes
> Sower of certainty and doubt
> Sender of pain and joy and grief
> You have chosen for me.
> How much you have hurt me.
> Have I not been saved yet
> Or have you forgotten me?
> Alas, you have forgotten me
> Have forgotten me
> Forgotten me.

Like other Egyptian intellectuals Abdel Sabur tended to withdraw from the unwelcome reality of the 1967 defeat and become more introspective. Nasser's untimely death was the desperate finale of this period of depression. As other poets, he wrote an apparently deeply felt yet rather occasional elegy on his leader's death, 'The Dream and the Song':

> Can he who gave to life die,
> Really die?
> What shall we do after him?
> What shall we do without him?
> Is he really dead?
>
> Have you died? No, for you will return when the broken
> people gather behind your bier,
> When they shout as though inspired
> Long live Egypt ... long live Egypt!
> Then you will live, for you are part of her soil.

Another leading poet Ahmad Hijazi (1935–) was born in a village in lower Egypt and moved to Cairo for his further education. In the capital he experienced great feelings of loneliness and alienation which influenced his early poetry. The title of his first collection, *City without Heart* (1956), lays bare his attitude which presumably represents the feelings of many Egyptian villagers who have left their homes to make a new life in the city. His poem 'Goodbye' begins:

> My friends
> How I dread the end of the road
> And the evening words of parting
> 'Goodbye'!
> 'Goodbye' and 'All the best' are painful.
> All expressions of farewell are bitter.
> Death is bitter
> And everything that steals man from man.

If the evening promises loneliness, the heat of the day offers little comfort:

The streets of the large city
Are abysses of fire
Which regurgitate at noon
The flames they have eaten in the morning.
How unhappy is the man who chances only upon their sun,
Only the buildings and railings, and the buildings and railings,
Only the squares, triangles and glass.
How miserable to be faced by a night of emptiness,
And a day of holiday
Empty of meeting.

However, Hijazi began to enjoy the company of other young people who inspired in him a belief in the virtues of Arab nationalism and socialism which compensated for his feelings of loneliness. He published in 1959 a collection entitled *Aurès* (the mountains in Algeria) inspired by the Algerian war of independence. In a preface he wrote:

My story with the [people of the] Aurès is my story of salvation. I began to write it after meeting some young men of the present blazing generation ... We used to meet in Cairo cafés and we have faith in Arabism and in working for it ... I love life and I found the young men from the East and West [of the Arab world] loving life too ... I sought sincerity and I found these young men to be living examples of the ideas they believed in.

He became a committed nationalist and began to write socialist anthems and poems on Nasser. In 'Song of the ASU' he sings words somewhat redolent of Soviet ideological poetry:

Be a family to me
Citadel of the poor peasants
For I have no family
Save men without names.
Be a capital for me
City of marvellous workers
For I have no homeland
Since I left the green earth.

Political affiliation has filled the void for him. His anthem of commitment rings out:

We are here and in our eyes is the homeland
And faces of fathers and sons, and memory and time.
In our breasts is the faith of our separation here.

Such deep identification with the system left the poet vulnerable to political changes and he was deeply affected by Nasser's death. His lines recall those of Abdel Sabur:

No he is not dead! We went wandering through the night of the city
Calling you; so come out to us and restore what we are calling for.
If you are thirsty we shall be a wind and river for you.
If you are hungry we shall be bread, salt, fruit.
If you are naked we shall be clothes and protection.

We are searching for you in its quarters.
The night was deep, the cafés still awake,
The faint lanterns and eyes
Staring as if we would see you appear from a balcony
Or from a radio your voice would shout loudly
Mocking what the allegers alleged
Or as if a man would come out crying into the night
'He has returned to life'!

Muhammad al-Faituri (1930–) was born in Egypt of a Sudanese father
and Egyptian mother and being black he identified with the fortunes of
Africa and with the position of the black man in a white-dominated
society. His collections bear such titles as *Songs of Africa, A Lover from
Africa* and *Remember Me, Africa*. The poems are vivid, deeply felt and
angry, and not submissive. In 'Sorrows of the Black City' he writes:

But when darkness builds up
On the city streets
Barricades of black stone
They stretch out their hands in silence
To the balconies of the morrow.
They are imprisoned cries for help
In an imprisoned land.
Their days are plague-ridden memories
Of a pestilential land.
Their faces are, like their hands, sad.
You see them bowed in silence
Gazing at the cracks.
You think them submissive
But they are on fire!

Radio, Television and Films

Whereas written literature and the theatre reach relatively small audiences,
the cinema and television screens and radio broadcasts are means of
presenting mass culture. The spoken word presents no problem to the
semi-literate or illiterate listener if it is in the Egyptian dialect and not
literary Arabic; radios are relatively cheap, and access to cinema and
television screens can be guaranteed by the government. Most states consider control of the means of mass communication, especially radio and
TV, essential to the development of their policies, enabling them both to
spread their own propaganda and stifle opposing views. They can be used
also to propagate education and culture and to introduce new ideas and

techniques. In Africa, Egypt has gone furthest in making use of radio broadcasts both inside and outside the country. In addition to news and entertainment programmes, the radio has been used to spread government messages, broadcast political speeches, and haltingly to introduce educational courses, which were dropped because of a lack of direction and planning. The radio comes first in importance in terms of numbers of listeners, followed by readers of newspapers and television viewers.

Television offers more direct entertainment and education than radio. It made its début in Egypt in 1960 since which time there has been a steady growth in the number of sets. Both TV and radio were arms of government controlled by the Ministry of Information. Sixty per cent of TV broadcasting time was devoted to entertainment, the population, especially the peasants, being particularly addicted to light entertainment and farce, which usually seems rather over-acted to Western taste. News, culture and religion took up most of the remaining time. The government used TV to propagate adult literacy campaigns and to try to orientate peasants towards modern methods in agriculture, hygiene and family planning. These courses were not too successful because of a lack of follow-up but various Ministries, especially of Health, Social Affairs, Culture and Education, continued to be encouraged to sponsor their own programmes. A Peoples Broadcasting System was opened in 1973 to produce educational programmes for students sitting examinations at all levels. TV sets were put in public places, co-operative centres, cafés and so on, to encourage greater audience participation and they often form part of the background to the chatter in a coffee house or even a shop. While programmes open endless vistas of the life of others with new concepts, methods and problems, both in Cairo and abroad, it is difficult to gauge exactly their impact. What is viewed on the screen can easily be taken as unreal and as having no relevance to the viewer's own life. Programmes which attempt to influence and educate others have to be produced with care and there is the danger that what is thought relevant in Cairo may seem quite irrelevant to the villager hundreds of miles away.

The cinema has a long history in Egypt, the first films being seen as early as 1905. Since that time there has been a substantial growth of cinemas and local film producers, and Egypt has now one of the most thriving film industries in the Third World. The films produced were made with financial success rather than artistic merit in view. The most popular type was the melodrama in which the rich man loved the poor girl, full of sentimentality, sexual frustration, seduction and suicide. Farces and musicals were also popular. A few serious novels were filmed. There was a strict censorship before the revolution which forbade films to attack foreigners, government officials, religion, or to show the true situation of peasants and workers, or anything favourable to socialism or unfavourable to monarchies. Some films took refuge in allegory, but it is difficult to blame producers for not producing more serious films under such conditions.

The revolution altered the situation. Themes changed radically. Censorship was relaxed in some areas, although extended in others. There were to be no apologetics for monarchies, the aristocracy or feudalism, and socialism was to be encouraged. Although the state did not exercise a total direction of culture, there was nevertheless a great increase in the number of social-realist films which portrayed the real conditions of the urban and rural poor, and of films with patriotic themes such as the Suez war. In addition serious novelists, such as Nagib Mahfouz, began to write film scripts and to have their novels filmed. As one student of the Egyptian film put it: 'The Egyptian cinema left the salon, the bedroom and the night club, to go in search of the real Egypt'.

The government made the decision to allow the public and private sectors to exist side by side after establishing a State Cinema Corporation whose main aim was to raise the quality of production even at the expense of box office success. In addition it sponsors young film makers and exports Egyptian films to Europe and elsewhere. The film industry is, however, commercially successful and Egyptian films, popular throughout the Arab world, are one of the main channels for the diffusion of Egyptian culture and even a knowledge of the Egyptian dialect. They seem to survive whatever the political vicissitudes.

Music and Popular Culture

Music to most Egyptians means accompanied songs sung by well-known artists either live or in recorded form. They are traditional in pattern with certain Western innovations and form the chief means of continuous, usually background, entertainment on the radio. They are the heirs of a longer tradition of singing and poetic recitals which were a chief form of public entertainment. Ballad singers performed at celebrations such as weddings, harvests and saints' days, singing traditional songs in the Egyptian dialect. Gypsy singers and other itinerant performers who travelled round villages and city quarters were held in low esteem yet were nevertheless popular. During the fast of Ramadan café owners would invite them to perform and to extemporise compliments. The ballads were usually well-known stories with texts which the singers modified with puns and contemporary references. The rural versions of the songs had punning rhymes incomprehensible to the town-dwelling *effendis*. There were also storytellers who would recite at similar celebrations familiar stories with traditional themes, lasting sometimes several nights. The audiences knew the story but nevertheless loved the performance and accompanied it (as with songs and poems) with shouts of 'Allah' or 'well done'. The children especially were spellbound by the hypnotic flow of words and events. The storyteller sometimes accompanied himself on the violin.

From these popular entertainments and from the tradition of religious songs there developed the modern popular song which has been given wide circulation on record and radio. Some of the songs of the 1920s and 1930s were of the music-hall type with intriguing titles such as 'Draw the Curtains so we can Enjoy Ourselves' sung before rowdy audiences. But at this period there came to Cairo a young girl who was to become a unique phenomenon in the world of Arab popular music. She was called Umm Kulthum (after the daughter of the prophet), the child of a religious shaikh in an Egyptian village. From the age of 5 the strength and beauty of her voice were recognised and she began to give concerts in local villages and later in Cairo. Her early repertoire was based on classical, religious songs of a limited appeal but she soon added an eroticism to her songs which gained a wider popularity. It was an eroticism which was an alliance of flesh and spirit in a religious context. She herself described them as 'the songs and poems which celebrate the dreams of religious love and the dreams of secular love'. She had a hard time beginning her career in Cairo as a country girl, as women – apart from European *artistes* – had not entered the entertainment field in any great numbers and singers were rather despised. However, because of her evident sincerity and the appeal of her material she eventually became the best known and most popular singer in the Arab world. She had a regular radio programme, made films, and her concerts were booked out months in advance. The Arab world, it seemed, came to a halt to listen to her programme on the first Thursday of the month. Her songs provoked an ecstatic reaction in her listeners. She sang solely for the Arabs, taking them back to their roots and singing of a landscape in which they recognised themselves. This was especially important at times of disaster and defeat. She became a legend, a friend of rulers, and half a million people attended her funeral in 1975. Egypt, it was said, was Nasser, Umm Kulthum and the pyramids. She gave great life and vitality to Arab music and was a socio-cultural phenomenon without precedent. She was also a symbol of Islamic upright-ness and, although she sang of love, would never allow herself to be kissed on the lips in films.

Her opponents accused her of encouraging physical and mental laziness in her listeners, who were content to be transported by her songs as a substitute for action. She was not a very enthusiastic supporter of Nasser's regime but she was patriotic and supported her country, especially in times of crisis, and the Palestinian cause. Her records and performances made her a millionairess.

Umm Kulthum represented popular culture and native Arab music, which appealed to thousands of listeners. The attempt to bring Western musical forms to Egypt is a more élitist undertaking and of more limited appeal. Ballet, opera and a symphony orchestra have been introduced and there are native Egyptians performing in all three spheres. An opera house was founded in 1869 and opened with a performance of Verdi's *Rigoletto*. It was unfortunately burned down in the early 1970s. A symphony orches-tra was formed in 1955 under an Austrian conductor and it is hoped that it will eventually consist entirely of Egyptian players. It plays works by Egyptian composers, some of whom try in their music to fuse the traditions of Europe and the Arab world.

Newspapers and Journals

Journalism has a long history in Egypt. The first newspapers appeared in 1798 since which time they have played an important role in politics, in the diffusion of knowledge and in the development of culture and literature. The best known newspaper, *al-Ahram* (*The Pyramids*) was founded in 1876 and still exists. It has been the most serious and respected paper in the Arab world and after the revolution had a unique role because of its editor's close links with Nasser. Muhammad Haykal became the second best known man in Egypt and was widely regarded as Nasser's confidant and spokesman. He became far more than a newspaper editor, acting as go-between and even negotiator with world leaders. His editorials in the Friday edition were considered as official comments on events or as the trial floatings of new ideas and policies. Haykal too made the *Ahram* much more than a newspaper; the headquarters in Cairo, housed in a uniquely clean and efficient building, contain research and documentation centres and its own publishing house. He was the head of a small and seemingly independent empire.

In 1960 the *al-Ahram* together with other daily newspapers and journals were placed under the supervision of the National Union – later the Arab Socialist Union – which was given wide powers over the publishing of these papers. It amounted to state censorship of the press and, in fact, no editor would step out of line for fear that his paper would be closed down. Well-known writers were appointed editors and a fair number of journals were published each with its own specialisation. *Al-Tali'a* (*The Vanguard*) was the organ of the left-wing theorists published by *Ahram*; *al-Magalla* (*The Journal*), edited by Yahya Haqqi, was a general cultural journal which included work by many of the leading writers; *al-Masrah* (*The Theatre*) was an interesting publication which printed both original plays and translations of Western dramatists. At times of a change of government policy or ministers some journals ceased publication, changed editor, reappeared under a different title, or confusingly the same title might be used for another publication. It was relatively simple using these methods to keep most of the journals in line if they tended to show any independence.

9 *The Life of the People*

This Chapter attempts to describe how the ordinary Egyptian sees life and the changes that he has had to face, whether he is a peasant or town-dweller, rich or poor. All developing nations are by definition changing and it is the individual, either alone or within a family or larger group, who has to deal with change and who reacts by adapting or sometimes by clinging more firmly on to the familiar and the traditional. Some changes are planned by modernising leaders, others happen through force of circumstances, but it is always the individual who may accept or reject change despite the urgings of government or leader. Western countries have had centuries to absorb 'modernisation' and the changes it can bring in all aspects of life such as the growth of secularisation, the weakening of family ties, different moral attitudes, the changing status of women, and despite the length of time involved tension and disruption have been unavoidable. Developing countries are having to accelerate the pace of change, some to an almost intolerable degree. Egypt has in some ways been more fortunate than her neighbours in having met and absorbed change earlier than they and yet there remain as elsewhere countless problems to overcome.

Islam

Islam has already been discussed as an aspect of government policy. The Islam of the Azhar mosque and of the religious leaders might be called 'official' Islam while at the same time there coexists the religion of the hearts and minds of the people, 'popular' Islam. An artificial distinction should not be made, however, for President Nasser using religion for purposes of state could appeal directly to the humblest believer, and there exists a continuum from the learning of the Shaikh of the Azhar to the almost instinctive beliefs of the unlettered. Despite rapid modernisation and the inflow of Western ideas Islam still maintains a secure place in Egyptian life.

For centuries in Islamic countries side by side with the religion of the mosque has existed the religion of the *sufi*[13] or mystic organisation. Orthodox religion was felt by some men to be too formalistic and they turned through mysticism to seek a more direct approach to God. Such men gradually banded together to form *sufi* orders (*tariqas* or paths) with their own organisation and practices. Followers or disciples were attracted to these movements which spread throughout the Islamic world. In Egypt in 1964 some sixty orders were registered in Egypt with the High Sufi Council, a body which attempted to guide *sufi* activities. The head of the Council was appointed by Nasser. The government was anxious to ensure that there were no strong centres for the people's loyalty other than the government and attempted to use the orders for its own purposes. However, it realised fairly soon that they were not a threat to the regime and that they were too conservative to be of much use in propagating modern socialist principles. It is difficult to suppress these orders as they derive from the religious instincts of the people which, as other regimes have found, are difficult to eradicate. Under Sadat they experienced a minor revival and were officially approved, seemingly as part of his policy to let all flowers bloom and to counteract the image of materialism and atheism of the previous regime.

On the whole the *sufi* order provides a source of comfort to those who either feel threatened by change and tension or do not want to change their traditional life-style. Those who join are mainly peasants and lower-grade workers, although some orders attract middle-class intellectuals and professionals into a kind of philanthropic activity in which all members are equal and receive help and comfort from one another. Comradeship is expressed in regular meetings which usually take the form of *dhikrs*. These are the typical mystical rituals at which the name of Allah and other phrases are repeated to the accompaniment of rhythmic movements and drumming. The purpose of such rituals in their ideal form is to achieve a state of mind and body in which union with God is achieved, but they can easily become debased into rather trivial affairs during which the participants in a state of trance lash and cut themselves or merely shuffle round mumbling formulae for the benefit of a watching audience.

The celebration of the birthday (*mawlid*) of a *sufi* saint can be the occasion for a great popular festival. The biggest of these is that of Ahmad al-Badawi who died in 1276 in Tanta, where every October his tomb becomes the centre of a popular celebration and fair. Many people visit the tomb to obtain blessing from the saint, to watch a *sufi* procession, and perhaps most of all to see the show – stalls, booths, cafés, firework displays and bands. This and other similar local *mawlids* have been one of the chief forms of popular recreation together with celebrations for the Feast of the Sacrifice (a religious occasion to mark the sacrifice of sheep during the pilgrimage to Mecca) and the ending of the fast of the month of Ramadan. The government was not averse to using such festivals for its own purposes. At Tanta in 1964 many tents were set up by the Arab Socialist Union and the centre of a government firework display was a portrait of Nasser. At other events festive arches bore the name of Allah in white lights over an illuminated picture of the President. This mingling of religion and state probably seemed entirely natural to most of those who witnessed it.

Another aspect of Islam in society is that of the law. Traditionally in Muslim societies the only law necessary is the *sharia* – the law based on the *Quran* and the traditions of Muhammad and their interpretation. This

law in theory covered all relevant aspects of life and society, although
in practice customary law has often modified its provisions. Modern
states have had to face problems undreamt of by Muslim lawyers and have
tended to introduce 'secular' laws alongside the Islamic. Egypt has had
such laws for the past hundred years which have regulated most aspects of
public life, especially commercial and criminal. Those of personal status
such as marriage, divorce and inheritance have been excepted. These
were the preserve of the *sharia* courts and yet even they were influenced
by a modernising society. Finally in 1956 the religious courts were incor-
porated into the national system, a move which did not seem to arouse
much opposition among the *ulama*. The Azhar went as far as to welcome
this 'liberating step'. Egypt now has a full system of courts ranging from
courts of the first instance to the single Court of Appeal. All come under
the Ministry of Justice and the High Judiciary Council of which the chairman is the president of the Republic. The pressures to re-introduce purely
Islamic law have been discussed earlier and the face-saving formula of
making the *sharia* the source of all legislation was introduced. It has not
in practice affected secular law, for example on banking or investment,
or even hindered the modernisation of the laws of marriage and divorce.
In fact in the latter case Sadat was pushed (by his wife?) against some
opposition in a direction away from traditional law.

As Westernisation or secularisation has increased there have also been
significant signs of a revival of interest in Islam. The political aspects of
this have been mentioned and the Muslim Brotherhood — and its more
extreme manifestations — continues to exert an appeal. Religion has
been a comfort in face of change and trouble. One of the largest squares
in Cairo is packed with thousands of believers at prayer during Ramadan,
kneeling in the street on specially laid out carpets. Another manifestation
of religious fervour has been what one Egyptian observer termed

sensational religion. Its most popular advocate is Shaikh Kishk[14]
whose Friday sermons are attended by thousands of bearded men
and veiled women and are taped and sold at prices more usually fetched
by the offerings of pop singers. His appeal is to the illiterate or semi-
literate and is based on intense emotionalism.

An Egyptian scholar has said that Egyptians have a tendency to become
disillusioned quickly and after the defeat of 1967 they turned to religion
and especially to making the pilgrimage to Mecca as a sign both of personal
faith and communal solidarity. The extreme aim of a religious revival
would be an Islamic revolution of the Iranian pattern and this is the goal
of the Muslim Brothers. There exists, however, in modern Egyptian society
a cleavage between those who look to a religious revival and those who
have turned their backs on Islam, perhaps after an education in the
West in the belief that Egypt's future lies in a secular, technological and

dustrialised society with its values based, according to conviction, in Marxist ideology or in universal humanitarian ideals. But not wishing to cut themselves off entirely from their heritage it is interesting to note that even some of those Egyptians who profess atheism or agnosticism may still view themselves as Muslim in a wide cultural sense.

The Copts

Egyptian society is basically homogeneous — Muslim and Arab. There is, however, a large minority. The Christian Copts are the descendants of the first Egyptian converts to Christianity and, therefore, of the original Pharaonic inhabitants. Throughout the centuries of Arab and Ottoman Muslim rule they have kept their faith, although they gradually abandoned the Coptic language (a development of ancient Egyptian) in favour of Arabic (Coptic is now only the language of the liturgy). The Copts have experienced the familiar difficulties of a minority — discrimination, periodic persecution, suspicion of collaboration with fellow Christian, yet European rulers — although the state has on several occasions proclaimed the official equality of all Egyptians regardless of religion or ethnic origin. They have survived by clinging to their church and a close family life, and by making themselves useful, often as clerks in the towns, as their literacy rate was usually higher than that of the Muslims. They have also been successful lawyers, doctors, engineers and businessmen. Some became part of the wealthy landowning aristocracy and suffered under the land redistribution schemes, as did the businessmen from nationalisation. In the villages the Coptic and Muslim peasants live side by side, sharing village life and even following each others' customs and festivals. For example, Muslim women in Upper Egypt observe the spring Christian festival, a week of ancient rites preceding Easter Sunday. Special foods are eaten and eggs are hardboiled and painted.

It has traditionally been difficult to estimate the numbers of Copts as peasant families tend to keep the number of their children secret. The government attempts somewhat to minimise the total while the Copts do the opposite. An estimate in 1974 put the number somewhere between 4 and 6 million. The Copts would like to think they comprise one-sixth of the population. Whatever the exact proportion the Copts complain with justification that they are not proportionately represented in national life. There were thirteen Coptic members in the 1960 National Assembly of 400, and it was reckoned that only three positions in the top 150 government posts were held by Copts. Nasser tended to regard the Coptic community with indifference; he was an Arab nationalist appealing chiefly to Muslims in Egypt and elsewhere. In 1956 he proclaimed Islam to be the religion of the state, although the Copts made great efforts to demonstrate their loyalty to him and to Egypt especially during times of crisis.

They claimed that he did not trust them and that there was discrimination and no true equality. This he strongly denied in public. However, the future of the Coptic community is unclear and there has been some emigration to Europe and elsewhere. With the growth of fundamental Islamic movements since 1970 there have been unwelcome clashes between Muslims and Copts. Bombs have been planted outside churches and leaders of the Coptic community protested in 1980 about harassment to President Sadat who rather unkindly told them to stop playing politics. In 1981 he even arrested the Coptic 'pope'. During times of tension fears of persecution and discrimination come to the surface very easily among all the Christian minorities in the Middle East.

Class and Society

Before the revolution Egyptian society ranged from the utter poverty of the landless labourers to the wealth of the large landowners and businessmen. If the revolution changed this system it did so by slightly closing the gap between the extremes – the labourers became a little better off, the top layer of the very rich was eliminated by land reform, sequestration and nationalisation.

At the bottom of society in economic terms there remain the *tarahil* – the migrant landless labourers who try to find seasonal labour on the land or elsewhere, who dig canals and build roads often in appalling conditions. Their ancestors dug the Suez Canal. As peasants their aim is to own a plot of land. It is estimated that they total about 1 million and they are essential to the Egyptian economy as long as mechanisation is absent. Their conditions have improved slightly since the revolution: they receive a minimum day's wage and work legal hours, their children go to school and some of them escape into the army. They complain that before 1952 they had been treated like animals and slaves: 'Now we feel like human beings', they say. Yusuf Idris in a novel set in a village ascribes to the peasants a poor view of the labourers: 'In their view, the *tarahil* were human scum who descended on their estate once or twice a year like an unavoidable plague'.

It is the possession of land which distinguishes the labourers from the peasants, whether the poorest owning one feddan (1·038 acres) or less, or the rich who may have twenty feddans or more. The peasants as a class make up the rural population scattered among some 7,000 villages. Some changes in the countryside have been brought about by the disappearance of the large landowners for whom the peasants worked, by a steady migration to the cities and by the state's attempts to introduce new local government in place of the traditional power structure.

In the towns and the cities there is the mass of the urban poor, doing menial jobs, if employed, as unskilled workers or trying to scratch a living by other means. Economically above these are those regularly employed, such as industrial workers, taxi drivers and minor government employees. Between a quarter and a third of the urban population constitute the lower middle class of the petty bourgeoisie, consisting of the vast numbers of the lower bureaucracy, school teachers and small-scale traders, perhaps together with less successful professionals such as doctors and lawyers. Most of this group would aspire to move up the social scale.

With the aristocracy virtually eliminated, those at the top constitute an upper middle class or state bourgeoisie made up of senior bureaucrats, prosperous lawyers, doctors, army officers and managers in industry. Many in this group profited from the revolution, especially army officers who often moved into government posts, and managers who were appointed to run new or newly nationalised undertakings. The group had strong economic foundations and means of action and developed its own lifestyle. Education, the army and technical training have brought about some social mobility — for example, Nasser was the son of a minor government employee, Sadat the son of a small farmer. With the liberalisation of the economy under the latter a middle class re-emerged consisting both of pre-revolutionary businessmen and others who received back property and land and moved again into business, and newcomers to the group who have exploited, in some cases corruptly, the new opportunities. Haykal named them a 'parasite class' with 'a . . . high pattern . . . of vulgar consumption'. The wealth that is obvious in Egypt causes resentment amongst those who are still have-nots and may eventually cause class conflict. The government has to be careful not to discriminate and give the urban poor any reason for discontent.

Social Life

In the whole of the Middle East the family is at the centre of society, despite differences between tribal and settled populations, between town and country. In Egypt the central role of the family is being modified by factors of change. Traditionally, the extended family has been based on consanguine rather than conjugal relationships, with the father or grandfather the fount of authority. The family looks after its members with a kind of inbuilt social service. Great affection is shown towards the children and the relationship between mother and son, especially the eldest, is close. The mother often takes the name 'mother of so-and-so' rather than her husband's name. The Egyptian extends his liking for company from the family to friends and acquaintances. A recent survey reported that 'What people fear most in Egypt is loneliness. They desire constantly to be surrounded by relatives and friends'. In a village school a researcher once drew an outline of a house and asked the children what was needed to make it complete. After doors, windows and so on had been added, one pupil shouted out that the neighbours were missing. In houses and flats, chairs are often placed round the edge of the room facing inward, curtains and shutters are often closed (not just to keep out the heat) so that any gathering feels intimate and cosily enclosed against the outside world. Officials' offices often have their doors open and there is a constant stream of visitors, both social and business. These officials conduct their business with several people at the same time in an atmosphere which is comforting and warm but does not necessarily promote efficiency.

Egypt feels a crowded country, its cities and towns, buses and trains, offices and universities constantly swarming with people. Because of the attitudes outlined above, there seems to be little resentment at continual human contact, although the increasing population poses severe problems for the available facilities and for economic development. The government has officially sponsored family planning in an attempt to limit rapid population growth, but the programme has been introduced with only limited success. Traditional and religious opposition remains to be overcome. In the villages and to a lesser extent in the towns a large family is a proof of the virility of the husband and the cessation of pregnancies through birth control could be too easily taken as a sign of impotence. This is important in a society where male dominance is still insisted upon. In addition children, especially sons, are taken as signs of God's blessing and are part of the peasant's capital where labour in the field is largely manual. If the woman were for example to take the pill without telling her husband the non-production of children could be a reason for divorce, and the wife might be afraid of losing her hold on her husband. Religious opposition to contraception has not been marked and there seems to be no absolute prohibition in Islamic law. On the contrary, some religious leaders have supported it on humanitarian and social grounds. In 1965 the government began the national family planning programme with medical centres distributing or fitting contraceptives. But although Nasser underlined that a population policy was essential to Egypt's welfare the programme has suffered both from a lack of money and of commitment among the uneducated population. It is one thing to establish a national policy in Cairo and quite another to ensure that a peasant woman follows it rigorously in the privacy of her own home. In two and a half years it was estimated that the centres had spread the use of contraceptives among 7 per cent of potential users. Even among urban educated families, although smaller families are common, there still lingers the feeling that many children are the natural order of things and that come what may, God will provide. The campaign was continued under Sadat although with complaints that it lacked real dedication and thoroughness. A newspaper editorial complained in 1980:

What is the point of a hoarding in Tahrir square [in Cairo] equating a small family with a 'better life' if a newly-wed couple don't know where to obtain family-planning advice or, if having obtained a supply of free contraceptives aren't quite sure how to use them, aren't sure if they work, and anyway don't see the urgency of deciding right now whether or not they really want a child.

In 1980 it was reported that birth control was practised by 23·5 per cent of married women and that 45 per cent were opposed to it.

Changes in the traditional way of life are being brought about by education, by migration into new locations where life often has to be lived without the benefit of family support, and by women's emancipation. The wife in the town has led a restricted life, remaining at home to run the household; the peasant wife runs the household and also takes part in most agricultural tasks. These roles are changing through education which widens the girl's horizons and takes her out of the home and, increasingly, by the economic necessity for the wife to go out to work herself. The position of women is at the very root of social change in the whole of the Middle East. The concept of the harem is basic to most people's notion of the Arab world with the woman segregated and veiled and playing no role in the male world outside the home. It is only in this century that the revolt against this system began; the first women's association in Egypt was formed in 1920 to demand political and social equality, education, and certain reforms in marriage laws and customs. Since that time Egyptian women have gained greater equality and freedom, although some say that progress in this direction is illusory and that men's attitudes towards them and their role have not changed much. (A comparison with Saudi Arabia can be illuminating, where women are still strictly segregated, forbidden to drive or to work openly with men, and where the husband has the legal right to forbid his wife to travel or to leave the country.)

In Egypt education is mixed, women take up many occupations in factories, or airlines, as doctors or office workers, or in university and government. The first Egyptian woman ambassador took office in 1979. For such women the traditional split between marriage and a career has almost disappeared. However, it is clear that Egyptian women feel there is still much to change. A recent work, *The Hidden Face of Eve* by an Egyptian woman doctor, Nawal Saadawi, gives an intimate inside picture of woman's position in Egypt, based on her many years' work as a doctor. She sees a woman's problems beginning at birth with the traditional preference for boys:

From the moment she is born and even before she learns to pronounce words, the way people look at her, the expression in their eyes, and their glances somehow indicate that she was born 'incomplete' or 'with something missing'. From the day of her birth to the moment of death, a question will continue to haunt her: 'Why?' Why is it that preference is given to her brother?

This discrimination, she believes, is carried on throughout the girl's life at school, in marriage, at work. She is educated into the ideas of obedience to men, of inferior status, and of accepting two sets of morals – one for men and one for women. This is particularly striking with regard to pre-marital chastity where, writes Dr Saadawi, there is the belief that chastity is important only for girls and not boys. To the family the virginity of the daughter is of supreme importance and an intact hymen more important than the loss of an eye or limb. The murder of unmarried girls known to have transgressed has traditionally been sanctioned in some areas, especially Upper Egypt. At weddings the display of a blood-stained cloth as proof of virginity has been (and sometimes still is) the climax of the ceremony. This kind of prejudice continues after marriage where 'sexual experience in the life of a man is a source of pride and a symbol of virility; whereas sexual experience in the life of women is a source of shame and a symbol of degradation'.

Marriages have traditionally been arranged, ideally within the family, and the couples rarely meet alone before the wedding. Some young people rebel against these customs but find it difficult to meet members of the opposite sex alone. Sometimes change is forced when the son leaves his village for the town or goes abroad to be educated.[15] Films, books and travel spread new ideas, especially about romantic love, and although love has certainly not been absent in many marriages, the boy-meets-girl situation has been very difficult. Romantic love and yearning have been a constant theme of Arab songs and films and this has caused a tension in society with traditional and religious values.

Marriage is naturally at the centre of life and its provisions have been closely governed by Islamic law. The ideal laid down by Egyptian text-books is that woman is made for marriage, that she should obey her husband, stay at home and love her children. The ideal husband should love his wife (no mention is made of love of the wife for him), treat her well and be responsible for her. 'God dislikes divorce' because permanence in marriage is of value to the children. Polygamy is not forbidden; neither is it encouraged. In practice, Egyptian women writers complain, marriage is still a very unequal partnership. Nasser's Charter of 1962 stated that

> Woman must be regarded as equal to man and must, therefore, shed the remaining shackles that impede her free movement so that she might take a constructive and profound part in shaping life.

Yet Dr Saadawi wrote 'that the laws governing marriage can be considered the most backward in the Arab countries'. Amina Said, a champion of women's rights and editor of a women's magazine, likewise complained in 1966:

If we look at the new Egyptian constitution which in my opinion is one of the leading documents in terms of women's emancipation, we find it rich in laws designed to assure equality between men and women, *except* in matters relating to personal status [that is] laws governing the family, divorce inheritance, marriage.

At the time they were writing a man could divorce his wife at will (by saying 'I divorce you' three times in her presence or not), could take other wives, was given custody of the children, boys at 9 and girls at 11, had to pay a limited amount of maintenance, and could use the police to force a runaway wife to return to him. Under ceaseless prompting from his wife, President Sadat finally agreed in 1979 to modify these practices. This he did by presidential decree (to avoid opposition in the Peoples Assembly) and used the Shaikh of the Azhar to reassure the country that Islamic law was not being contravened. According to the new decree, a husband must inform his wife that he is divorcing her and also notify the local Muslim official who registers marriages and divorces. There are now provisions for maintenance payments (for life after fifteen years' marriage) and custody of children who can remain with the mother − girls until marriage, and boys until age 15. A husband must ask his wife before taking a second wife and if she objects she can ask for a divorce.

It is still too early to know how these laws will be received by the Egyptian male and whether attitudes will change. The divorce rate has been high (about 1 in 4·5 marriages) and Egyptian women maintain that in the majority of families the role of wives has been one of complete submission, that the man stubbornly holds on to his traditional domestic sovereignty and refuses to participate in household chores. Economic necessity is forcing change. More women need to go out to work to supplement the family income and this only seems to add another burden to their already full-time occupation. The woman may be educated for a career, and yet still subject to her husband's domination and veto. In the villages women have always worked alongside the men in the field, unveiled and unmolested, but in the town only 7−10 per cent of women take outside work. After 1952 there was no longer a stigma on women who worked; the problem was to find suitable employment, especially for the well-educated girl. In labouring work there are more difficulties such as unequal pay, lack of promotion (few men would be willing to work under a woman), lack of facilities such as child care centres and adequate maternity leave. In addition, she has to face the outside world, so different from the sheltered, dependent and socially confined home. Women going to work in a factory near Cairo at 5.00 a.m. complained that they could not go out alone as they were continually harassed and propositioned by men in the street.

On the positive side, Egyptian women have made considerable progress. They have had the vote since 1956 and the right to be elected to all publicly elected bodies. In 1972 the ASU established a women's secretariat and in 1975 the ASU Feminist Organisation was founded to 'raise the standard and capability of the Egyptian woman'. After some apparent initial faltering by Sadat he seemed resolved on a progressive campaign for women. Following a series of riots by fundamentalist Egyptian young men demanding a stricter Islam, he replied that 'women would not be forced to revert to dressing in "tents". They must live as equals'. His wife said even more forcefully:

> The rebuilding of the Egyptian human being is the first challenge confronting Egypt now. But the men alone cannot meet this challenge; women have a by no means lesser role ... if we wish woman to participate with all her energy and capacity in the battles posed by the challenge, we must first accord her equal treatment and we must give her the complete conviction that our society believes in her stature and her role in society. We must accord her her rights under the liberal *sharia*.

However, Dr Saadawi's conclusion is that

> Despite the fact that in Egypt we have a woman Cabinet Minister since 1962 and six women members of parliament, the vast majority of Egyptian women are still poor, ignorant, illiterate and riddled with disease, and spend long hours of the day and part of the night toiling in the factories, offices, fields, and homes. They live a life of exhaustion, inhuman and pitiless, a prey to the autocratic domination of a father, a husband, a brother, or any other male member of the family. Even the small minority of women, usually from the middle class, who have had a higher or university education are still prisoners of old traditions, exposed to the vagaries of the man or men in the family and to the weight of a new burden, that of a full-time or part-time job with all the extra effort it entails.

Amina Said makes the additional important point that

> One of the most important challenges facing the Arab woman today is that of trying to equate her inner self, her thoughts, and attitudes and feelings, with the contemporary social reality about her ... Society may move at an astonishing speed but the mind is not able to keep up with the pace, and this applies especially to matters related to women.

Village Life

Peasants comprise about 56 per cent of the Egyptian population. They live in villages (which can be large with up to 15,000 inhabitants) scattered in the Delta and along the Nile, following a way of life that has developed over the centuries. It is a life bound to the soil and the river, an inward self-centred life that has haltingly opened itself to the outside world. The radio, television and cinema depict new horizons, and education and migration disrupt traditional patterns of behaviour and thought. It is, nevertheless, the most traditional of societies and probably the most difficult to change. The peasant does not adopt change for change's sake. He has to be convinced of its benefit and usefulness. Recent studies have shown a growing awareness of the peasant of what is happening in Cairo and other towns, but not a disposition to do anything. Such apathy is the result of a healthy scepticism. The revolution turned its attention to the village and attempted to convince the peasants of the value of its new ideology, of land reform, of socialism and new methods of local government. Nasser admitted that this was a daunting task. Even totalitarian governments have found collectivisation difficult (in Poland, for example, private ownership of land is still common) and there was never any attempt by the government, or the will, to impose a Russian or Chinese type solution. Nasser believed that:

> the *fellah* is too individualistic, too atached to his secular dream of acquiring a plot of land to agree [to nationalization] ... Besides, the traditional mistrust of the *fellah* for his government is such that we ought to avoid giving him the impression that we are seeking to make him a state functionary.

Change had to be gradual and justified at every step.

Egyptians, even those who spring from the village, have fixed ideas about the peasant. Taha Husain, who grew up in a village, wrote:

> He was a *fellah* with all the besetting sins of his kind, hunger for land, miserliness over money, an overweening anxiety to be the gainer in any and every transaction.

Ali Sabry, a member of the Revolutionary Command Council: Our peasantry is not yet 'sufficiently enlightened to take up a leading role'. Another Egyptian observer: 'The *fellah* as a rule cannot be hurried into new ways of doing things'. The peasant is suspicious of, yet subservient to, authority which believes he is trying to cheat it, quick to anger especially where irrigation rights or family honour are concerned. When so minded he can relapse into a state of wakeful passivity known as *kaif* when he does, says or thinks nothing. To the outsider it can be taken as a sign of stubbornness or of perfect patience. It can be a way of abating suffering.

In the past, villages have been closed communities which have regulated themselves according to their customary law and inherited customs and manners. They have tried to settle feuds and disputes internally in order to avoid calling in the outsider, a government official or policeman who is regarded with deep suspicion. Villages provided their own headman, watchman, mosque and even jail. Belief and value systems have grown up within villages and a formal observance of Islam is often supplemented by other beliefs — in unseen forces, genii, the power of the evil eye (children are left dirty and unwashed in the hope that this will ward it off), the effectiveness of sorceresses and holy men. In places in Upper Egypt close proximity to ancient monuments has kept alive a belief in the power of the ancient Egyptian gods. Within the system women have been relatively free, although strictly forbidden to transgress clearly defined limits. Any who do may be ostracised or even murdered.

There are different attitudes amongst Egyptians towards the peasant and village life; there may be a feeling of disgust at the squalor and of despair of improvement, or a romantic view of the peace and security. President Sadat was a strong proponent of the latter view. He grew up in a village and wrote:

I could never tear myself away from the life of the village. It was a series of uninterrupted pleasures. There was something different to look forward to each day: the seed-sowing season; irrigation time; the wheat harvest and harvest celebrations... It was an inexhaustible source of happiness.

In his later life he believed that:

the feeling that I am a peasant gives me a rare self-sufficiency. Indeed, the land is always there... I control my fate... A man's village is his peace of mind. All villagers have peace of mind, however lowly, poor or weak they may be, because each has a home, or rather a sense of home, even if his actual dwelling consists only of one room, a bath-room and *mastaba* [bench].

Town dwellers are not so sanguine. They see dirt and primitiveness and a great gap is fixed between their way of life and that of the peasant. They have no desire to live and work in the villages away from the city and it is difficult to persuade young doctors and teachers and bureaucrats to move into the countryside. Conscription or compulsion, a possible solution, does not produce dedication or good work. Under Sadat there was a 30 per cent shortfall of medical personnel in rural areas. This is a world-wide problem where there is often a surplus or sufficiency of doctors for the urban middle classes and less than one doctor per village. (Egyptian doctors also emigrate to Europe and America and to oil-rich Arab countries.)

To try to solve the problem, the concept of 'Combined Units' was evolved at the end of the Second World War. These units were to contain

gle complex doctors, teachers, agricultural experts and social
who would provide a given area with their services and attempt
standards of efficiency, hygiene and education. The new regime
took up this project with the aim of providing a unit for every 15,000
people. It was estimated that some 850 would be needed in 1954 for 13
million people. (The figure at present would be about 1,600 units.) A
development programme was launched by Nasser in 1955 which was the
start of the 'social revolution' — what he called 'our true revolution'.
By 1967 about 300 units were said to be functioning, greater progress
being hampered by lack of finance and personnel. Those in operation, if
functioning efficiently, can be a source of inspiration to the people they
serve and provide suitable conditions for doctors and others to work in.
The basic problem remains that of convincing the peasant of the need for
a change in his attitudes. One example may demonstrate the root problem, the clash between innovation and tradition. Bilharzia is a debilitating
worm disease afflicting the *fellah* through a snail which breeds in the Nile.
It can be cured by inoculation and the cycle of the disease broken if the
peasants urinate away from the canals. One doctor in a village explained
at length the hazards of the disease and the villagers agreed to be inocu-
lated and to be more hygienic. In this way the disease would finally be
eliminated. Yet after three months it returned to the area. The boys had
resumed their swimming in the canals as it was so hot; pure water was
said to be tasteless and impotent compared with canal water; and the
villagers told the doctor they had to bathe and urinate in the canal as a
ritual ablution before praying in the mosque. The doctor inevitably
felt discouraged and frustrated and unwilling to try again. The peasants
had not yet been persuaded that health was more important than ingrained habits.

In addition to trying to improve health, agriculture and education,
Nasser embarked on a campaign to weaken the traditional political structure in rural areas and to create new political and social relationships
which would endorse his ideas for change in a socialist framework. Based
on a strong central authority, plans were drawn up for new elected village
councils and for executive committees to run the Combined Units and
other village affairs. The headman of the village, the *umdah*, was to be
elected by the villagers; he had to be an active member of the Arab Socialist
Union and it turned out that he was usually a member of a powerful local
family. This would probably ensure that his authority would be accepted
by the village as a whole. The councils were to consist of elected and
ex-officio members who would also be ASU members. Once again progress
was hindered by the lack of trained personnel and cash, and by natural
differences of approach between young administrators or advisers coming
in from outside the village and the *fellah*, or by clashes between doctrin-
aire socialists and experienced leaders. The villagers would often offer
servile flattery to the officials, while nevertheless still clinging to their own

traditions. It was estimated that by 1970 about a quarter of the villages had functioning local councils while the rest still had only the traditional *umdah*.

But despite opposition and traditionalism, change has come to the Egyptian countryside, much of it unplanned and spontaneous. Rural areas benefited under the revolution from a rise in the relative share of public expenditure. Electricity and paved roads are being introduced. The peasants accepted the leadership of Nasser and believed that he, perhaps in spite of the fumblings of the bureaucrats, sincerely wished to better their lot. Perhaps most of all the High Dam has changed the very basis of their existence. In one case study of an Upper Egyptian village a young peasant, Shahhat, has the following thoughts while looking at the Nile, which seem to sum up the situation:

> To Shahhat, the Nile was *el-Bahr*, the sea, the giver of life. This was the month of August, when the river always rose to flood its banks. Now...the High Dam at Aswan had held back these waters. The Nile would never flood again. Shahhat wondered what his life would have been like if the river had not been tamed. Poorer, but lived in the old natural rhythms and certainties. For the dam had brought the incessant field work, even in the hottest summer. It had brought diesel pumps, the fight to load sugar cane, the feuds, the frustrations. It had created inspectors...

Town and City

In 1937 the urban population comprised about 27 per cent of the total. By 1976 this proportion had risen to 44 per cent of a total population of 38 million, an increase which has resulted in enormous pressure on urban facilities. The population of Cairo alone is now thought to be some 8 million. Rich and developed states find large, populous cities difficult to run with housing, traffic, public transport and other problems (exemplified by New York's descent into near bankruptcy). Large cities in the Third World pose almost insuperable problems. It is difficult to forecast how Cairo will or can develop with an estimated population of 12–16 million in the year 2000. The optimum population for the city's present facilities is put at 1·5 million. The pressure which is at present generated would conceivably bring a Western city to a standstill if not to revolt. Cairo by a process of osmosis seems to absorb its new citizens by continuously lowering its standards. It would seem inevitable that one day this process must come to a halt. Housing and transport already lag far behind demand.

The major problem is the over-concentration on Cairo which acts as a magnet for all Egypt. This is a result of the complete centralisation of government and other facilities in the capital. In consequence Cairo takes up a disproportionate share of the country's resources; no other city exerts the same attraction, nor makes the same demands. Cairo takes 27 per cent of the nation's electricity, 40 per cent of vegetables, fruit and meat, has 33 per cent of all doctors, 66 per cent of TV sets, 30 per cent of secondary school students, 58 per cent of graduate civil servants. Most cultural facilities are located in the capital. To modern Egyptians, Cairo's name is *Misr* — that is, Egypt. The magnetism of the city is reinforced by the need to migrate from the villages where the growing population is confined to a static or shrinking area of agricultural land, and where the mud brick construction of village houses does not allow vertical expansion. So the villager looks to Cairo. More than one third of the population now consists of immigrants who are shaping the culture of the city as much as adjusting to it. They move into already overcrowded areas, creating a density in some parts of over 260,000 to the square mile (New York with its skyscrapers has a density of 25,000 per square mile), and the city remorselessly expands to embrace surrounding villages and agricultural land. Observers speak of the ruralisation of Cairo rather than the urbanisation of the population and the bourgeoisie fears the changes this brings to their city. Some areas remain like villages with unpaved roads, low mud brick dwellings and animals wandering in the streets. The expansion of Cairo, and to some extent of Alexandria, is such that some planners envisage in the future a possible linear megalopolis stretching between the two cities.

The immigrants move into the poorer areas of the city, increasing congestion and overcrowding. Families live in one room and share facilities as there is never enough housing to accommodate the increased numbers. It is estimated that to keep up with the growth some 62,000 housing units are needed per year. This figure is more than double the annual rate of 30,000 units for the whole of Egypt during 1960–70. So the density increases. People build shacks on the roofs of other dwellings, or some 1 million of them squat in the tombs and houses of the City of the Dead — a large cemetery area where Cairenes traditionally bury their dead and which they visit to be near their late relatives on holidays and festivals. Other areas of Cairo gradually decline through lack of maintenance, and because of lack of finance it has been officially recognised that some areas cannot conceivably be reclaimed. Local revenue covers only a quarter to a third of Cairo's expenses leaving nothing for development, yet housing for the poor has to be provided by the government. Private developers build only for those who can afford high rates. The poor could never pay enough to give them any return on their investment, so the good areas of Cairo are monopolised by higher government employees, doctors, engineers and the like, and foreigners. The government has tried hard to cope with housing, building thousands of flats for industrial workers and lower-grade government clerks, but leaving the poor untouched. Thus they are caught in a trap. It is estimated that 75 per cent of the families living in Sayyida Zaynab, a densely-populated poor area, earn less than

£E20 per month. This level of poverty can be numbing to the outsider.

The divide between city and country has been mentioned; the migrant into the city has to cross this divide into a new life and a new atmosphere and to try to make the necessary adjustments. In some ways this process is eased by the 'ruralisation' of areas of Cairo where rural life can to a certain extent be duplicated. The link with the native locality has, however, been broken and the advantages of village life, such as solidarity, mutual help, familiarity and security, cannot easily be recreated. Peasants from the same village or area do tend to go to the same part of Cairo, to meet in a certain café, to go to the same mosque and to form friendship and benevolent societies. In this way the newly arrived peasant, often a young man, can meet those he knows and perhaps be helped to find employment. If whole families migrate they find quite severe changes. The home is usually one room instead of a house; the 'outside' is just the street without a village centre or meeting place. The women probably feel more isolated, having to do the washing alone at home rather than in a gossiping group at the village water supply. They no longer have to work in the fields and must search out different employment. Life as a whole becomes more impersonal and anonymous. Festivals and celebrations no longer involve the whole of one community.

Two types of young men migrate, the have-nots and the bright young men in search of education and opportunity. The former are more numerous. The educated youth often finds village life confining, lacking suitable employment which is only to be found in the cities and towns. The have-nots, squeezed off the land or landless anyway, usually seek out manual work which can prove to be even more taxing than agricultural labour. It is regular, not confined to seasons, carried out more in groups and perhaps less satisfying. Some migrants seek work with those from their village who have 'made it' in small businesses, or they become self-employed peddlers, shoe-shiners, tea makers or domestic servants. The children of first generation migrants clearly have fewer problems of adjustment and become regular city dwellers, perhaps still looking, as did President Sadat, upon one village as their home.

Migrants as well as all other Cairo dwellers have to move about the city and transportation is second only in importance to housing in making a city pleasant to live in. Cairo falls badly short on both counts, although what would surely cause total breakdown in a Western city seems to be accepted almost cheerfully in Egypt. Within the city there are trains, trams and buses. The trams run in the older areas and do not cross the Nile. Trains run to two suburbs only and are often crowded with passengers who sit on the roofs and occasionally and disastrously hit the overhead cables. Buses are the only means of transport for the majority of people who cannot afford private cars or taxis. In the early 1970s there were some 1,200 serviceable buses attempting to carry 3·5 million passengers per day. (In comparison London Transport runs some 6,500 buses, which *together with* the underground trains carry 5·75 million passengers per day.) The resulting overcrowding has to be seen to be believed. Passengers crowd inside and cling outside on to every available foot and handhold. Consequently the vehicles soon deteriorate through inadequate maintenance, with doors and windows ripped out and a permanent tilt to the side. Yet for many commuters they are the only alternative to walking and must constitute a daily misery. There are relatively few private cars by Western standards but together with taxis, horse- and hand-drawn carts, they soon cause traffic jams in many areas of the city. The rush hour seems to last most of the day. New roads and bridges benefit mostly the affluent with the private car, and although there are plans and surveys for new trains, tram and underground lines little has yet been done. A long-term Western observer accurately and without exaggeration describes the transport situation:

> One finds in Cairo's streets a hodgepodge of lopsided buses, meandering taxis, streams of pedestrians, over 100,000 private automobiles, plodding donkey- and horse-carts, pushcarts, mobile restaurants, trolleys, trams, garbage carts, and street sweepers. The side-walk becomes a parking lot, recreational facility, dormitory, and workshop. The result is the transportation crisis of a poor city in a poor country.

In the Western world migration to the cities has usually occurred together with industrialisation. The traditional systems of rural industry have been affected (for example, the introduction of mechanical spinning and weaving) or new industrial developments have offered the opportunity of employment, and the villager has moved to a new place of work. As has been shown, migration in Egypt has rarely been from village to factory, although this process has occurred indirectly, usually after a few years' residence in the city or in the first generation after migration. The step from seasonal traditional agricultural work or from employment to regular skilled or semi-skilled work is great and requires both training and psychological adjustment. The government has recognised this and has established a number of vocational schools and apprentice training schemes. Some students are sent abroad to be trained in industrial or agricultural establishments. It is interesting that in a 1966 survey secondary school students listed engineer (35 per cent) as their first career choice, followed by military officer, doctor, dentist, down through lawyer, scientist to a mere 2·7 per cent who wanted to become secretarial or industrial workers. As there is no government direction into industry (as there was an attempt to place engineering graduates according to demand), it follows that there is a shortage of skilled workers in Egypt.

In some factories, for example the steel works at Helwan, a suburb of Cairo, in-plant training has been undertaken. There have been vacancies or deficiencies at most levels, especially in the lower management group. Initially, the factory recruited unskilled and semi-skilled labour from the local villages and found that absenteeism and turnover were affected by the seasonal pattern of agriculture on the neighbouring lands. The management was pessimistic about the ability of the plant to change the mentality of the farmer to that of an industrial worker. The policy was, therefore, adopted of hiring as workers only those who had completed military service and whose attitudes had presumably been moulded by army discipline. In 1967 a newspaper quoted from a survey made of industrial workers:

> Outside the textile industry all our industries are recent ... and have been able to recruit only among peasant workers ... The industrial worker still reasons as a man of the soil; this newcomer is uprooted.

Obviously, this is a passing phase in any industrialising society. As a part of the larger society the factory worker is beginning to be recognised as an important, though small, part of society. He may be envied by his contemporaries who still work in agriculture or as artisans for the improved conditions of his employment. The tide is turning in his favour as industrialisation increases. The number of factory workers rose from 600,000 in 1959 to over 900,000 in 1970. There exists, however, a deep cleavage between these workers and the petty bourgeoisie of the city who regard them with some prejudice, despite the fact that Nasser in the Charter assigned a leading role in the revolution to the labour force:

> Industry develops the shape of society in a far-reaching manner ... The worker has become master of the machine and not a cog in industrial activity ... The position of workers in the new society will be measured solely in terms of success in industrial development.

Nasser believed that workers had achieved 'great success' and, therefore, they were given certain rights in the socialist laws of 1961. Unions organised by industry were legalised although they were given little freedom of action and subjected to political and administrative controls. In return for this tight control the government brought in some compensatory benefits such as a shorter working week, minimum wages, sick pay, holidays, and social insurance and even profit-sharing and membership of factory boards. Strikes were made illegal, or said to be unnecessary in a socialist society, although some collective bargaining was allowed. It became very difficult to dismiss workers, especially from the nationalised industries and if the Arab Socialist Union defended them. While this improved the security of the worker, it did not necessarily improve the efficiency of the factory. There were few signs of unrest among factory workers until 1968 when the demonstrations took place in Helwan in protest against the aftermath of the 1967 defeat. These expressed political frustration rather than economic discontent. However, compared with other Middle Eastern states a trade union movement did begin to take shape and to make itself felt in Egypt.

A looming aspect of Egyptian society is the bureaucracy. A strong centralised government encourages the growth of a bureaucracy and Egypt has had this tradition since Pharaonic days. Two factors turned this growth into a flood. Nationalised enterprises and numerous government agencies needed many administrators to run them, and the government introduced a policy of guaranteeing all graduates posts in the administration or the public sector. This humane policy has often meant in practice that Parkinson's Law has operated. One man's job is done by two and so on. It is common to see in Egyptian offices four or five people seated round one table with no visible means of occupation. Work has to be created for them and Egypt is notorious for form filling and rubber stamping.

It is estimated that the number of government posts increased from 310,000 in 1947 to over 1 million in 1967, excluding the army. It is difficult to believe that efficiency increased in proportion. In addition, a strict bureaucratic hierarchy engenders an unwillingness to accept responsibility and a lack of initiative. Many small decisions can often be taken only by the minister concerned. This leads to delays and frustrations for the ordinary citizen or for the foreign business trying to obtain an import licence or contract. When President Sadat took office in 1970 he estimated that '20 per cent of our energy is lost because of administration'. An Egyptian newspaper complained bitterly in 1980 of a 'wholly selfish lack of commitment' amongst senior bureaucrats and of a 'sea of apathy, narrow-minded cynicism and ·ignorance'. The citizen seems patiently to accept the system and jokes about it. In Tawfiq al-Hakim's play *The Sultan's Dilemma* the following exchange takes place. A judge is attempting to discover a man's profession and says:

'Tell me something about this person ... What does he do?' 'Nothing' is the reply. 'Has he no profession?' 'Allegedly, yes but that is not the case.' 'He is alleged to have a profession, but does not work.' 'That is so.'

The judge concludes:

'Then he must be a civil servant!'

The bureaucrats tend to consolidate their power and to acquire economic and social privileges. An acute student of the Egyptian bureaucracy has written:

Members of this new bureaucratic élite...are, unlike in the West, more affluent and more educated than most of their clientele; the Egyptian public 'servant' is actually more of a master.

To reform the bureaucracy is a daunting undertaking, involving a root and branch change of ingrained attitudes and traditions and questions of motivation and incentive, and it is something that affects most aspects of life in the city and smaller urban centres. Change can only come through education of trainee bureaucrats *before* they enter the service and through the adoption of more efficient methods. There has been no lack of suggestions and plans for streamlining the administration. The student quoted above writes: 'People do, on the whole, know the 'proper' way of getting something done, but many of them do not feel inclined to do it'. This is the basic problem of motivation. When a project engages the attention of a sufficient number of enthusiastic men, red tape and delay can be overcome – the building of the Aswan Dam, the running and widening of the Suez Canal, the military crossing of the Canal in 1973 all demonstrate that.

One aspect of Egyptian society in which change and development have come about is the army. It has provided a means of education and social mobility and of reaching the top in politics. It has emphasised the concepts of discipline and service and under Nasser in many ways was the embodiment of state. It has fought at least four campaigns or wars in which national prestige was at stake. In 1955 the regime introduced a Military Draft Law which made military service, with a few exceptions, compulsory for every able-bodied male. In 1980 a law was introduced to increase service from eighteen months to two years for secondary school leavers in order to train them to handle ever more complex weaponry. Army life has brought together Egyptians from every level of society, although clear distinctions remain. The *fellah* and poor urban classes have traditionally provided the privates and NCOs and are those for whom military life is the greatest change. Some peasants have traditionally tried to avoid service by mutilating themselves, buying an exemption or trying to register as a student. After 1952 escape was not so easy and anyway the peasants were not unaware of the changes that took place in a returned soldier and this helped to break down resistance to recruitment. The junior officers mainly came from the lower-middle-class city dwellers. Graduates of universities and technical schools have received direct commissions and have been favourably treated. Several were sent to the Soviet Union for training and returned to form an élite officer corps. Nasser favoured this group as the backbone of his regime together with those who had engineered the coup with him. A career as an officer was keenly sought after. Young pilots, tank commanders and technical specialists became the symbols of the new society. They had officers' clubs, good pay and privileges, better facilities in academies and staff colleges. This treatment maintained the gap between private soldier and officer and the army has been criticised for a lack of *esprit de corps*, even for a certain contempt for the lower ranks on the part of the officers.

Some of the worst aspects of the Egyptian army were demonstrated in the 1967 war — lack of organisation and initiative, stubborn adherence to previously drawn up plans, poor maintenance and communications. Some of the best were shown in the storming of the east bank of the Suez Canal in 1973 — meticulous planning, innovation and bravery. Sadat after the crossing built up army prestige, giving it a place of honour in society while at the same time discouraging its participation in politics. It is deeply ironic that his assassination took place during a military parade celebrating the anniversary of the 1973 achievement.

10 *Mubarak's Middle Way*

Internal Developments

Political leaders usually suffer a certain reassessment of their achievements after their death. President Sadat has undergone such a reassessment. The last months of his regime have been criticised as a period of spreading corruption when those around him exploited economic liberalisation for personal profit, and as a period of his growing megalomania and indifference to the real problems of Egypt. He was beginning to go astray, suffering from physical frailty and the pressures of having to live up to his image. So committed to his own ideas was he that he termed any who disagreed with him 'unbelievers'. As the pressures mounted he retreated more into isolation. While still admired by the West, he was viewed with deepening indifference or hostility by his own people and he was hated by other Arabs. His wife who had been much in the public eye had to share his unpopularity. The growth of corruption particularly irritated young Muslim fundamentalists, those who had adopted and developed the ideas of the Muslim Brothers. A group of them in the army decided that Sadat had to be punished for his errors. Through careful planning they managed to join the military parade that Sadat was to review on the eighth anniversary of the crossing of the Suez Canal. They were together in a truck which they ordered to stop opposite the reviewing stand. Two or three jumped out and ran, firing machine guns and throwing grenades, towards Sadat who was standing to salute the marchpast. He died instantly. Seven others in the stand also died and twenty-eight were wounded.

Those involved in the plot were arrested and their leader, Lieutenant Khalid al-Islambuli, confessed: 'I killed him but I am not guilty. I did what I did for the sake of religion and of my country. I killed the pharaoh.' One of his companions added: 'I had come to the conclusion that the man ought to be killed and I was praying to God that *I* would be given the honour of making the tyrant pay for his sins'. The assassins belonged to a group in the *Jihad* movement, one of the extreme Islamic groupings that appeared in Egypt under Sadat. Their thinking and the motives for their actions were entirely and consistently Muslim. They had obtained a *fatwa* (a legal ruling) from a religious judge (*mufti*) which declared that it was legal to kill a ruler who disobeyed the ordinances of God. Sadat had corrupted Islamic society and so had to die. They were not afraid to die themselves and on the Day of Judgement they were convinced they would be judged solely according to their intentions.

In the eyes of the state they had committed treason for which there was no justification. Death sentences were passed and in April 1982 two of the conspirators were shot and three hanged. They remained quite impenitent to the end.

Many Egyptians welcomed Sadat's disappearance and few came onto the streets to mourn his death. His funeral was a sombre occasion, attended by foreign statesmen — a very different affair from the emotional and chaotic scenes of Nasser's burial. Egyptian commentators claimed that this demonstrated the very low ebb to which Sadat's popularity had sunk. Feelings may now have come full circle in that there appears to be developing a nostalgia for the days of Nasser. Yet despite Sadat's mistakes the fact that the transfer of power was smooth showed a great stability in the system.

Husni Mubarak was a rather shadowy figure, an unknown quantity whom Sadat had appointed vice-president of the state in 1975 and of the ruling National Democratic Party in 1978. He was born in 1928 in Northern Egypt and spent his career in the armed forces. He was not, though, a member of the Free Officers' movement. He trained as a pilot in the Soviet Union and as an airforce officer he must have felt deeply the defeat of the Egyptian air force in 1967. He became airforce chief of staff in 1969 and deputy war minister in 1972. He had obviously been a loyal lieutenant to Sadat and on taking power was eager not to deviate too radically from his predecessor's policies. By nature cautious, almost his first public words were that he would never make a promise he could not fulfil — an admirable aim for a politician, but one which could be an excuse for inaction.

In a speech to the People's Assembly in November 1981, he outlined the principles of his government's policy and spoke about the future he wanted for Egypt. Economically, he would bring benefits to the poorer members of the society in order to counter the conspicuous consumption and profiteering of the 'fat cats' of the country. *Infitah* (the opening-up of the economy) would continue with no return to the restrictive days of Nasser, but it had to be an *infitah* of production rather than consumption, which would benefit all society and not the rich few. The state could not stand idly by. The all-important food subsidies, the cutting of which caused the violent riots under Sadat, would remain for those in need and imports of unnecessary luxury goods would be curtailed. Most importantly, the peace treaty with Israel would be observed while Egypt was ready to deal 'without complexes' with anyone who did not meddle in Egyptian affairs — a signal that he would welcome approaches from other Arab states as long as they made no prior conditions. His immediate concern in the aftermath of the assassination and in the religious fervour was to ensure that 'the internal front was totally secure and that the security forces were guarding the peace'. Sadat's death was a warning to Egypt 'to cleanse itself of the plague of religious extremism'. This could be achieved only with social justice. 'Egypt is for all society — not a privileged few or the chosen elite or the sectarian dictatorship.' Opposition parties would be allowed but opposition should be about 'differences not conflict, without creating confusion; it should be an exchange of views not an exchange of accusations'.

Thus Mubarak explained his vision of Egypt's future. It was in some ways a synthesis of the policies of Nasser and Sadat, an attempt to select the best of both. The Egyptians were on the whole ready to let him try his solution as an antidote to the last frantic years of Sadat.

In political life there have been two opposite but not contradictory processes. While there has been a clamp down on the religious extremist opposition there has also been an opening up of party politics. Sadat made some moves towards establishing democracy but soon discovered that he deeply disliked any strong opposition to his policies. Mubarak has cautiously allowed more overt political activity. Slowly the parties and their news-papers have come back to life as Mubarak gradually released the hundreds of political opponents imprisoned by Sadat. The politicians were eager to participate in a political debate, trusting that Mubarak would welcome constructive criticism, although it was clear that, in his eyes, they occasion-ally went too far and he uttered disturbing threats: 'I hope freedom is not used to an extent that would damage national security. If it is I will not be lenient with anybody.' This kind of remark demonstrates the difficulty of identifying one man with the state and its policy. Criticism is taken as personal and critics are dealt with personally by the head of state.

Some five parties have been allowed to function in addition to the rul-ing National Democratic Party (of which Mubarak is president). The left wing opposition is the National Progressive Union Party, a grouping of socialists led by one of the few remaining Free Officers, Khalid Muhyidin, and the Socialist Labour Party. Interestingly, the Wafd surfaced yet again and won a court case against its prohibition. One religious party, the *Umma* has been licensed and, although it states its main policy to be 'the proclamation of the Sunni Islamic *sharia* (law) as a political, social and cultural system for society and the state as an immediate and radical remedy to our problems', it is not extremist. Officially unrepresented are the communists, religious groups such as the Muslim Brothers, and avowed Nasserists, although all three tendencies are represented in other parties. The policies of the main parties differ in emphasis on such matters as the place of *infitah* in the economy and of the *sharia* in legal matters. Four of the six are against the Camp David peace process and wish it to be stopped and reversed. (The two in favour are the ruling party and, perhaps more surprisingly, the *Umma*.) For the election in 1984 a system of proportional representation was established with the proviso that only those parties gaining 8 per cent or more of the total vote could be represented in the Assembly. Any votes gained below this percentage would be forfeit to the majority party. The smaller parties saw this as an attempt to stifle them. Nevertheless, at present Egypt has the most open political system of any Arab state and a determined attempt is being made to foster a democratic society. In the election to no one's surprise the National Democratic Party received over 70 per cent of the votes (390 seats) leaving the Wafd as the only other party with any seats (58). The Progressive

Union obtained 7 per cent of the votes and consequently lost them all to the NDP. There were some complaints that the ballot was rigged but on the whole there seemed to be little interference. In any case it was the most open election in Egypt for several decades. Haykal placed it clearly in its context: '[It] was not a return to democracy, but rather a good rehearsal for it. Mubarak has passed his first examination well. Now he faces a more important one – will he show himself capable of tolerating the winds of change?'

So democracy began its halting progress. Once an opposition is legalised and open debate permitted there is virtually no end to the demands for further freedoms. The ultimate goal is that of the freedom to dismiss electorally the man who has brought in greater democracy. Mubarak has not been willing to contemplate this possibility and has always been ready to limit what he considered too outspoken criticism. In the National Assembly the opposition tries to make debating points or to embarrass the government but with the National Democratic Party's large majority the government is in a position to reject any opposition demands. The opposition frets under these conditions. The judicial authorities keep a strict eye on electoral practices and when a court ruled on certain irregularities in nominating candidates in the 1984 elections, new elections were called for April 1987. Mubarak acted quickly in order to forestall any pressure from the opposition.

The same parties moved into gear in slightly different formations. The atmosphere was lively and some 15,000 candidates stood for the 448 seats. There were many electoral meetings of intense debate, despite the fact that a large portion of the population showed little faith in politicians' ability to change their living standards or in the political process. Free elections were not yet deeply embedded in the people's consciousness. The National Democratic Party was again the front runner, embodying for most people the legitimacy of the state under Mubarak. It was a network of business men, contractors, high officials, rural grandees and others who often benefited from government policies. The Wafd was the party of small businessmen and claimed to be the sole heir of the 1952 revolution. In 1984 it had campaigned with the Muslim Brothers; this time it ran alone. The Brothers joined an Alliance for the election with the socialists and liberals (with the slogan 'Islam is the solution'), and the main leftist opposition was again the National Progressive Union (Tagammu). In addition nearly 400 independents stood for the 48 seats allotted to them.

Mubarak encouraged the secular opposition both on the left (Tagammu) and the centre-right in an attempt to prevent the religious factor from becoming too dominant. He also tried to encourage the more moderate Muslims (the Brothers) who had been allowed to form the Alliance in defiance of the electoral laws banning religious parties from standing. The elections passed off quite peacefully although the opposition accused the government of intimidation and anyway the National Democratic Party had the greatest access to the media and officially sponsored rallies and propaganda. There were also accusations that the results, which surprised no-one, were falsified. Only a quarter of those eligible voted and elected 309 members of the National Democractic Party, 56 of the Alliance and 35 of the Wafd. The main left received only 2 per cent of the vote and obtained no seats. No real independents were elected as the 48 seats were captured by National Democratic Party sponsored candidates. In the new parliament the opposition was more diversified although the left remained without any real voice.

The government had retained the initiative and under Mubarak was still not quite sure what to do with it. He was elected president for a second six-year term in 1987, the sole candidate endorsed by the Assembly with its National Democratic Party majority. In the referendum he received 97 per cent of the votes cast. Despite this overwhelming support his critics accuse him of not really using his power; he has inherited it without utilising it. He is blamed for not carrying out his good intentions and for only acting as arbitrator among competing forces, giving the impression that he is still groping for a direction. The bitter joke is: 'Mubarak hasn't done anything wrong. But then again he hasn't done anything'.

The courts continued to monitor the electoral process and in May 1990 decided once again that the 1987 elections had been invalid as the rules regarding independent and women candidates had not been observed. A new electoral law was passed in October with independent and all party candidates to stand in the various constituencies without restriction. The referendum approving the dissolution of the Assembly was approved in October by 94 per cent of the votes and once more the country prepared to go the polls. The first round took place in November and initially nine parties were going to run candidates including a new Green Party and the revived Young Egypt Party. In the end the Wafd and the Alliance decided to boycott the elections as they had unsuccessfully demanded more concessions including the lifting of the state of emergency. The first result showed that inevitably the National Democratic Party had gained a large majority although several 'real' independents had been elected including the ex-Free Officer Khalid Muhyidin.

Covert or illegal opposition has continued to be widespread, some of it very violent. Large numbers of religious extremists have been arrested, tried and imprisoned. The regime has felt very threatened by the growth of extremism and has tried hard to contain it. The Ministry of the Interior has acted toughly, torturing those arrested and clamping down on demonstrations, some of which have had to be dispersed with live ammunition. Numerous deaths have resulted. The opposition thrives on confrontation and the creation of martyrs. The government's stated policy is that of 'trying to contain the fundamentalists by persuasion. The police only resort to violence when they come under attack.' Leaders of the Azhar mosque have said that reform depends entirely on dialogue and that they utterly reject violence. The particularly tough and hated Minister of the Interior, Zaki Badr, was sacked by Mubarak in January 1990 in an attempt to appease the protesters but his successor, Abd al-Halim Musa, believed to be more moderate has had to face numerous violent demonstrations and has reacted quite strongly. Equally worrying have been the sectarian disturbances in which Muslims have gone on the rampage against Christians and Christian property, unsettling the fragile balance between Copts and Muslims.

Mubarak has been worried by these signs of intolerance and has with difficulty held back from reining in all opposition more tightly. He genuinely wishes to see a wider democractic system which is introduced by consensus and responsibility. He has been very wary of demands for the introduction of a legal system based solely on the *sharia*. The Assembly rejected calls for the imposition of Islamic law and instead voted to review the legal code gradually and scientifically and to revise any provisions that were seen to contradict the Islamic code. In general the appeal of religion has not noticeably lessened since Sadat's death. The wearing of Muslim dress by women is prevalent and spreading and the attitudes of the wearers seem to be strengthening. These affect other members of society. Numbers of students insist on segregation, some refuse to study 'Western' subjects; Egyptair no longer serves alcohol on its flights. In a legal case a court refused a lawyer permission to make his son and daughter equal heirs as this was contrary to the *sharia*. Judges sometimes apply the Islamic law and not the civil, claiming that it is *the* source of all legislation.

Sometimes there is stronger resistance or movement the other way. The leader of the *Jihad* was arrested for calling for the death of the author Nagib Mahfouz, the Nobel prize-winner, as he had written a novel (*Children of our Quarter*, see page 144) which he considered anti-Islamic. There was strong reaction against this anti-Salman Rushdie type of behaviour. The author refused police protection and is still alive. The *Jihad* leader languished in prison. The sensitive matter of marriage, divorce and polygamy has been tackled carefully after the resentment felt against the law of personal status brought in by Sadat (under his wife's prompting). The law recognising certain women's rights was reinstated but polygamy was still allowed.

Fear of assassination by extremists was naturally great after the murder of Sadat. There have been many attempts, one at least succeeded and sent shivers through the establishment. In October 1990 a group of five gunmen shot at an official car outside a large hotel in central Cairo. The passenger was killed immediately, Rifaat al-Mahgoub, the speaker of the National Assembly. Although he had frequently quarrelled with Muslim Brothers over the application of the *sharia* it was eventually suspected that he had been shot in mistake for the Minister of the Interior who had passed the same spot a few minutes earlier. He would have been a prime target for the killers who were identified as members of *Jihad*, the group which had earlier assassinated Sadat. The killing was followed by yet another crack-down on Islamic fundamentalists of whom some 3,000 were arrested. The atmosphere remained tense.

In 1986 the establishment was shaken by a violent mutiny which broke out amongst the Central Security Force. This is a paramilitary organisation of men who had failed to reach the requirements for full military service and their black clad figures are common in Cairo on traffic duty or on guard outside embassies. The Force had been built up as a means of control particularly after the bread riots of 1977 and numbered 300,000 men. They were miserably paid – £E6 a month – and in February the rumour circulated that their term of compulsory service was to be increased from three to four years. In anger thousands of the conscripts went on the rampage in Cairo setting fire to hotels and nightclubs and anything that smacked of wealth and corruption. There was rioting elsewhere and great damage was caused. Tension had been mounting in the country, the price of food had risen and there had been workers' strikes over pay and benefits. Resentment was widespread over Mubarak's policies and his ties with Washington. The President reacted angrily and warned that Egyptians could be much worse off under another leader. The army reacted quickly to the rioting and contained the situation. The rumour of the extra year's service was firmly quashed. The conscripts returned to their barracks and by early March the curfew was lifted. The outbreak had demonstrated how fragile the social situation in Egypt was and how dependent was the state on the army.

Mubarak has had to tread warily in another area. While trying to continue many of Sadat's policies he has also had to face the corruption that had become rife under his predecessor. A distinction had to be made between policies and those who corruptly benefited from them. Sadat's brother Ismat was brought to trial almost as a scapegoat. He was accused of making millions of pounds through corrupt deals and of having acquired property worth nearly 150 million dollars. He was found guilty, jailed for one year and his property sequestrated. During the trial many charges were made against Sadat's administration including the accusation that ministers and officials were guilty of not having prevented Ismat's corrupt actions. Mubarak drew back and refused, as he said, to put the whole of Sadat's regime on trial (especially as he had been an integral part of it). Ismat was released after six months, although his property was still held, and the drive against corruption lost some of its urgency. Cynics shrugged their shoulders and wondered why.

Foreign Relations

Sadat's two main legacies in foreign affairs were the agreements with Israel and the rapprochement with the United States. Both countries waited anxiously to discover whether Mubarak believed in continuity or change. Almost immediately he assured Israel that he would honour the peace process. For Egypt this meant primarily regaining the Sinai peninsula; for Israel the full 'normalisation' of relations. There was some apprehension in Jerusalem that once the withdrawal from Sinai was completed Egypt might reject the treaty or that relations would worsen. In fact it was Israeli actions which caused a deterioration. The withdrawal was completed on schedule in April 1982. In Sinai there were left various installations that the Israelis had constructed, in particular two military airfields. The settlement of Yamit on the coast was dismantled and the settlers, much to their dismay, were forced to return to Israel. A Multi-national Force and Observers took up position to monitor the peace. One Egyptian army division was allowed to be stationed in Sinai.

Gradually relations improved; ambassadors were exchanged; Israeli tourists were visiting Egypt; communications by air and land were established; Egypt became Israel's largest supplier of crude oil. But many Egyptians were cautious, as if fearing the day when they would have to justify their actions before their Arab colleagues. Then in June 1982 Israel invaded Lebanon with apparent American approval. Egypt condemned the invasion but was otherwise helpless. It was the greatest possible embarrassment for Mubarak and although the other Arab states (apart from Syria) offered little other than verbal opposition Egypt was blamed for having opted out of the Arab/Israeli confrontation, thus allowing Israel a free hand on her northern borders once Sinai had been made safe.

Israel named the invasion 'Peace for Galilee', an effort to prevent Palestinian attacks over the border. However, under the forceful leadership of General Sharon, the move soon broadened into an attempt to expel the whole of the Palestine Liberation Organization from Lebanon. The outskirts of Beirut were reached amid much loss of life and destruction. Egypt was compelled to show much greater disapproval and withdrew her ambassador from Tel Aviv. Other contacts were kept to a formal minimum. Mubarak said that full diplomatic relations would be restored only when Israel withdrew from Lebanon and peace returned to the area. The Egyptian Foreign Minister added that any Israeli action which affected an Arab country affected normalisation between Israel and Egypt. As a result of the invasion he said, 'Normalisation was no longer normal'. The United States and Israel further concluded a strategic pact which outraged Mubarak. It was a 'catastrophe' for him and a humiliation before other Arabs.

After the massacres of Palestinians by Christian Lebanese in Sabra and Chatila camps, unhindered by the Israeli forces, Egypt said that her relations with Israel were 90 per cent frozen. A period of cold peace has followed. Israel has continued to anger Mubarak with the violent repression of the Palestinian *intifada* uprising on the West Bank and in Gaza, with the continuing spread of settlements in the occupied territories and massive Soviet immigration. The world was heartened when the Palestinian National Council decided in November 1988 on a guarded recognition of Israel and announced the establishment of a Palestinian state. Mubarak has since called for a peace conference with Israel, the United States and the PLO, and while America has talked to the PLO, Israel has steadfastly refused to do so in any setting. All these Israeli actions embarrassed Mubarak although to date, despite opposition and external Arab pressure, he has refused to go back on the peace treaty.

Mubarak has slowly mended his fences with the Arab world after the isolation brought about by the Camp David accords. Gradually the Arab leaders have welcomed Egypt back into the fold. Yasir Arafat, the Chairman of the PLO, met Mubarak in Cairo in December 1983, quite a significant move as he had just been expelled from Lebanon under Syrian pressure. He seemed to be moving towards the 'moderate' Arab wing, those who might be willing together with Egypt to recognise Israel.

In January 1984 at a meeting in Morocco Egypt was unconditionally readmitted to the Islamic Conference Organization. In November 1987 Iraq and Morocco restored links with Egypt and in 1989 King Fahd of Saudi Arabia visited Cairo to set the stamp of approval on Egypt's return to acceptability. Further moves included the setting up in April 1989 of the Arab Cooperation Council of Egypt, Iraq, Jordan and North Yemen to stimulate cooperation in trade, defence and security but like so many of its predecessors it has now been overtaken by events.

At the Arab summit meeting in Casablanca in May 1989 Mubarak spoke of his pleasure at being back: 'The Arab people of Egypt are very happy in the unification of the ranks after separation'. He added with terrible unknowing irony that 'We welcome the fact that fraternal Iraq through the wisdom of its leadership has proved its true intentions *vis-à-vis* the establishment of a just and permanent peace on the basis of good neighbourliness, respect of national sovereignty and the territorial integrity of all the states of the region'. Thus politicians have to eat their words, yet at that time a period of unity did seem to be in prospect.

The headquarters of the Arab League returned to Cairo and even Syria, the bitterest of Egypt's critics, unconditionally (i.e. without demanding a rejection of Camp David) reestablished diplomatic relations and in May 1990 Mubarak visited Damascus to discuss an Arab summit which would have had Lebanon and the PLO on the agenda.

reign policy in general he has aimed to restore a balance in relations he believed that Sadat had relied too heavily on the United States. He has tried to work more closely with the Soviet Union although the great changes in Russia and Eastern Europe with the ending of the Cold War have meant that the Third World countries can no longer play the superpowers off against each other and Moscow is a broken reed as far as substantial military or financial aid is concerned.

The Arab world was shaken to its core by the Iraqi seizure of Kuwait in August 1990. It was a betrayal by Saddam Hussain of Arab unity and a violation of a brother Arab state. Mubarak was not prepared to stand idly by and at a summit meeting in Cairo he forced through a resolution backing Kuwait and condemning Iraq. Three states voted against and five abstained or expressed reservations. In addition, Egypt immediately decided to send troops to Saudi Arabia to participate in the international force on the Kuwaiti border. The Egyptian troops fought well in the brief but bitter war. Egypt will have an important role in any inter-Arab post-war settlement.

The Economy

Mubarak has tried to achieve balance and moderation in domestic politics and foreign relations. In the economy he has sought a middle course between socialist rigidity and capitalist free for all. Serious efforts have been made to correct the faults of the previous government. He is a cautious leader and he has warned that no miracle cure can be expected to their economic problems. He brought in new ministers to replace those associated with Sadat's policies and gave them the task of making *infitah* more attractive to Egyptian and foreign investors alike. There has not been, however, any sudden change in policy. Sometimes friends and opponents both believe Mubarak is too cautious and urge him without much optimism to exhibit more decisiveness. But he is very circumscribed in his field of action.

The momentary balance of payments surplus soon disappeared and the country has been falling deeper into debt. The current account trade deficit was expected to be $7,500 million in 1990, having risen from some $5,430 million in 1987–88. There was some hope in 1989 as not all was gloom; revenue was rising from Suez Canal dues ($1,300 million), tourism ($1,000 million) and non-oil exports ($1,500 million). Remittances from the many Egyptians working abroad remained stable. They ranged from peasants farming in Iraq to doctors and surgeons in private practice. While their remittances proved vital to the economy their absence inevitably lowered the standard of some of the professions in Egypt.

The oil sector see-sawed with variations in world prices. Revenue in 1988 of $755 million had more than doubled in 1989 to $1,651 million.

Production in 1988 was 870,000 barrels per day of which 190,000 were exported. Exploration continued apace and many new concessions were awarded. Finds were made in the Gulf of Suez and there was hope of further discoveries in the Western Desert. There was an increase in the amount of natural gas exploited. A factor affecting the oil supply was the continuing low level of the Nile which meant more fuel was needed to generate electricity as the water flow was not sufficient to work all the generators at the Aswan High Dam. The level of the river was expected to reach about the average in 1990.

Like many Third World countries Egypt is crippled with heavy foreign debts and is hard pressed even to pay the interest on them. The debt began to be contracted after the Camp David accords, when loans were given as a reward but at a time when interest rates were high. Egypt is always struggling to increase foreign earnings and throughout the period talks have been taking place with the International Monetary Fund/World Bank in an attempt to reschedule repayment of debts totalling some $18,000 million. The IMF always lays down conditions in such cases, economic reform, liberalisation of trade and price regulations, promotion of the private sector, lifting or reduction of subsidies, all things which Egypt approved in principle but which are very hard to implement on the ground. The overwhelming poverty of the country makes most price rises simply impossible to contemplate. Despite the worrying deterioration in the balance of payments the IMF has been convinced that some progress is being made in economic reform and agreement has been reached on an interim rescheduling of the debt.

Mubarak is deeply concerned about the effect any price rises or cutting of subsidies would have on the population. He has in mind the bread riots and he sacked a prime minister whom he thought was going too far to meet the demands of the IMF, fearing that the proposed price increases would cause civil war. Nevertheless, in 1989 and 1990 price rises were brought in for electricity and some petroleum products, fuel and flour and oil. It is very difficult to touch the food subsidies (costing in 1986 $3.8 billion) and Mubarak is confused by the problem. In 1989 the IMF stressed that Egypt could not afford to pay everyone's food bill but Mubarak replied that Egypt could not afford not to; yet a year later he said that the state could not indefinitely subsidise basic foods and services and that living standards were likely to fall. The IMF does understand these problems and welcomes even the most halting moves in the right direction.

The IMF also pushes for greater privatisation of state run businesses. A presidential adviser, Abu Ghazala, who had as Minister of Defence built a whole network of army enterprises (in weapons, housing, even agriculture), was made responsible in 1990 for selling off some of these businesses to the private sector, leaving untouched the major state industries such as iron, steel and textiles. There has been a great debate on the merits of the economic policies of the regimes of Nasser and

Sadat, for or against nationalisation and privatisation. The journalist Haykal claimed that Sadat's policy of *infitah* had been a disaster.

All economic progress is still hamstrung by the alarming growth of the population which increases by one person every thirty seconds or one and a quarter million a year. The forecast for the year 2000 is 70 million people. Cairo itself is growing by 300,000 annually. The present fertility rate is just under five children per mother. This puts enormous pressure on existing facilities, housing, schooling, hospitals and education. (It is ironic that the rising birth rate is the result of better medicine.) Housing never catches up with demand and there is need to create nearly half a million jobs a year just to prevent the present 20 per cent rate of unemployment from rising. Universities and schools remain desperately overcrowded and the illiteracy rate remains high at 50 per cent (in 1970 it was 56 per cent).

The situation has been worsened by the enforced return of Egyptian migrants from Iraq. This began with the end of the Iran–Iraq war. Jobs held by Egyptians were wanted for Iraqi ex-soldiers and Baghdad restricted the remittances allowed to be sent home. Many Egyptians were actually killed in mugging and other attacks by ex-soldiers on the loose. Bodies were returned to Cairo in a scandalous atmosphere. About one million of the estimated 2 million Egyptians had gone home by the time of the outbreak of the Gulf crisis. This had a severe impact on the Egyptian economy with the loss of remittances and the need to help financially those who returned. After August 1990 the return of migrants turned to a flood. Thousands of the 150,000 Egyptians in Kuwait and of those still in Iraq struggled home penniless, having lost jobs, possessions and money. The crisis affected other aspects of economic life too. There was an inevitable decline in aid from Kuwait, in trade with Iraq, in tourism, in Suez Canal dues. On the other hand oil prices were higher. One estimate put the total loss to Egypt for the year at $9 billion. However, Egypt's role in the crisis and the hardship caused were recognised abroad and some $14 billion of debts were cancelled by United States creditors and others and additional help was promised by the European Community, Japan and the Gulf states.

11   *Conclusion*

In the course of this book many of Egypt's problems and the various solutions proposed have been described. Fallible men have tried in their own ways to surmount what sometimes appear to be insurmountable obstacles. The experience of the West has shown that the most complex and developed societies cannot avoid disasters, failures and wrong turnings. At each parliamentary election new policies are put to the people, and in turn each new government discovers that there *are* no easy solutions and that most policies have to be modified in the face of economic, social or international realities. A country trying to develop rapidly faces its problems in a more acute form.

Egypt is basically a stable country and during thirty-two years there have been only three men at the helm. Although a leader is not a country, where there are no fixed political institutions it is difficult to avoid making the identification. Nasser and Sadat gave very different complexions to Egyptian society, starting from the basis of different conceptions and personalities. Nasser was suspicious, mistrustful and a conspirator by nature, unwilling to share power — and he left an Egypt shaped in his image. He was, however, an overwhelming personality, a visionary, destined from youth to lead his country into a new stage of development. Floundering Arab leaders around him forced him into a wider role. A Syrian statesman claimed of him that he had

> no right to choose, but was fated to lead the way, to receive all the shafts of the enemy, to be happy or unhappy depending on the state of the nation . . . He who leads a whole historical process must inevitably take up this stand.

Thus placed in history, Nasser, instead of solving problems, chose to incarnate them. According to Qaddafi of Libya he again had little choice:

> Nasser tried hard to make the masses . . . believe in themselves. But the harder he tried, the more they clung to his person.

Tawfiq al-Hakim saw a sinister willingness on Nasser's part to take on the leader's role:

> He made us feel that there existed in Egypt and the whole Arab world only one power, one personality . . . Nasserism rested on the . . . basis of the destruction of minds and wills, other than the mind and will of the leader . . . He is a lesson we must heed well in order to oppose everyone who puts himself forward for the leadership of the Arabs.

Nevertheless he left behind an Egypt and an Arab world very different from what they had been when he assumed power; he led a breakthrough from one era to the next. He had to live through a period of historical changes which often posed problems too great for one man. He expelled the British, yet brought the Russians in; he fought for Arab unity, yet fought other Arabs in doing so; he crushed a corrupt regime, yet built up a restrictive police state; he destroyed a government system, yet left few institutions in its place. The contrast between hope and achievement became greater in the 1960s when he came to reap the whirlwind. In the words of one critic, they were a decade 'of great expectations and tragic failures, of glories and sufferings on an unprecedented scale'; in the words of another: 'a decade of confusion, contradiction and crisis . . . a tragic decade'. But he was worshipped and respected, and he brought Egypt back to the Egyptians. Egypt basked in his reflected glory. He was a colossus.

He did not succeed in building permanent institutions; during his rule he produced three political organisations, five parliaments of two years each, six constitutions, and his cabinets lasted about thirteen months. He did not plan ahead very much. He admitted that he often reacted to rather than led situations, sometimes not seeing where his tactics were leading. 'Really', he once said to the British ambassador, 'I have no plan'. Haykal said that he always reacted (to real or imagined slights) with pride and anger. The Russians called him impulsive and hot-headed. Sadat said that Nasser was too preoccupied with his own security to have a clear vision of the future. Yet he was a world statesman and in a real sense *was* Egypt, and only if he had been a lesser man would he perhaps have been easier to deal with and would have made fewer mistakes.

On his death the Egyptian people clung to his body and to his memory, only gradually feeling some relief at the passing of an overwhelming man and becoming prepared to face the future under a less awesome figure. Sadat in the beginning was no less committed to Egypt's welfare than was Nasser, but he had to face a quite different set of historical circumstances. He was also of very different character. He analysed what he considered to be Nasser's mistakes and proposed his own solutions. With political astuteness and determination he came to dominate Egypt and pursued certain clear objectives. He made his country for a time a more open society and inheriting few institutions he experimented with his own. Towards the end of his life, however, he was losing his way, closing his mind and hitting out blindly at any he believed to be opponents. In this he was again different from Nasser who in the last three years of his life had become more open, more ready to listen and to experiment. This late change of direction under Nasser was something that Sadat was initially able to build upon. .

Mubarak inherited a bitter and divided country. After ten years of rule many problems remain unsolved. How can the Islamic fundamentalists be integrated into society in a non-disruptive manner? In which direction will democracy develop? How will it ever be possible to solve the overwhelming economic problems? Where will Egypt stand in the world that will emerge in the aftermath of the Gulf Crisis? Whatever the answers may be, the future development of Egypt presents a challenge which will tax to the utmost the ability and wisdom of its leaders.

Notes

1   A hotel advertisement in an Egyptian newspaper in 1980 described one of these areas as 'where the grands live'.
2   The last British shares were sold in 1979.
3   Mahmud Fahmi Nuqrashi (1888–1948), originally a member of the Wafd who had been imprisoned by the British for suspected activities against them. In 1937 he left the Wafd to form his own anti-Wafdist political grouping.
4   After Sadat's negotiations with Israel the League left Cairo in March 1979 for Tunis and expelled Egypt as punishment for her behaviour.
5   Strictly his given name was Gamal and his father's name Abdel Nasser, in English 'the servant of the victorious (God)'. He is best known in the West, however, as Nasser.
6   He died in 1965 in Rome, the remnant of a rather notorious and pathetic playboy.
7   Although the name Egypt was officially dropped it will continue to be used here, always remembering that the UAR continued as the name of the country until Sadat changed it to the Arab Republic of Egypt.
8   Some Egyptians objected strongly to the disappearance of the ancient name of their country.
9   Anwar el-Sadat published his autobiography *In Search of Identity* (London: Collins, 1978) which is useful but which has to be taken with a handful of salt. It was written to justify his policies and therefore is almost totally unself-critical.
10 Perhaps not so ridiculous. At the Madrid conference on détente in 1980 the clock was stopped at just before midnight in order to try to reach agreement on the agenda before the midnight deadline!
11 Since the 1967 occupation of the West Bank of Jordan, Zionist settlements had gradually been established throughout the area. Some extremists argued that the territory was Judea and Samaria, an integral part of Israel, never to be returned to the Arabs and to be totally settled by Jewish immigrants.
12 Some sources say only two. The party's own account claims four.
13 The term is derived from *suf*–wool from which the cloaks of the earliest mystics are supposed to have been made.
14 He was at one time imprisoned by Sadat.
15 There is now even quite a flourishing business in newspaper advertising for potential partners. The usual qualities for partners are sought, with the addition of a subtle colour discrimination. Women describe themselves in descending order of desirability as white, 'wheaten' colour, dark, and deep brown (black?).

Bibliography

This listing is very selective. It includes the books I found most useful in writing this study and it points to some which may aid further reading. Several of them also contain useful bibliographies.

History and Politics

Baker, R. W., *Egypt's Uncertain Revolution under Nasser and Sadat* (Cambridge, Mass: Harvard University Press, 1978).
Baker R. W., *Sadat and after: Struggles for Egypt's Political Soul* (London: I. B. Tauris, 1990).
Kerr, M., *The Arab Cold War 1958–64* (Oxford: Oxford University Press for Chatham House, 1965). A study of Iraqi-Syrian–Egyptian negotiations and interesting for the verbatim quotations.
Rejwan, N., *Nasserist Ideology: its Exponents and Critics* (published for the Shiloah Center, Tel Aviv by Wiley, New York, 1974).
Springborg, R., *Mubarak's Egypt: Fragmentation of the Political Order* (Westview Press: Boulder and London, 1989).
Tripp, C. and Owen, R. eds, *Egypt under Mubarak* (Routledge, London and New York: 1989).
Vatikiotis, P. J., *The Modern History of Egypt*, 2nd edn (London: Weidenfeld & Nicholson, 1980).
Waterbury, J., *The Egypt of Nasser and Sadat: The political economy of two regimes* (Princeton NJ: Princeton University Press, 1983).

Society

Abu Lughod, J., *Cairo: 1001 Years of 'the City Victorious'* (New Jersey: Princeton University Press, 1971).
Ammar, H., *Growing up in an Egyptian Village* (New York: Grove Press, 1954).
Ayrout, H. H., *The Egyptian Peasant*, trans. from French by J. A. Williams (Boston, Mass.: Beacon Press, 1963).
Ayubi, N. N., *Bureaucracy and Politics in Contemporary Egypt* (London: Ithaca Press, 1980).
Carré, O., *Enseignement Islamique et Ideal Socialiste* (Beirut: Dar el-Machreq, n.d.).
Critchfield, R., *Shahhat, an Egyptian* (New York: Syracuse University Press, 1978). A fascinating attempt to look inside the 'mind' of an Egyptian village.
El Saadawi, N., *The Hidden Face of Eve: Women in the Arab World*, trans. by S. Hetata (London: Zed Press, 1980). By a leading Arab doctor and feminist.

Gilsenan, M., *Saint and Sufi in Modern Egypt: an Essay in the Sociology of Religion* (Oxford: Oxford University Press, 1973).

Harik, I., *The Political Mobilization of Peasants: a Study of an Egyptian Community* (Bloomington, Ind.: Indiana University Press, 1974).

Hill, E., *Mahkama! Studies in the Egyptian Legal System* (London: Ithaca Press, 1979). A study of Egyptian law courts in action.

Mayfield, J. B., *Rural Politics in Nasser's Egypt* (Austin, Tex.: University of Texas, 1971).

Mitchell, R., *The Society of Muslim Brothers* (London: Oxford University Press, 1969). The best study, although not now up to date.

Wikan, U., *Life Among the Poor in Cairo*, trans. A. Henning (London: Tavistock Press, 1980). First hand observations.

Economy

Cooper, M. N., *The Transformation of Egypt* (London: Croom Helm, 1982). On the political economy of Nasser and Sadat.

Mabro, R., *The Egyptian Economy 1952–1972* (Oxford: Clarendon Press, 1974). The best short study of the Nasser period, which has to be supplemented by articles on the Sadat policy. It has a good bibliography.

Radwan, S., *Agrarian Reform and Rural Poverty 1952–1975* (Geneva: International Labour Office, 1977).

Work by Egyptians

A few participants in events have written their memoirs, and a leading commentator and journalist, Mohammed Haykal (Heikal), has published inside accounts.

Heikal, M., *Autumn of Fury: The Assassination of Sadat* (London: Andre Deutsch, 1983). A bitter attack on Sadat and his method of government.

Heikal, M., *Nasser, the Cairo Documents* (London: New English Library, 1972). A study of Nasser's relations with other leaders.

Heikal, M., *The Road to Ramadan* (London: Collins, 1975). The events leading to the 1973 war.

Heikal, M., *Sphinx and Commissar: the Rise and Fall of Soviet Influence in the Arab World* (London: Collins, 1978).

Nasser, G., *The Philosophy of the Revolution* (Cairo: Ministry of National Guidance, 1954). A not very illuminating guide to Nasser's thought.

Neguib, M., *Egypt's Destiny: a Personal Statement* (London: Gollancz. 1955). The ousted president's apologia.

Sadat, A., *Revolt on the Nile* (London: Wingate, 1957).

201 Egypt: Politics and Society 1945–1990

Sadat, A., *In Search of Identity: an Autobiography* (London: Collins, 1978). Totally un-self-critical and therefore interesting.

Biographies of Nasser and Sadat

Several biographies of Nasser appeared soon after his death. Among the best are:

Lacouture, J., *Nasser*, trans. by D. Hofstadter (London: Secker and Warburg, 1973).
Stephens, R., *Nasser: a political biography* (London: Penguin, 1971). A detailed and straightforward account.
Vatikiotis, P. J. *Nasser and his Generation* (London: Croom Helm, 1978). A good study by a keen observer of the Egyptian scene.

A critical biography of Sadat was published only a month or so after his assassination:

Hirst, D. and Beeson, I., *Sadat* (London: Faber, 1981).

Suez Affair

Many books have been written on the Suez war by soldiers, statesmen, journalists and academics. A number of political memoirs cover the subject with varying degrees of frankness, notably those by Eden, Selwyn Lloyd, Dayan and Pineau. Each adds something to our knowledge of the affair. A good general survey is:

Love, K., *Suez, the Twice Fought War* (London: Longman, 1969).

Arab–Israeli wars

Each war has produced a large number of studies and memoirs and military analyses. One covers them all and includes a brief bibliography.

Depuy, T. N., *Elusive Victory: the Arab–Israeli Wars 1947–1974* (London: Macdonald and Jane's, 1978).
Herzog, C., *The Arab-Israeli Wars: War and Peace in the Middle East from the War of Independence to Lebanon* (London: Arms and Armour Press, 1984). The Israeli side by a former general, now president of the state.

Literature

A considerable number of poems, plays, short stories and novels have now been translated from Arabic into English. Many of these are listed in M. Badawi's article 'Modern Arabic Literature' in *Middle East and Islam: a Bibliographical Introduction* (ed. D. Grimwood-Jones). (Zug: Inter-documentaton Company, 1979).

Index

Index